STO

Contemporary Sociological Theory

MARGARET M. POLOMA

The University of Akron

MACMILLAN PUBLISHING CO., INC.

New York

COLLIER MACMILLAN PUBLISHERS

London

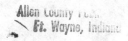

Macmillan Publishing Co., Inc.
866 Third Avenue, New York, New York 10022

Collier Macmillan Canada, Ltd.

Library of Congress Cataloging in Publication Data

Contemporary sociological theory.

  Bibliography: p.
  Includes index.
  1. Sociology. I. Poloma, Margaret M.
HM51.C599   301'.01   78-24392
ISBN 0-02-396100-7

Printing: 1 2 3 4 5 6 7 8   Year: 9 0 1 2 3 4 5

Preface

Contemporary Sociological Theory is designed as a text to introduce un-
dergraduate students of sociology to some of the noteworthy theorists in
the field. It is intended to provide a survey of the salient perspectives
in theory by using an exemplary theorist as an illustration of a particular
approach. Although some criticisms of each theory will be presented, this
text is not intended as a critical work. Other books exist on the market
to provide detailed critiques of contemporary theory for advanced students who are familiar with the basic outline of a theorist's work or a
particular school of thought. Although references to classical theory will
be made as deemed necessary, this text is not intended as a history of
social thought. It would be helpful for the student to be familiar with the
works of Durkheim, Weber, Simmel, Marx, and other classical theorists,
but such knowledge is not a prerequisite for understanding the materials
discussed here. *Contemporary Sociological Theory* is intended to provide
a framework and a basic overview of contemporary theory, enabling the
student to approach with understanding the writings of those who may
well be included among the classical theorists of tomorrow.

Ideally this text will be used in conjunction with primary sources or
as a preliminary overview to enable students to approach primary works
of contemporary theorists on their own. A secondary source such as this
cannot be a replacement for firsthand experience with the writings of
sociological theorists. If the history of social thought is taught within the
same course as contemporary theories, *Contemporary Sociological Theory*
could be used with another work dealing with classical theory to demonstrate how contemporary scholarship is indebted to the past.

The text is divided into three major parts: (1) a discussion of the
naturalistic, or positivistic, ideal type theory; (2) a discussion of the
humanistic, or interpretative, theory; and (3) a discussion of the evaluative, or applied, ideal type. These three broad classifications are intended only as heuristic devices within which major theorists may be
compared and contrasted. The student is periodically reminded that these
classifications are ideal types, with each theory under discussion possessing traits of the other classifications as well. Each theorist's work is
placed with the typology according to underlying assumptions about the
nature of person, society, and theory discussed within each chapter.
These assumptions are the basis for having categorized a particular perspective as "naturalistic," "interpretative," or "evaluative."

Each chapter (with the exception of the introductory first one) cen-
ters on a particular theorist representing an approach that is significant
in modern sociological theory. The author is convinced that the beginning student finds it easier to deal with the "person approach" to studying

theory than with the "conceptual approach," the "school-of-thought approach," or the more recent "paradigm approach." Although each of these models is valuable in subsequent efforts to integrate the theorists' works or as a supplemental approach within a course, the author has found that the person approach presents the best base upon which to build a student's knowledge of theory.

The organization of each chapter consists of an introduction, a synopsis of the theorist's main works, and a discussion of underlying assumptions. The introduction will serve to place the theorist within a particular perspective, relative to the materials covered within the text and relative to the history of social thought. The main section of each chapter will deal with a summary of the primary works of the theorist. The aim has been to provide a brief, noncritical summary of the theory, usually focusing on one or two of the theorist's most significant contributions. The last section of each chapter will discuss the theorist's (1) image of person; (2) image of person with regard to image of society; and (3) view of sociological theory. These three sets of assumptions form the basis for classifying a theorist as naturalistic, humanistic, or evaluative. A special attempt has been made within each chapter to define the concepts that provide the building blocks of the theory. The glossary at the end of the text will serve as a reference for the salient concepts.

I would like to thank all of my former students and my colleagues who have encouraged me by listening to my thoughts and by reading drafts of this manuscript. Among those earning my special gratitude are Irwin Deutscher, Barbara Gartland, Larry Isaac, Mary Minard Moynihan, and Samuel A. Mueller, as well as anonymous reviewers chosen by Macmillan to review all or part of earlier versions of the manuscript. Deepest appreciation to my husband and colleague T. Neal Garland, who shares with me the problems and joys of being part of a two-career family. My thanks also to my editor at Macmillan, Kenneth J. Scott, without whose patience and support this book would never have become a reality. Finally, I would like to thank Susan Greenberg and Margaret Ritchie for the fine job of copyediting and for making *Contemporary Sociological Theory* more readable than it otherwise would have been.

M. M. P.

Contents

part *III*. Contributors to Evaluative
            Sociology

CONTEMPORARY SOCIOLOGICAL THEORY

1

The Quest for Sociological Theory

Like it or not, and know it or not, sociologists will organize their researches in terms of their prior assumptions, the character of sociology will depend on them and will change when they change. To explore the character of a sociology, to know what a sociology is, therefore requires us to identify its deepest assumptions about man and society. For these reasons it will not be to its *methods* of study to which I will look to an understanding of its character, but rather to its assumptions about man and society. The use of particular methods of study implies the existence of particular assumptions about man and society. (Gouldner, 1970:28)

Although they may not be stated formally, all sociological theory rests upon assumptions about the nature of man and the nature of society. These assumptions form foundations upon which the structures of the various theoretical perspectives are built. As Gouldner implied in the quotation just cited, sociologists are often blind to the assumptions contained in their theoretical formulations, partly, as we shall see, because of the image that many sociologists have of themselves and their discipline.

In an attempt to establish sociology's academic credibility, much attention was given to idealizing it as a science that must aim for scientific neutrality and detachment. This image of sociology as science is not particularly accurate; nevertheless, until recently it served as a base upon which much contemporary American sociology rested. As we see from the quotation from Gouldner, the feasibility of a value-free sociology is being seriously questioned. Different theoretical perspectives utilize different assumptions—although sociologists may fail or refuse to recognize them. In being deluded by the myth of a value-free discipline, sociologists until recently paid little attention to the assumptions about the nature of man and the nature of society that were contained in differing perspectives. Students of sociology are today becoming more and more aware that theories about society cannot be easily merged into a single theory. Com-

1

petitive and conflicting assumptions abound regarding the image of man and the related image of society in contemporary theory.

The major dichotomy in sociology has been expressed in different ways. Catton (1966) discusses "animistic" versus "naturalistic" sociology. Giddens (1976) sets up a distinction between "positivistic" and "interpretative" sociologies. Martindale (1974) discusses the historical roots of "humanistic" versus "scientific" sociology. All of these terms have been used and abused to the point where theorists may be reluctant to wear any such label. Dennis Wrong, for example, is willing to be counted among the humanistic sociologists, if the term is understood as he intends. Because it often is not, Wrong (1976) attempts to avoid misunderstanding and calls his approach to sociology "skeptical sociology." It appears, however, that in theory there is a single dichotomy with "animistic," "interpretative," "humanistic," and "skeptical" on one side and "naturalistic," "positivistic," and "scientific" on the other.[1]

We wish to emphasize at the onset that such dichotomizing is necessarily an attempt to make use of what a master of classical sociological theory, Max Weber, refers to as an "ideal type." As we describe one polar type as "naturalistic" or "positivistic" and the other as "humanistic" or "interpretative," keep in mind that polar types do not exist in reality. They are abstractions, derived from reality, that enable sociologists to discuss social phenomena. As we shall see in discussing each theory, each tends to be more or less positivistic or more or less humanistic. The heuristic value of such a typology to the comparison and contrasting of theoretical assumptions should become more apparent as detailed attention is given to various theories representative of these types.

The Nature of Naturalistic or Positivistic Theory _____

Naturalistic or positivistic sociology is committed to the idea that sociology is a science just as the natural sciences are science. Among the naturalistic sociologists are those who use physics and biology for models as well as those who are committed to the unity of all science, natural and social alike, without reducing any discipline to another. Catton (1966)

---

[1] In this text we choose to use the terms *positivistic* and *naturalistic* interchangeably, ignoring the many attempts to define and redefine and the criticisms of the misuse and abuse of both concepts. The same holds true for *humanistic* and *interpretative*. We shy away from the term *animistic* because of its disparaging use. Because all sociology claims to be "scientific," in one form or another, it is also meaningless to use this term to refer to one of the polar types.

acknowledges that physicalism (merging sociology into the study of physiochemical science) and mechanism (using physical mechanical principles to help explain social phenomena) are compatible with naturalistic sociology. He further observes the strong empiricist bent of naturalistic sociology with its insistence on verifiable data. Perhaps one of the most important traits in naturalistic or positivistic sociology is the belief that social phenomena are patterned and are subject to deterministic laws much as are the laws governing the natural sciences. Sociological theory then becomes a quest for laws similar to the law of gravity or the law of material density in physics.

This approach to theory produces a simple yet rigorously demanding definition of sociological theory. Philosopher of science Richard Rudner (1966) has defined a theory as "a systematically related set of statements, including some lawlike generalizations, that is empirically testable." Such a definition calls for a precise definition of concepts or variables, which in turn yield statements or propositions and which must be interrelated to form a scientific theory. It is only after a theory has been subjected to numerous tests and has been found empirically sound that it may be elevated to the realm of a scientific law. Rudner's definition of a theory merits closer scrutiny if we are to understand the nature of naturalistic theory, particularly regarding defining concepts, forming propositions, and interrelating propositions into theory.

The basic unit of a theory is a sociological concept or variable that provides the base for empirical testability. Émile Durkheim, the early sociological theorist who produced classic works upon which naturalistic theory rests, referred to such concepts as "social facts." A social fact is a concept that has an empirical reality outside a person's imagination. For Durkheim such social facts included marital status, age, religion, economic conditions, and suicide and crime rates. Contemporary sociologists refer to such social facts as *variables* or concepts that have variable properties. For example, suicide rates may increase or decrease; a person may be single, married, divorced, or widowed; and religious identification includes groups of Protestants, Catholics, and Jews as well as a residual category of "other." Such social facts or variables are concrete, observable, and capable of being measured. Upon them rest much of the philosopher of science's dictum that a theory must be "empirically testable."

Variable concepts and their precise definitions are the bricks from which theory is constructed. These analytical bricks, however, must be mortared together through the construction of propositions. Very simply stated, a *proposition* is a generalized statement of relationship among social facts or variables. The statement that agnostics have a higher suicide rate than do devout Jews, Catholics, or Protestants is an example of a proposition. It shows a relationship (greater than) between religion (social fact or variable) and suicide rates (another social fact). Another propositional statement based upon Durkheim's study of suicide is that suicide rates tend to increase during times of rapid economic change. In propositions, sociological concepts are linked together into the statements called for in Rudner's definition of a theory.

Propositions are not in themselves theories any more than mortared bricks are a building. Building materials must be arranged in accord with a blueprint; so must propositional statements be interrelated to form a theory. Going back to Rudner's definition, we see that a theory is "a systematically related set of statements." In his classic study of suicide, Durkheim took propositional statements such as those cited and out of them derived a theory of social solidarity. Durkheim demonstrated that social solidarity or group cohesiveness can be empirically measured through observable social facts, including religious affiliation and marital status. For example, Durkheim found that Jews formed a more tightly knit community than did Protestants who tended to be more individualistically oriented. Married couples with children were more tied to a social group than were single adults. In the case of both married couples and Jews of Durkheim's day, the suicide rate was less than for unmarrieds or for members of other religious groups. It was through the interrelation of empirically observable statements that the theory was formed.

Naturalistic theory is committed to precision in theory construction, yet it would be fair to assert that there are varying degrees of such commitment. In the chapters that follow, we will see that some naturalistic theorists emphasize the development and definition of concepts that are arranged in categories or taxonomies. These theorists are committed to the position that the conceptual level of theory construction may not be bypassed quickly (cf. Parsons, Chapter 8). Other naturalistic theorists quickly define their concepts and then move on to developing propositional statements (cf. Coser, Chapter 5). Because theory is defined as a set of interconnected propositions, some theorists have not only defined concepts but developed propositions and attempted to interrelate them into a single theory (cf. Homans, Chapter 3). Still other theorists are more concerned about critiquing theory in light of their understanding of the naturalistic model than about developing theory themselves (cf. Merton, Chapter 2). Each of these four emphases—concepts, propositions, interrelated propositions, and metatheories—represents a varying type of commitment to the development of naturalistic theory.

There is still another approach to naturalistic theory. It not only uses an analogy between the natural sciences and the social sciences but is committed to the unity of all science. Such a position asserts that there must be a unified theory of society (rather than competing theories) and that ideally this theory is to be incorporated into a unified scientific theory. Although we are nowhere near approaching such a unified body of knowledge, scientists should keep this model in mind while working within their respective disciplines. General or modern systems theorists (discussed in Chapter 8) provide an illustration of this approach. General systems theory stresses the need for a common language and a common model to facilitate the communication among the scientific specialists in order to work toward a unified natural science and social science theory.

In summary we may say that naturalistic theory advocates that sociology fashion itself in the image of the natural sciences. In terms of the concrete application of this model, however, there are varying degrees and types of adherence to naturalistic theory. In reality we would find very little naturalistic theory in sociology if we were to apply the strict requirements set down by the philosophers of science regarding interrelated propositions and empirical testability. This is a persistent sociological dilemma—a discrepancy between the ideal theory and the real theories that we find both in the history of social thought and in the works of contemporary theorists. In many ways, because of the complexity of our subject matter our sociological products have not yet reached our scientific aspirations.

NATURALISTIC SOCIOLOGY'S ASSUMPTIONS ABOUT PEOPLE AND SOCIETY

Although naturalistic sociologists would deny that they have any value assumptions regarding the nature of man, careful reading of their works suggests otherwise. Implicit assumptions about man are present that may be correlated with assumptions about the nature of society: men and women are fallen creatures whose redemption is made possible by an ordered social world.

The image of a person as a fallen creature is not a new one. It may be found in biblical writings as well as in philosophical treatises. Thomas Hobbes, a seventeenth-century British philosopher, presented a model of man and society that may be viewed as a base for naturalistic sociology's unexpressed assumptions. For Hobbes, human action is determined by passions and greed, which manifest themselves in violent conflict situations. In addition to such passion, however, men and women are endowed with reason. Reason allows this fallen state of nature to be overcome and permits violent conflict to be transformed into nonviolent cooperation. This feat is accomplished through the establishment of a political state that provides protection for its people from their own greedy, passionate nature. Thus, for Hobbes, people are selfish and warlike but in need of security. Society evolves to constrain man's passions and to socialize men and women into submission.

Within Hobbes's theory we find the assumptions that men and women are naturally egoistic, determined creatures, yet capable of rational action—assumptions that have been built into much naturalistic theory. Although most naturalistic sociologists would be reluctant to express the view that man is inherently egoistic, they would imply that society is necessary to constrain persons. People are viewed primarily as creatures who are products of the social order rather than as creatures who are capable of fashioning and designing their world. Like Hobbes, naturalistic sociologists observe rationality in men and women—a rationality that will employ the necessary means to secure the desired goals. Both the means and the goals, however, are inherent within the social order. We will see this interrelated image of people and society time and again as we focus on individual theorists and the assumptions underlying their respective theories in the chapters that follow. It is ordered society that prevents man from falling victim to what Hobbes termed a "war of all against all" where man's passions rule.

The Nature of Humanistic or Interpretative Sociology

Humanistic sociology stands in contrast to naturalistic or positivistic sociology on three important issues. First, unlike naturalistic sociology, humanistic sociology accepts "common-sense notions about the nature of human nature" (Catton, 1966:57), attempting to confirm and build on them. For example, concepts like *self*, emphasis on language and meaning, questions of human freedom versus determinism, all of which are too elusive for most precise naturalistic sociologists, are the essence of sociological concern for humanists. Second, humanistic sociologists share the conviction that "these common-sense notions can and should serve as the premises from which more elaborate sociological formulations are to be derived" (Catton, 1966:57). Thus theory building in sociology starts with the seemingly obvious, the everyday, the commonplace. Third, humanistic sociology "arises out of concerns shared with the humanities rather than from an effort to apply methodological prescriptions allegedly based on the natural sciences to the study of human affairs" (Wrong, 1976:1). In other words, sociology differs from the natural sciences and errs when it strays too far from the humanities in its fascination with the scientific.

Perhaps the most persistent debate between naturalistic and humanistic sociology involves methodology, or the procedure for doing sociology scientifically. We have noted that whereas naturalistic sociology is committed to the assumption that sociology must be a science in the vein of the natural sciences, humanistic sociology is critical of such a stance. Naturalistic sociology's emphasis on "science building" looks to the natural sciences for a model of theory construction and precision in sociological research. Many have become very mathematically and statistically oriented in this quest for precision. Humanistic sociology, on the other hand, stresses the properties in human behavior that make men and women unique in the realm of creation. One of the most significant differences is that people attach meaning to what they encounter. Such meaning or interpretation of social phenomena must be studied, claim interpretative sociologists, in accord with its own properties (which cannot be reduced to the laws of natural science). Fascination with a deterministic or naturalistic sociology has led to a neglect, they charge, of the colorful mosaic that is the result of man's interpretative action.

HUMANISTIC SOCIOLOGY'S ASSUMPTIONS ABOUT PEOPLE AND SOCIETY

Humanistic sociology rests on very different assumptions about the nature of people and society. Although the specifics of the assumptions vary from theorist to theorist, there appears to be a consensus that men and women are at least partially free to shape their own personal worlds, if not the larger social world of which they are a part. Giddens (1976:155) summarizes some additional assumptions or "insights" of the interpretative school. First, "the social world, unlike the world of nature, has to be grasped as a skilled accomplishment of active human subjects," and second, "the constitution of this world as 'meaningful,' 'accountable' or 'intelligible' depends upon language, regarded however not simply as a system of signs or symbols but as a medium of practical activity."

Thus the interpretative sociologist tends to stress a more creative and freer person than allowed for by the naturalists. Although the interpretative sociologist is aware of the potentially constraining power of our social institutions, he/she focuses on the creative abilities of men and women to shape them.[2] When dealing with "institutions" or "social struc-

---

[2] Most interpretative sociology tends to be micro- rather than macrosociologically oriented. Wagner (1964:751–784) has effectively argued that this emphasis on the interactional process has made it difficult to analyze anything but small groups. He acknowledges that there is an "apparent inability of 'interpretative' sociologists to transfer their interactional conceptions effectively from micro- to macrosociological areas." This stress on microsociology, we will see in subsequent chapters, makes interpretative sociology different from naturalistic theory, which emphasizes the study of large-scale organizations and structures. We argue, however, that it is possible for the naturalistic sociologist to focus on the individual (as does Homans) and for the interpretative sociologist to deal with larger structures (as does Berger).

tures," interpretative sociologists are likely to express an awareness that social reality, rather than being a finished product, is always in the process of being constructed. Men and women are free actors in the social world and yet, to some extent, are simultaneously shaped by the social world that is already in existence. In interpretative or humanistic sociology, the emphasis tends to be on the interaction in and the interpretation of the world rather than on the nature of the structure.

The Rise of Evaluative Sociological Theory

In contemporary American theory, naturalistic or positivistic sociology has been the predominant model, with interpretative or humanistic theory providing an alternate approach. The popularity of the former may be demonstrated by the term "standard American sociology," with the latter taking the position of the "loyal opposition" (Mullins, 1973). Both are committed to the science of sociology, but because of contrasting assumptions about people and society, each produces theories that are at odds with the other's.

Yet there is still another set of assumptions that cuts through both naturalistic and interpretative sociology. These assumptions center on what has been referred to as the "self-image of the sociologist." Friedrichs (1970) uses a religious analogy to discuss the sociologist's self-image as being either "prophet" or "priest." A religious prophet is one who is critical of his/her social world and who heralds a need for conversion to avert an impending catastrophe. Just as biblical prophets were often at odds with their own people as they called for religious renewal, so too have sociological prophets been at odds with the practices of their own discipline. Sociology was born from the loins of a secular philosophical (rather than a religious) prophecy. Its putative founder, Auguste Comte, sought to establish sociology as a religion of humanity that would scientifically discover the secret to perfect social harmony and the perfectability of man (Friedrichs, 1970:69–70). But just as prophets fail to beget other prophets in religion, sociology all too soon lost the prophetic thrust that separated it from the existing social world, which it purported to study. With an attempt to establish sociology as a respected academic discipline came the institution of a sociological priesthood. Sociologists of the priestly mode, like their religious counterparts, were more likely to accept the existing social order and to preach to uphold it. Whereas a prophetic sociologist would be concerned with critiquing the social world and offering plans for its redemption, the priestly sociologist would emphasize the institutional nature of the sociological profession. In other words, prophetic sociologists call for some change in the larger social world, and priestly sociologists call for an academic discipline to study social reality objectively.

Just as priests have outnumbered prophets in religion, sociological priests have also outnumbered sociological prophets. In sociology this has been true in both naturalistic and humanistic sociologies, and the admonition that sociology must be value-free has therefore predominated. Although the meaning of such neutrality is far from agreed upon, it has contributed to the growth of the priesthood and its commitment to scientific detachment. Some prophetic voices, however, may be heard within contemporary theory, insisting that sociological endeavors be relevant to the affairs of the world. (Other otherwise priestly sociologists may on occasion join such prophetic utterances, but usually they take care to separate their role of "value-free sociologist" from that of "concerned citizen.") Such prophets question whether it is possible to be value-neutral or value-free. They argue that the sociological priests also have value-laden assumptions within their work, but are often blinded by them.

The prophets suggest not only that it is impossible to be truly neutral in terms of values but also that such neutrality may not be at all desirable. We have already noted how assumptions about people, society, and sociology are an inherent part of both naturalistic and humanistic theory. Being blind to these assumptions and perhaps to even more important ones about the implications of their theories, argue the prophets or evaluative sociologists, does not make sociology value-free. Evaluative sociologists might echo the position of German sociologist Ralf Dahrendorf (1968:18) when he asserts that it is "more important to warn against the radical separation of science and value judgments than to warn against their commingling." Sociologists have a responsibility to examine the consequences of their scholarly activity.

Dahrendorf (1968:259–271) demonstrates this need of sociologists to be aware of the entire context in which their work is conducted and to assess the political and moral consequences of research and theory in his discussion of the failure of Project Camelot. Project Camelot was proposed as a $4 million to $6 million research project sponsored by the Special Operations Research Office of the U.S. Army enabling social scientists to study the causes of internal upheavals and revolutions in developing countries. The amount of money was phenomenal for any social science project and was able to buy the services of some outstanding sociologists. By failing to address the potential consequences of the project in terms of hidden values, some of these sociologists failed to recognize that funding by the U.S. Army was the Achilles' heel of the project. For a number of reasons, mostly stemming from a mounting opposition to the U.S. military's sponsorship of the research, Project Camelot was canceled.[3] Dahrendorf, among others, has questioned the appropriateness of sociologists' working for the U.S. Army to study revolutions. Although the expressed intent of the sociologists might have been couched in the value-free terms of the development of knowledge, the intent of the American military was a value-laden one of suppressing revolutions. Being aware of the entire context of the research project makes it apparent that values were very much a part of Project Camelot, and a good sociologist may not ignore them.

It is important to note that evaluative theory, with its prophetic rather than priestly thrust, may be either naturalistic or humanistic.[4] Auguste Comte, whom Friedrichs categorizes as a prophet, advocated that sociology develop along naturalistic lines. His contemporary, Karl Marx, on the other hand, may be viewed as a prophet in the humanistic ranks. So too within contemporary theory, prophets are arising within the naturalistic as well as the humanistic camp.

Organization of Text

Based on the underlying assumptions about the nature of people and society as well as on the sociologist's self-image as priest or prophet, an ideal type emerges in the four-cell typology depicted in Figure 1.

Part I of the text will deal with standard American sociology, which has tended toward the priestly–naturalistic mode. Part II will deal with the priestly humanists, who have served as a loyal opposition to the dominant school. Part III will cover four noteworthy evaluative sociologists from both naturalistic and humanistic camps who are prophetic in their attempts to deal with the social issues that confront modern society.

As we have attempted to demonstrate in this brief introduction and will continue to do during the presentation of the various theories, the

[3] For further discussion of Project Camelot, see Irving L. Horowitz (1967).

[4] Wagner (1963) posits three types of theory: positive, interpretative, and evaluative. We are using the term *evaluative* somewhat differently from his usage, where evaluative theorists are necessarily ideological and deliberately value-laden. We assume that values are present in both positive and interpretative sociologies, with evaluative sociology developing in both camps. We attempt to demonstrate throughout the text that no theory is "value-free," in that all contain and rest upon unproven assumptions. Those theorists who recognize this and opt to work with social-problem-related issues need not flaunt any disdain for science. Evaluative theorists share the vision of a sociology engaged in social prescriptions based upon either naturalistic or humanistic scholarly theories.

SOCIOLOGIST'S SELF IMAGE

		Priest	Prophet
NATURE OF THEORY	Naturalistic	Robert K. Merton George C. Homans Peter M. Blau Lewis Coser Ralf Dahrendorf Gerhard Lenski Talcott Parsons	Amitai Etzioni
	Humanistic	Erving Goffman Herbert Blumer Harold Garfinkel Peter Berger	C. Wright Mills Daniel Bell Alvin Gouldner

FIGURE 1

quest for sociological theory is not a unified enterprise with all scholars in agreement as to its essence. Points of view and attempts to construct theory vary within the discipline.[5] There is no one theoretical model that appeals to all sociologists nor is there one that can be used to approach all questions of sociological interest. Underlying this variety are different assumptions about the nature of people and the nature of society. Given the basic differences in such assumptions, as well as differences in opinion as to the role that sociologists should play in the larger society, the debates in sociological theory will continue to rage. These controversies, rather than being received as problematic, may be seen as a sign of vitality and growth. Each theory contributes to the mosaic of a better understanding of men and women and the social world in which they live.

References _____

CATTON, WILLIAM R., JR.
  1966 *From Animistic to Naturalistic Sociology.* New York: McGraw-Hill Book Company.
DAHRENDORF, RALF
  1968 *Essays in the Theory of Society.* Stanford, Calif.: Stanford University Press.
FRIEDRICHS, ROBERT W.
  1970 *A Sociology of Sociology.* New York: The Free Press.

[5] It is our position that there is no way the diverse contemporary perspectives can be reconciled into a single theory. Any attempt to unify the theories presented in contemporary sociology fails to do justice to the often conflicting assumptions underlying them. For a detailed discussion of the conflicting and competing cognitions in sociological theory, see Strasser (1976).

GIDDENS, ANTHONY
  1976 *New Rules of Sociological Method: A Positive Critique of Interpretative Sociologies.* New York: Basic Books, Inc., Publishers.
GOULDNER, ALVIN W.
  1970 *The Coming Crisis of Western Sociology.* New York: Basic Books, Inc., Publishers.
HOROWITZ, IRVING L.
  1967 *The Rise and Fall of Project Camelot: Studies in the Relationship Between Social Science and Practical Politics.* Cambridge, Mass.: The MIT Press.
MARTINDALE, DON
  1974 *Sociological Theory and the Problem of Values.* Columbus, Ohio: Charles E. Merrill Publishing Company.
MULLINS, NICHOLAS C.
  1973 *Theories and Theory Groups in Contemporary American Sociology.* New York: Harper & Row, Publishers.
RUDNER, RICHARD S.
  1966 *Philosophy of Social Science.* Englewood Cliffs, N.J.: Prentice-Hall, Inc.
STRASSER, HERMAN
  1976 *The Normative Structure of Sociology.* London: Routledge & Kegan Paul Ltd.
WAGNER, HELMUT R.
  1963 "Types of Sociological Theory." *American Sociological Review* 28 (October):735–42.
  1964 "The Relationship Between Small and Large Sociological Theories." *American Journal of Sociology* 69 (May):571–84.
WRONG, DENNIS
  1976 *Skeptical Sociology.* New York: Columbia University Press.

CONTRIBUTORS TO
NATURALISTIC
SOCIOLOGICAL THEORY

part I _____

2

Structural Functionalism As Theory: The End of an Era?

> The aspects of sociology that have been taken to provide the signs and symptoms of crisis are of a familiar kind: a change and clash of doctrine accompanied by deepened tension, and sometimes abrasive conflict, among practitioners of the craft. The clash involves the strong claim that existing paradigms are incapable of handling problems they should, in principle, be capable of handling. (Merton, 1975:22)

The study of the structure and the functioning of society is a sociological concern permeating the works of founding fathers and contemporary theorists alike.[1] This approach has its sociological origins in the works of its founder, Auguste Comte. Sociology, according to Comte, was to study social statics (structure) as well as social dynamics (process/function). In discussing the structure of society, Comte accepted the premise that "society was like a living organism," but he made little attempt to develop this thesis. It was a British sociologist of the mid-nineteenth century, Herbert Spencer, who discussed specific differences and similarities between biological and social systems. Spencer's (1895:436–506) discussion of society as a living organism can be summarized in the following points.

---

[1] Functionalism, as a perspective, is certainly not a new approach to the study of society. In considering the question, "Who was the first functionalist?" Goode (1973:66) answered that this person was "very likely the first man who ever thought systematically and somewhat objectively about human society."

15

1. Both societies and living organisms experience growth.
2. Both "social bodies" and "living bodies" increase in structure as they increase in size; that is, the larger the social structure, the more parts there are, just as the larger the biological system, the more complex it becomes. A lower animal, such as an earthworm, has few distinguishable parts as compared with a higher-level animal, such as man.
3. The parts that develop in living bodies and in social bodies each serve a function or purpose: "they grow into unlike organs having unlike duties." The liver in higher animals has a structure and function different from the lungs; similarly, the family is an institutional structure with different purposes than the political system or the economic system.
4. In both living systems and social systems, a change in a part affects other parts and ultimately the whole. An alteration in the political system from a democratic to a totalitarian government affects the family, education, religion, and so on. The parts are interdependent.
5. The parts, although interdependent, are microstructures that may be studied separately. Thus the circulatory system or the respiratory system has been focused on by biological and medical specialities, just as the political system or the economic system may be the subject of intense scrutiny by political scientists and economists, respectively.

Spencer was cautious to point out that this was a model or an analogy that should not be reified. Societies are not exactly like living organisms; there is a very important difference. In an organic system, the parts are bound together in close contact; in societal systems, intense contact may not be apparent, with the parts being widely dispersed. The basic assumptions of sociological functionalist thought began in Comte and continued in Spencer's work, namely, that society may be visualized as a system made up of interdependent parts.

The rise of structural functionalism as a distinct perspective in sociology received its greatest impetus through the writings of the classical French sociologist, Émile Durkheim. Durkheim viewed modern society as an organic whole having a reality of its own. This whole has needs or functions that must be met by the member parts in order for it to exist in its "normal" state. If certain needs are not met, a "pathological" condition develops. For example, the economic function is one need that must be met in a modern society. If there is a severe fluctuation in the economy, it effects other parts of the system and ultimately the whole system. A severe depression may collapse the political system, alter the system of the family, and cause changes in the religious structure. Such a jolt in the system is viewed as a pathological state, which ultimately will work itself out so that a normal state may be regained. Contemporary functionalists have termed the "normal state" *equilibrium,* or a balanced system, whereas the "pathological state" represents disequilibrium or social change.

The functionalism of Durkheim was kept alive and expanded by two twentieth-century anthropologists, Bronislaw Malinowski and A. R. Radcliffe-Brown. Both Radcliffe-Brown and Malinowski were influenced by sociologists who view society as a living organism, and both contributed statements on the nature of functional analysis built on the organic model. In his defining of some of the basic concepts of functionalism in social science, Radcliffe-Brown's (1976:503–511) understanding of structural functionalism is basic to contemporary functional analysis:

> The *function* of any recurrent activity, such as the punishment of a crime, or a funeral ceremony, is the part it plays in the social life as a whole and therefore the contribution it makes to the maintenance of the structural continuity. (Radcliffe-Brown, 1976:505)

Malinowski's contribution to functionalism, although different in some ways from Radcliffe-Brown's,[2] supports this basic conception of functionalism. The anthropologist was to analyze culture by looking at "anthropological facts" and the part such facts play within the cultural system (Malinowski, 1976:511).

Although Durkheim was an influential sociologist on the European continent at the turn of the century, his writings did not have a great immediate impact on the course of American sociology. Sociology in the United States during the time Durkheim was active in France was heavily reform- and action-oriented, closely allied to the ministry and social work. As it developed as an academic discipline, American sociology pursued a path in social behaviorism, attempting to combine the study of both objective and subjective realities. This blend of sociology and psychology was not in the tradition of Durkheim, who in his intellectual works tried to demonstrate the need for sociology—a need that could not be met by psychology. It was not until the late 1930s that Durkheim began to have a direct impact on the course of the discipline in the United States. This was accomplished largely through the efforts of Talcott Parsons (see Chapter 8), who was influenced by his own study with functionalist anthropologist Malinowski. Parsons, in turn, influenced numerous students (including Robert Merton, whom we will discuss at length in this chapter), many of whom became leading sociologists in the United States.

In discussing the history of structural functionalism, Alvin Gouldner (1970:138–157) reminds his readers of the milieu in which Parsonian

---

[2] For a brief discussion of Malinowski's and Radcliffe-Brown's respective contributions to functional analysis, see Turner (1974:21–25).

functionalism developed. Although it was during the economic upheaval of the Great Depression both here and abroad, Parsons's functionalist theory revealed a faith in the revamping and the survival of the system. His was an optimistic social theory in the midst of a depression. But Parsons's optimism seemed vindicated by the success of the United States in World War II and the return to affluence following the Great Depression. For those living through seeming chaos in the system, followed by a recoupment and a further development, Parsons's optimistic theory rang true. As Gouldner observed (1970:142): "To see society in terms of firm, clearly defined structures, as Parsons' new theory did, was not dissonant with the collective experience, the shared personal reality of daily life."

Although structural functionalism had many leading spokespersons who were not always of one theoretical mind, it did propose that sociology was a study of social structures as units made up of interdependent parts. Coser and Rosenberg (1976:490) have observed that structural functionalists differ in their definitions of sociological concepts. It is possible, however, to produce a definition of the two key concepts based on standard sociological usage. *Structure* [3] refers to "a set of relatively stable and patterned social units" or a "system with relatively enduring patterns." Social institutions such as the family, religion, or government are examples of such structures or social systems. Each is made up of interdependent parts (norms governing status roles) according to some pattern. Coser and Rosenberg (1976:490) define function as "those consequences of any social activity which make for the adaptation or adjustment of a given structure of its component parts." *Function* thus refers to the dynamic process within the structure. It raises the question of how the social norms governing statuses enable the statuses to interrelate with each other and with the larger system.

For several decades structural functionalism reigned as the dominant paradigm or theoretical model in contemporary American sociology. In 1959 Kingsley Davis, in his presidential address to members of the American Sociological Association, went as far as to assert that structural func-

---

[3] Structural functionalists often use the concept *system* when discussing social institutions or structures. A system is simply an organization of interdependent parts that make up the whole. This can be illustrated by an electrical system (the subject matter of physics and engineering), a respiratory system (the concern of biologists), or a social system (the domain of sociologists). A social system includes a structure of interrelated statuses or positions held together through reciprocal role expectations. For example, the statuses of husband, wife, and child interrelate (because of expectations and performance of each of these roles) to form an institution we call the family. Structures of institutions are interrelated to form a larger social system, perhaps a town or a city. These systems are subject to change, but change is a very gradual process as the system tends toward equilibrium, or balance.

tionalism was indistinguishable from sociology itself. Within the past ten years, however, structural functional theory has come under increasing attack, forcing even its leading proponents to curb their assertions about its potential as a unifying theory in sociology. Robert K. Merton, who perhaps more than any other theorist has developed a clear and basic statement of functionalist theory, is one such proponent making more limited claims for this perspective. Acknowledging that this approach has led to an advancement in sociological knowledge, he also concedes that it may not be able to solve all sociological problems (Merton, 1975:25). At the same time, Merton remains a staunch defender of functional analysis, which he describes as generating "a problematics I find interesting and a way of thinking about problems I find more effective than any other I know" (Merton, 1975:30). Merton's structural functional model is, in the words of Coser and Rosenberg (1976:492), "the most sophisticated treatment of the functionalist approach now available."

The Salience of Social Structure in Merton's Functionalism

Merton's model for functionalist analysis is an outgrowth of his comprehensive knowledge of classical theorists. He has utilized writers as diverse as Max Weber, W. I. Thomas, and Émile Durkheim as a basis for his own work.[4] It might appear on the surface that Merton has no unified theory of his own, that he has simply written essays elaborating on aspects of classical writings. There is, however, a salient theme that runs through his articles, namely, *the importance of focusing on the social structure in sociological analysis.*

Merton's early works were heavily influenced by the German sociologist Max Weber, as demonstrated in his doctoral dissertation analyzing the rise of science in seventeenth-century England. In it Merton investigated the relationship between Protestantism and the rise of science in much the same way that Weber's classic work showed a correlation between the Protestant ethic and the rise of capitalism. In analyzing the

---

[4] For a discussion of Merton's reliance on classical European sociologists, see Coser (1975). Coser praises Merton's ability

> to hearken to many of the voices that spoke to him from the European past but never to pay homage at any shrine exclusively. . . . Merton has succeeded in transmitting to us a multifaceted and many colored fabric of ideas, both European and American; which he has managed to incorporate into the rich texture of his own lifework by harnessing them to his own creative purposes.

writings of the British Royal Society, Merton found that "certain elements of the Protestant ethic had pervaded the realm of scientific endeavors and had left their indelible stamp upon the attitudes of scientists toward their work" (Merton, 1936:3).

The influence of Weber may also be discerned in Merton's discussion of bureaucracy. Following Weber, Merton (1957:195–196) observes the following points regarding modern bureaucratic organization

1. It is a formal, rationally organized social structure.
2. It involves a clearly defined pattern of activities.
3. These activities are ideally related to the purposes of the organization.
4. The offices of the organization are integrated into the whole bureaucratic structure.
5. The statuses of the bureaucracy are hierarchized.
6. Obligations and privileges of persons in the bureaucracy are defined by limited and specific rules.
7. Authority resides in the office and not in the person.
8. Relations between persons are formally defined.

Large-scale organizations, including the student's own college or university, provide good illustrations of this model of bureaucracy described by both Weber and Merton.

Merton does not stop with a description of the structure but goes on to discuss personality as a product of this structural organization. The bureaucratic structure exerts pressure upon an individual to be "methodical, prudent, disciplined." This pressure sometimes leads to a blind following of regulations without regard for the purposes or functions for which the rules were originally established. Although such rules may function for the efficiency of the organization, they may also become negatively functional by causing overconformity. This may lead to a conflict or tension between the bureaucrat and the very persons his/her institution has been established to serve. Probably every student has encountered some problem with the bureaucracy of his/her own institution. Consider the student who asks to take out a book on reserve at the library when the library closes and promises to return it the next morning at library opening time. The librarian, who refuses the request, is following a rule that reserve books are not to circulate outside the library. The student is baffled because no one else will be using the book after the library has closed for the night. Yet rules are rules, and the personnel feel that they must adhere to them. The bureaucratic structure may create a personality type that adheres to the letter of the law rather than to the spirit in which the rules were established. Merton urges an empirical study of the impact of the bureaucracy on personality that would demonstrate the interdependence of social organization and personality formation.

The influence of the institution or structure on personal behavior is a theme that permeates Merton's writings. This theme is further illustrated by another of Merton's often-cited articles, which deals with the "self-fulfilling prophecy," an elaboration on Thomas's classic statement: "If men define situations as real, they are real in their consequences." Merton observes, "The self-fulfilling prophecy is, in the beginning, a *false* definition of the situation evoking a new behavior which makes the originally false conception come true" (Merton, 1957:423). Again, it is the structure that accounts for people's behavior. For example, the failure of the banks during the crash of 1929 was in part due to a definition of the situation that caused a run on the banks and ultimately a bank failure. Merton extends this same principle to evaluations of ethnic groups and the social effect of this evaluation by the in-group on the out-group. Just as the Federal Deposit Insurance Corporation and other bank legislation stilled public panic and prevented subsequent widespread bank failure, so too institutional controls may be used to regulate ethnic-group encounters. The self-fulfilling prophecy, Merton points out, "operates only in the absence of institutional controls."

This theme of the impact of the institution on the lives of its members is also illustrated in "Social Structure and Anomie" (1938). Here Merton attempts to demonstrate "how some social structures exert a definite pressure upon certain persons in the society to engage in nonconformist rather than conformist conduct" (Merton, 1938:672). *Anomie* (a concept taken from Durkheim's writings) is a result of a disjuncture between cultural goals and the institutionalized means available to obtain these goals. In our society, monetary success as evidenced by conspicuous consumption may be cited as a culturally defined goal. The institutionalized means may be a good-paying job. Anomie, says Merton, does not exist as long as the society provides the institutionalized means for obtaining the cultural goals it sets. What we have generally is a situation of *conformity*, where legitimate means are employed to secure the desired ends. But if cultural goals and institutional means do not coincide, *anomie* or nonconformity may result. Much of what we call "crime" is an example of anomie. The lower-class young man who turns to pushing drugs in order to buy a new sports car and flashy clothes, the bookkeeper who embezzles to provide a new, modern home for his family, and the college-educated call girl who has learned that luxuries could be part of her daily life through her illegal profession are all examples of nonconformity. The "ends" desired by the young man, the bookkeeper, and the college-educated girl are promulgated daily in advertisments in the media. The "means" to these ends are viewed as criminal or anomic behavior. Thus *anomie* is not a psychological concept to be explained through psychological theory; rather it is a cultural and structural problem requiring a sociological explanation.

Although Merton's sociological interests are varied, we have attempted to illustrate how many of his essays have been concerned with the focus on structural concerns. His interpretation of classical theorists with a focus on social structure is but one demonstration of his structural orientation. Another is Merton's classic paradigm for functional analysis.

Merton's Paradigm for Functional Analysis

As we have seen in Chapter 1, those committed to naturalistic theory emphasize the need for precision in constructing theory. Of utmost importance is a precise definition of concepts that enable the construction of clearly stated hypotheses. Merton begins his treatment of functional analysis by pointing out its imprecise vocabulary as well as some ambiguous assumptions or postulates that are contained in this theory. Merton laments the fact that "too often a single term has been used to symbolize different concepts, just as the same concept has been symbolized by different terms" (Merton, 1967:74). Concepts must be defined clearly if they are to serve as building blocks for testable propositions. Moreover, propositions must be stated clearly and without ambiguity. Merton's model attempts to define some basic analytical concepts for functional analysis and to clear up some of the ambiguity found in functionalist postulates.

Merton cites three *prevailing postulates* [5] in functional analysis and then proceeds to modify each. The first postulate is the functional unity of society and may be defined as "a condition in which all parts of the social system work together with a sufficient degree of harmony or internal consistency, i.e. without producing persistent conflicts which can neither be resolved or regulated" (Merton, 1967:80). Merton asserts that complete functional unity of a society is "repeatedly contrary to fact." He cites several examples of social usages that may be *functional* for one

[5] Merton asserts that these postulates have been held by functionalists but that they are "debatable and unnecessary to the functional orientation" (1967:79). Merton believes that Radcliffe-Brown has most explicitly stated the postulate of the functional unity of society and cites Malinowski for contributing to the postulates of universal functionalism and indispensability. He does not limit his critique to these two anthropologists. Merton believes that the postulates have been adopted by both sociology and anthropology often enough to warrant criticism.

group (that is, contributing to the integration and cohesion of the group) while *dysfunctional* (contributing to a group's breakdown) to another. For example, religion had been viewed by the founding fathers of sociology as an important (if not essential) ingredient in society. We have numerous instances where religion has furthered the cohesiveness of a society, but we also have cases where religion has had disintegrative consequences. The Catholics and Protestants fighting each other on the streets of Belfast certainly give little evidence of the "functional unity" brought about through religion. Merton's paradigm would assert that dysfunctions (disintegrative elements) may not be ignored just because one is fascinated by the positive functions (integrative elements). He also notes that what is functional for one group (e.g., the Catholic society or the Protestant society in Belfast) may not be functional for the whole (the city of Belfast). The boundaries of the group being analyzed must thus be specified.

The second postulate, that of universal functionalism, is related to the first. Universal functionalism "holds that all standardized social or cultural forms have positive functions" (Merton, 1967:84). As we have already seen, Merton introduces the concept of *dysfunction* as well as *positive function*. Few social practices are unequivocally dysfunctional. Merton suggests that the cultural elements be considered according to a *net balance of functional consequences*, which weigh both positive and negative functions. In terms of our example of religion in Northern Ireland, a functionalist must seek to examine both its positive and negative functions and then must determine whether the balance reveals a primarily negative or a primarily positive function.

The third postulate, of *indispensability*, completes the trio. It states that "in every type of civilization, every custom, material object idea, and belief fulfills some vital function, has some task to accomplish, represents an indispensable part within a working whole" (Merton, 1967:86). Merton observes that this postulate is ambiguous. It is not clear whether the function (a societal need, such as the reproduction of new members) or the item (a norm, such as the nuclear family) is indispensable. Merton states:

> In short, the postulate of indispensability as it is ordinarily stated contains two related, but distinguishable, assertions. First, it is assumed that there are certain functions which are indispensable in the sense that, unless they are performed, the society (or group or individual) will not persist. This, then, sets forth a concept of functional prerequisites or preconditions functionally necessary for a society, and we shall have occasion to examine this concept in some detail. Second, and this is quite another matter, it is assumed that certain cultural or social forms are indispensable for fulfilling each of these functions. (Merton, 1967:87)

The first, that of functional prerequisites, must be empirically tested rather than simply assumed before it is incorporated into theory. In response to the second, Merton introduces the concept of *functional alternatives*. In other words, one functional item may be replaced or substituted by another, and the societal need will still be met.

An example may enable the student to better understand the problem of a crude postulate of indispensability. Even where a functional imperative is established (and there are few instances that cannot be challenged), more than one cultural item may be used to meet the societal need. The functional prerequisite of biological reproduction is essential, in the final analysis, to all societal groups. People grow old, die, and must be replaced for the society to continue. The cultural item through which this reproduction is achieved, however, does vary. Even the norm of reproduction within some type of marriage is being challenged in the 1970s, as some women express the desire for motherhood without the institutional ties of marriage.

In challenging these three postulates Merton is saying that (1) we cannot assume the complete integration of society; (2) we must acknowledge the dysfunctional as well as the positively functional consequences of a cultural item; and (3) the possibility of functional alternatives must be considered in any functional analysis.

In addition to the postulates refuted above, Merton notes still another problem in crude functionalism, specifically the confusion between "conscious motivations" and "objective consequences." In a Durkheim-like fashion, Merton asserts that the prime concern of the sociologist is not motivation but objective consequences. These consequences, however, may be *manifest* or *latent:* "Manifest functions are those objective consequences contributing to the adjustment or adaptation of the system which are intended and recognized by participants in the system; latent functions, correctively, being those which are neither intended nor recognized" (Merton, 1967:115). The concern of research has typically been directed toward the study of manifest functions, but study of manifest functions, to the neglect of latent functions, is misleading. There are numerous instances where the identification of the manifest function has not been nearly as sociologically significant as the discussion of latent consequences. For example, Veblen's theory of "conspicuous consumption" (where liberal spending of money for luxuries enhances one's status) demonstrates the importance of identifying latent functions. Although the manifest function of purchasing an automobile might be transportation to and from work, purchasing a Mercedes Benz serves a latent function of displaying wealth and status in a society. Any cultural practice may be analyzed from the perspective of latent as well as manifest functions. Merton himself uses the example of a political machine. Political machines, which tend to block the free operation of a democratic government, have been viewed dysfunctionally; that is, they make a negative contribution to local government by hampering the democratic process. Although this may be true on the manifest level, there are latent functions that have been ignored in such an analysis. For example, during the 1930s, when political machines were at their height, they served the local people who were hard hit by the Depression. The political machine provided many of the services that are today performed by welfare agencies. The latent function in this example may be more sociologically important than the manifest dysfunction. A sound functionalist analysis will not only observe functions and dysfunctions but will also be alert for latent as well as manifest functions.

After reviewing the problems of crude functionalist analysis, Merton presents a compact model or paradigm to be used in avoiding such pitfalls. This paradigm may be used to guide a functionalist by raising questions to be answered in analyses. Such questions include:

1. What is the nature of the system under analysis? Is it a particular cultural or ethnic group, a small group (such as a friendship group or a family), or a larger organization (such as a bureaucracy)? This is important to determine, for, as we have seen, what may be functional for one group need not be functional for another.
2. Are there latent as well as manifest functions that are to be considered in the net balance of consequences? As we have illustrated through Merton's example of the political machine, functions are not always intended, nor are they necessarily recognized by the participants in a system.
3. How can we determine whether a "functional requirement" exists for a particular system? Merton is unwilling to assume that all systems have a set of functional needs that must be met for a system to survive. In raising this query, Merton alerts functional analysts to the importance of watching for functional alternatives.
4. Does the interest of functionalists in the issue of order prevent them from seeing disequilibrium? In introducing the concept of dysfunction, as well as positive function, Merton advises functionalists that social change is possible and probable when a cultural practice or norm works against the social system. Not only are some items dysfunctional, but they may well allow for change in the group under study.

What Merton's paradigm attempts to do in addition to clarifying concepts and exposing fallacies in crude functionalism is to raise some questions that must be answered by those pursuing functionalist analysis. In order to answer them, the functionalist must remember that what may be functional for one group may be dysfunctional for another. Moreover the sociologist must take care not to overlook latent functions while being blinded by the more obvious manifest ones. In analyzing the functionality of a practice, a researcher must be alert to the probability of a norm's having multiple functions. Because cultural practice may be neither totally integrating nor disintegrating, assessment of its functionality must be viewed in terms of a net balance of consequences.

Critique of Functionalism

Merton first developed his paradigm in 1948 to encourage research using structural functional theory. His presentation became the model for the development of theory—theory ideally wed to sociological research. Structural functionalism, sometimes unfairly, has come under attack from numerous sources, including conflict theorists and social psychologists. We will consider some of the general assumptions asserted to be inherent in functionalism and the criticism that these assumptions generate. We will then relate these assumptions to Mertonian functionalism.

Structural functionalism, like all theory, rests on particular assumptions about the nature of society and the nature of human beings. These assumptions tend to be conservative; that is, they focus on the existing social structure rather than on social change. Society is assumed to be comprised of parts that are interrelated in an orderly fashion. Although Merton's paradigmatic scheme is an improvement over earlier functionalism, it still exaggerates the unity, stability, and harmony of social systems (for a critique see Zeitlin, 1973). This problem became particularly apparent in the 1960s, when cities were burning, students were rioting, workers were striking, and war was raging. Unity, stability, and harmony did not appear to be characteristic of American society.

Although Merton has argued that "functional analysis may involve no *intrinsic* ideological commitment although, like other forms of sociological analysis, it can be infused with any one of a wide range of ideological values" (Merton, 1967:93), the fact is that structural functionalism has tended to be a conservative social theory. Using its descriptive powers, it has focused on the structure of the society, emphasizing the status quo. Because of this emphasis on a harmonious structure, one leading conflict theorist, Ralf Dahrendorf (whom we will discuss in Chapter 6), termed functionalism a study of Utopia rather than reality. Functionalism, despite claims to the contrary, did not adequately reflect the conflict side of society.

Not only does structural functionalism rest upon certain assumptions about an orderly society, but it also reflects certain assumptions about the nature of people. In functionalism, human beings are treated as abstractions that occupy status or roles that form institutions or social structures. In its extreme form, structural functionalism implicitly treats human beings as enacting a predesignated script according to established norms or rules of society. In the Durkheimian tradition of avoiding psychological reductionism, persons are viewed as determined products of norms and the institutions that enshrine these norms. This view has led to criticism of sociology's "oversocialized conception of man" (Wrong, 1961) and the admonition to "bring men back" into sociological analysis (Homans, 1964). The person presented by functionalism is determined by social constraints or norms with little room for creativity and choice.

Structural functionalism, as a dominant sociological perspective, has drawn these and other attacks from its critics—so much so that sociologists are becoming reluctant to wear its theoretical label.[6] It may well be that no single functionalist really held to all the assertions made in its name, meaning that some of the criticisms of its conservative bias and inability to deal with change were directed against a composite theory that never existed in reality. This assertion takes on some credence as we go on to consider Merton's own image of people, of society, and of sociological theory.

Merton, like most naturalistic sociological theorists, holds that persons are shaped by the social structures in which they live. We have attempted to emphasize the importance Merton attaches to the analysis of social structure. Merton's image of people, however, is not one of rigid determinism. As Stinchcombe (1975:12) has observed, "the core process that Merton conceives as central to social structure is *the choice between socially structured alternatives*." In other words, there are patterns of behavior that are part of the institutional order (thus allowing sociology to develop as a science), and there are also alternatives (allowing for some voluntarism on the part of persons). People have some choices in their actions; these alternatives, however, are socially established with corresponding normative demands. Merton's actors, therefore, are neither free spirits doing as they please nor automated robots whose actions are completely predetermined. As Coser comments (1975:98):

> Merton's actors face role- and status-sets with often contradictory expectations and are continuously navigating between them. They attempt continuously to avoid the Scylla of overconformity and the Charybdis of deviance, while often falling prey to the lures of one or another.

[6] In an essay contribution to a book honoring Merton, Talcott Parsons pointed out Merton's objection to the phrase "structural functionalism." "He particularly did not like having it labeled an 'ism' and suggested that the simple descriptive phrase 'functional analysis' was more appropriate" (Parsons, 1975:67). Parsons concurs with Merton, asserting that functional analysis is an integral part of all sociological theory.

This statement may be illustrated by Merton's treatment of anomie as well as by his discussion of the bureaucratic personality, both of which have been briefly discussed in this chapter.

Merton's conception of society is not unlike that of a founding father of structural functional analysis, namely, Émile Durkheim. Social structures are integrated and their norms control their members. They do exist and are properly the subject matter of sociology. This may be seen in the priority Merton gives to structural analysis in sociology. But Merton's social structure does not assume the static nature deplored by many critics of structural functionalism. Merton's (1975:31–37) stipulations for structural analysis include an acknowledgment (1) that "social structures generate social conflict by being differentiated," (2) "that *sociological ambivalence* is built into normative structures in the form of incompatible patterned expectations," and (3) "that social structures generate both change within the structure and change of the structure." Although Merton's social structure clearly has a reality of its own—a reality that influences those who occupy the status roles that comprise it—it is not static. It is dynamic in its allowance for structural sources of conflict and deviant behavior. This principle may be demonstrated by Merton's treatment of "dysfunction" and "anomie" as catalysts of change—both concepts having been discussed earlier in this chapter.

Merton recognizes that his proposed structural functional analysis is but one approach to sociology, albeit the best one available. He acknowledges that the *ideal* is a unified comprehensive theory but feels there are problems "when the ideal is mistaken for the current thing" (Merton, 1975:29). Although Merton remains committed to the development of naturalistic sociological theory in general and structural functional analysis in particular, he cautions against premature closure in accepting a single theoretical paradigm. As Merton (1975:28) expresses his position:

> Were I called in as a consulting physician to review not only the diagnosis but also the recommended therapy, my opinion would be this: that the chronic crisis of sociology, with its diversity, competition and clash of doctrine, seems preferable to the therapy sometimes proposed for handling the acute crisis, namely, the prescription of a single theoretical perspective that promises to provide full and exclusive access to sociological truth.

Summary

Functionalism was, until recently, the dominant perspective in American sociological theory. Its tradition can be traced back to the founder of sociology, Auguste Comte, through Herbert Spencer and Émile Durkheim. Malinowski and Radcliffe-Brown, two distinguished anthropologists, built on Durkheim's theories and, in turn, influenced the American sociologist Talcott Parsons. As a young instructor at Harvard, Parsons introduced his student Robert K. Merton to the works of Émile Durkheim and to the functionalist perspective.

Merton has spent his sociological career in providing a structural functionalist bent for earlier sociological writings and in presenting a model or paradigm for structural functional analysis. He refuted postulates of crude functionalism that promulgated notions of the "functional unity of society," "universal functionalism," and "indispensability." Merton introduced the concepts of dysfunctions, functional alternatives, net balance of functional consequences, and manifest and latent functions, which he wove into a functionalist paradigm. Although this model moves beyond the postulates of early functionalism, problems still remain. Society is treated as an entity in and of itself, greater than and different from the sum of its parts. The individual is still left in an abstract position as occupant of status roles that comprise the structure. This abstractness contributes to charges that the paradigm is not testable.

George C. Homans, himself a former functionalist, argues that what sociology must do to get away from unreal abstractions is to return to seemingly obvious facts. Homans advocates a return to a study of human behavior grounded in psychological theory as a base upon which sociological theory is to build. The work of Homans and its relation to functionalism is the subject of the following chapter.

References

COSER, LEWIS
  1975 "Merton and the European Sociological Tradition." Pp. 85–100 in
       Lewis Coser (Ed.), *The Idea of Social Structure*. New York: Harcourt
       Brace Jovanovich, Inc.
COSER, LEWIS A., and BERNARD ROSENBERG
  1976 "Structure and Function." Pp. 490–492 in Lewis A. Coser and Bernard
       Rosenberg (Eds.), *Sociological Theory: A Book of Readings* (4th ed.).
       New York: Macmillan Publishing Co., Inc.
DAVIS, KINGSLEY
  1959 "The Myth of Functional Analysis as a Special Method in Sociology
       and Anthropology." *American Sociological Review* 24 (December):
       757–772.
GOODE, WILLIAM J.
  1973 *Explorations in Social Theory*. New York: Oxford University Press.
GOULDNER, ALVIN W.
  1970 *The Coming Crisis of Western Sociology*. New York: Basic Books, Inc.,
       Publishers.

HOMANS, GEORGE C.
    1964 "Bringing Men Back In." *American Sociological Review* 29 (December):809–818.
MALINOWSKI, BRONISLAW
    1976 "Functionalism in Anthropology." Pp. 511–524 in Lewis A. Coser and Bernard Rosenberg (Eds.), *Sociological Theory: A Book of Readings* (4th ed.). New York: Macmillan Publishing Co., Inc.
MARTINDALE, DON
    1960 *The Nature and Types of Sociological Theory*. Boston: Houghton Mifflin Company.
MERTON, ROBERT K.
    1936 "Puritanism, Pietism, and Science." *Sociological Review* 28 (January): 1–30.
    1938 "Social Structure and Anomie." *American Sociological Review* 3 (October):672–682.
    1957 *Social Theory and Social Structure*. London: The Free Press of Glencoe.
    1967 *On Theoretical Sociology*. New York: The Free Press.
    1973 *The Sociology of Science*. Chicago: University of Chicago Press.
    1975 "Structural Analysis in Sociology." Pp. 21–52 in Peter M. Blau (Ed.), *Approaches to the Study of Social Structure*. New York: The Free Press.
PARSONS, TALCOTT
    1975 " 'Structural-Functional' Theory in Sociology." Pp. 67–83 in Lewis A. Coser (Ed.), *The Idea of Social Structure*. New York: Harcourt Brace Jovanovich, Inc.
RADCLIFFE-BROWN, A. R.
    1976 "On the Concept of Function in Social Science." Pp. 503–511 in Lewis A. Coser and Bernard Rosenberg (Eds.), *Sociological Theory: A Book of Readings* (4th ed.). New York: Macmillan Publishing Co., Inc.
SPENCER, HERBERT
    1895 *Synthetic Philosophy*. New York: D. Appleton and Company.
STINCHCOMBE, ARTHUR
    1975 "Merton's Theory of Social Structure." Pp. 9–20 in Lewis A. Coser (Ed.), *The Ideal of Social Structure*. New York: Harcourt Brace Jovanovich, Inc.
STRASSER, HERMANN
    1976 *The Normative Structure of Sociology*. London: Routledge and Kegan Paul.
TURNER, JONATHAN H.
    1974 *The Structure of Sociological Theory*. Homewood, Ill.: The Dorsey Press.
WRONG, DENNIS
    1961 "The Oversocialized Conception of Man in Modern Sociology." *American Sociological Review* 26 (April):183–193.
ZEITLIN, IRVING M.
    1973 *Rethinking Sociology: A Critique of Contemporary Theory*. New York: Appleton-Century-Crofts.

3

Behavioral-Exchange Theory: A Proposed Explanation for Social Structure

If sociology is a science, it must take seriously one of the jobs of any science, which is that of providing explanations for the empirical relations it discovers. An explanation is a theory, and it takes the form of a deductive system. With all its talk about theory, the functionalist school did not take the job of theory seriously enough. It did not ask itself what a theory was, and it never produced a functional theory that was in fact an explanation. . . . If a serious effort is made to construct theories that will even begin to explain social phenomena, it turns out that their general propositions are not about the equilibrium of societies but about the behavior of men. (Homans, 1964:818)

As evidenced from this statement of George C. Homans, functionalist theory, although providing descriptions of social reality, failed to develop adequate explanations for structural developments. In fairness to functionalism, however, the seeds for such explanations may be found in the concept of *reciprocity*, which has been an important concept in sociology for functionalists as well as for nonfunctionalists. This term has been utilized by early anthropologists—including Malinowski, to whom American functionalism is greatly indebted. This concept, moreover, is central to Homans's own theory of social exchange. Few concepts, however, have been acknowledged so universally yet remained so obscure and ambiguous in sociological usage (see Gouldner, 1960, for a theoretical development of the concept of reciprocity).

This ambiguity has given rise to irreconcilable differences within exchange theory, a perspective that has developed around the concept of reciprocity. It is important to note at the outset that there is no single theory of social exchange; rather there are several theories based on the phenomenon of reciprocal expectations, each rooted in somewhat different assumptions about the nature of people, society, and social science. (For a detailed discussion of different theories of social exchange see Heath, 1976.) Yet in spite of basic differences in perspectives, theories of social exchange do share some common assumptions about the nature of social interaction.

Social-exchange theories are based upon an elementary principle in economic transactions: people provide goods or services and expect to receive desired goods or services in return. Exchange theorists share the simple assumption that social interaction is analogous to economic transactions. They acknowledge, however, that social exchange cannot always be measured in terms of dollars and cents, for in social transactions both the tangible and the intangible are exchanged. For example, a worker interacting with co-workers in a factory may cooperate extensively hoping to attain the tangible reward of a large Christmas bonus. At the same time, however, intangible rewards of friendship and goodwill may elicit similar behavior even when economic hard times make the bonus unlikely. The model of reciprocity remains, with people giving and expecting to receive in return.

Although the rudiments of exchange theory may be found in the writings of functionalist anthropologists and sociologists,[1] the full-scale development of a sociological theory of exchange is credited to George C. Homans, with subsequent modifications made by Peter M. Blau. Homans was eager to correct what he felt were deficiencies in functionalist theory. One of the criticisms of functionalism that we discussed in the last chapter was its neglect of the study of people in society. The focus of functionalism rests with either large or small systems, their organization or structure, and their purposes or functions. The individual is dealt with simply as filling a status or position and as performing a role dictated by this status or position. This stress on the structure stems from the Durkheimian tradition, which attempted to demonstrate the need for sociology as a discipline apart from psychology. Thus structural functionalism rep-

---

[1] For a discussion of exchange theory and its relation to anthropological functionalism, see Ekeh (1974:83ff.). Some commentators on sociological theory view exchange theory as a simple offshoot of structural functionalism. Some theories of exchange do warrant this assumption. There are, however, vast differences among the assumptions found in the exchange theory of behaviorist George C. Homans (the theorist dealt with in this chapter), the structural exchange theory of Peter M. Blau (Chapter 4), and the more social psychological orientation of J. W. Thibaut and H. H. Kelley (1959).

resented a kind of pure sociology as opposed to the hybrid of sociology and psychology that played an important part in the development of American sociology during the 1920s and the 1930s. As the pendulum swung away from social psychology, it reached the opposite extreme of downplaying the importance of people as actors in society. Exchange theory was one attempt to move the pendulum of theory away from extreme sociologism and toward a reevaluation of the role of the individual in the social system.[2]

What Homans emphasized was the need to bring men and women back into sociological analysis. Beginning his career as a structural functionalist, Homans broke with this theoretical perspective during the 1950s. We will briefly examine Homans's functionalism and his criticisms of this approach before considering his contribution to a behavioral-exchange theory.

The Human Group: *Homans's Contribution to Functionalist Theory*

As we have already noted, Homans began his career in the structural functionalist tradition that was assuming theoretical dominance during the 1940s. Homans's work *The Human Group* (1950) focused on the abstract concept of system as represented by concrete studies of small groups, with an interest in the structural composition and the operation of such groups. The work was widely acclaimed as a leading functionalist treatise. Of it Robert K. Merton (1950:xxiii) wrote, "not since Simmel's pioneering analysis of almost half a century ago has any single work contributed so much to a sociological theory of the structure, processes, and functions of small groups as George C. Homans's *The Human Group*." Yet despite such praise and acclaim, Homans broke with the functionalist tradition because of its failure to explain social phenomena.

Homans's functional analysis of groups is essentially of primary groups, rather than larger secondary groups or organizations. Homans

---

[2] Although the individual was brought into sociological theory again by behavioral exchange theory, as we shall see, the image of man was much in accord with the deterministic image presented in structural functionalism. This type of thinking led to Wrong's (1961) criticism of the "oversocialized conception of man" in contemporary sociological theory. Both functionalism and exchange theory appear to share a view of the person who is presented with choices that are structurally determined, leaving little room, if any, for creative action.

(1950:1) defines a *group* as "a number of persons who communicate with one another often over a span of time, and who are few enough so that each person is able to communicate with all the others, not at secondhand, through other people, but face-to-face." This definition is derived from the classic sociologist Charles Horton Cooley's concept of "primary group," and it represents one dimension of structural organization. Studies already existed on various groups fitting this definition, and Homans utilized five such studies to develop his sociological theory of small groups.[3]

Homans explicitly describes his method of constructing scientific theory in *The Human Group*. First, it represented a functionalist perspective in that Homans views the group as an organic whole, made up of interdependent parts. This whole or social system exists within a larger environmental system. Second, the theory must be somewhat abstract and removed from individual concrete examples. In the creation of such a theory, some concrete facts will inevitably be left out in the attempts to develop a theory that may be generalized beyond the single phenomenon under study. Third, a theory is arrived at *inductively;* that is, specific facts are used (in this case, data from studies of five small groups) to build a more general theory applicable to all groups. This inductive method is in contrast to *deduction* (which Homans employed in his later behaviorist theory of exchange), in which the theorist develops a general theory logically, setting forth propositions that remain to be tested through empirical observations. Homans thus begins with specific empirical facts and develops a more general theory of human groups from these facts.

Even in such inductive analysis, however, a conceptual vocabulary must be agreed on. As we saw in Chapter 1, concepts are the blocks out of which propositions are made; propositions are the matter from which theories are derived. Homans, in accordance with procedures of theory construction, advances a conceptual scheme that defines his key concepts. He then uses the vocabulary he had advanced to analyze each of the five studies in an attempt to derive propositions from the empirical studies selected.

We will briefly report on Homans's use of one study—that of the bank wiring room—as an illustration of his functionalist analysis. In this study, fourteen workers were selected from the larger Western Electric Company for a phase of the research project. In this project the work habits and the friendship patterns of the workers were closely observed and subjected to research analysis. Homans reconsiders the data presented

[3] The studies used are the bank wiring observation room from Roethlisberger and Dickson (1939); the Norton Street gang from Whyte (1943); the family in Tikopia from Firth (1936); the social disintegration of Hilltown from Hatch (1948); and the social conflict in an electrical equipment company from Arensberg and Macgregor (1942).

in this research report with an eye toward structural configurations that may apply to other groups besides that of the bank wiring room.

Homans's analysis, based on available data from the group, yields a description of what he terms the *internal system* and the *external system*. The *internal system* is the whole group made up of member parts, in this case the fourteen members of the bank wiring room. The *external system* is the layout of the room within which a group works. The internal system is thus the group as a whole, and the external system consists of the separation of the internal system (which is under close consideration) from its larger environment. The behavior of individuals within the internal system is guided by *norms*, that is, ideas "that can be put in the form of a statement specifying what members or other men should do, ought to do, are expected to do, under given circumstances" (Homans, 1950:130). Conformity to the group's norms is rewarded; nonconformity is punished.

The intended result of analyzing the bank wiring room was the development of some structurally oriented hypotheses regarding group formation and elaboration. After such hypotheses were induced from the study of the bank wiring room, they were reconsidered and modified in light of reported results of two other existing small-group studies chosen by Homans for inclusion in *The Human Group*. These hypotheses were to be general enough for all groups and were to be interrelated in an attempt to derive a unified theory of the structure and functioning of groups.

It is clear that for Homans all of society is organized into systems, based on the smallest of social systems, the group. Studying small groups, as Homans has done, leads to an understanding of larger groups and civilizations. For Homans, the laws of development, structure, and functioning of civilizations are identical to the laws operating in smaller groups. The advantage of studying smaller groups, such as those used in *The Human Group*, is that such groups can be much more easily researched than larger groups or entire civilizations.

Homans, although recognizing the contribution of functional analysis, later became critical of the functionalist approach, including his own failure "to explain much of anything" (Homans, 1974:6). What functionalism tried to do was to classify empirical observations (through the development of precise concepts) and to develop propositions describing the interrelationship of such classificatory concepts. Homans (1974:7) asserted that functionalism provided "some degree of intellectual organization" but that theory must go beyond such limited attempts. As he observed, "Any science has two main jobs to do: discovery and explanation. By the first we judge whether it is a science, by the second, how successful a science it is " (Homans, 1969:20). Structural functionalism thus represented an attempt to discover and describe, but it failed to explain. In the late 1950s, Homans modified his theory to include provisions for what he hoped would be the explanation of social structure through the principle of social exchange.

Exchange Theory: The Movement from Durkheim to Psychological Reductionism

Homans, in departing from structural functionalism, began to stress the importance of psychology to the explanation of social phenomena. In doing so, he was challenging the writings of sociology's classic scholar, Émile Durkheim. Durkheim spent much of his academic career demonstrating that sociology was an independent discipline. Its social facts (or variables) could not be explained by psychology; therefore sociology could not be reduced to a subfield of psychology. Durkheim's taboo against psychological reductionism is still very much alive today, but Homans set out to challenge this norm by arguing that all explanations of social behavior are at their roots psychological ones.

Yet it is not with psychology but with economics that Homans begins his theory. Homans's exchange theory rests on the assumption that persons engage in behavior either to earn rewards or to escape punishments. This exchange of behavior for reward is a basic principle of simple economic transactions. A person may exchange his or her services for a weekly paycheck. With this money, a person may purchase groceries, pay the rent, and buy membership in a tennis club. Each of these expenditures may be looked upon as an example of economic exchange. Homans views all social behavior—not just economic behavior—as a result of such exchange. For example, employment not only provides the extrinsic reward of a salary but may also provide the intrinsic rewards of friendship, satisfaction, and enhanced self-esteem. It also enables the worker to avoid the stigma of being unemployed. Homans assumes that people act in such a way as to minimize cost (e.g., punishment) and to enhance profits (i.e., the rewards minus any costs).

Economics may describe exchange relationships and sociology may describe social structures in which exchange takes place, but it is psychology that holds the key to explanation. The specific theory in psychology that Homans found suitable for explaining social structure is one of behavioral psychology, specifically the formulations of B. F. Skinner. Homans (1962:48) notes the following:

It [Skinner's theoretical propositions] consisted of contingent propositions and not just of categories. The propositions were ordinary causal statements, not teleological ones. They were of high order; whatever the future might hold, they could not at the moment be derived from more general propositions. They were of wide scope: they could be used to explain many findings other than those I was interested in. . . . Of course behavioral psychology could not explain everything, but I became convinced that its failures could be accounted for by lack of data or by the difficulties in tracing out long and complex causal chains rather than by any inherent inapplicability of its propositions. Sociology *was*, Durkheim to the contrary, a corollary of psychology.

Clearly Homans has utmost faith in the ability of behavioral psychology to meet the prerequisite of any scientific theory, namely, explanation.

Skinnerian behaviorism is, of course, but one particular brand of psychology. It asserts that an understanding of animal behavior would yield an understanding of human behavior. Behaviorists are uncomfortable with concepts such as mentality because it is impossible to observe the mind directly. Just as animals seek positive rewards and seek to avoid punishment, so do human animals seek to maximize profits and minimize costs. For exchange theorist Homans, it is not simply the functionalist status-role that provides the link between the individual and his/her structure; rather such structures or institutions are comprised of individuals in the process of exchanging both material and nonmaterial goods (Homans, 1958:597–606).

Homans believes that this process of exchange may be explained through five interrelated propositional statements borrowed from Skinnerian psychology. They are the success, stimulus, value, deprivation–satiation, and approval–aggression propositions. Through them much social behavior may be explained. Each proposition warrants some consideration.

The Success Proposition:

For all actions taken by persons, the more often a particular action of a person is rewarded, the more likely the person is to perform that action. (Homans, 1974:16)

In this proposition, Homans asserts that once a person succeeds in obtaining a reward (or in avoiding punishment), he/she is apt to repeat that action. Psychologist B. F. Skinner found this principle to hold in his study of the behavior of pigeons who were rewarded with corn when pecking at a particular object. Homans believes that this same elementary principle applies to human action. Daily life is made up of behavior that persons have found rewarding. We can expect a paycheck at the end of a hard week of work, we learn that studying for exams results in better grades, or we find that flashing a smile often elicits a warm greeting in return. Yet this proposition must be modified with others. Obviously not all individuals choose to work, not all students study before midterms, and not everyone smiles. Of itself, the success proposition is merely a half-truth that would not be able to withstand empirical testing.

The Stimulus Proposition:

> If in the past the occurrence of a particular stimulus, or set of stimuli, has been the occasion on which a person's action has been rewarded, then the more similar the present stimuli are to the past ones, the more likely the person is to perform the action, or some similar action, now. (Homans, 1974:22–23)

What the stimulus proposition addresses is the object or action that elicits the desired reward. Let us use a student who desires a good grade for this course to illustrate the proposition. The student has learned that he/she must keep up with coursework and set aside several hours for concentrated study in order to do well in an exam. Our student has specifically found it beneficial to devote the previous day to studying alone prior to taking an exam. He/she has been rewarded in the past with good grades and recognizes the importance of studying as the stimulus that brings about the desired reward. Over the years, however, the student has learned that he/she may do the time of concentrated study two days before the exam and with the same results as studying the day before, but he/she has also found that group study sessions are not beneficial. If the student has the opportunity of choosing a group study session or individual study, he/she would probably select the stimulus of an individual study session. Stimuli may be more or less similar to past ones, and Homans's proposition suggests that more similar ones are selected to bring about desired rewards. In this case, individual study (done either one or two days before an exam) is preferable to the dissimilar stimulus of group study.

The Value Proposition:

> The more valuable to a person is the result of his action, the more likely he is to perform the action. (Homans, 1974:25)

This proposition deals specifically with the rewards or punishments that result from action. The success proposition informs us that a student will study in order to earn good grades. The stimulus proposition acknowledges that particular kinds of studying may be more likely to bring about success than others. What the value proposition addresses is the degree to which a person desires the reward offered by the stimulus. Let us assume that our student has the opportunity to see a favorite performer in concert at the same time that he/she has set aside for study. Let us also assume that his/her schedule is such that if studying is not done at that time, no other block of time is available. The question then becomes one of values: Is a good test grade more valuable to the student than the enjoyment of attending the concert? Homans's proposition assumes that the student will perform the action that brings the desired reward.

The Deprivation–Satiation Proposition:

The more often in the recent past a person has received a particular reward, the less valuable any further unit of that reward becomes for him. (Homans, 1974:29)

The deprivation–satiation proposition further modifies the conditions under which the performance of a particular action is likely. If we continue the example provided for the value proposition, we will see that this is the case. The value proposition does not specify why a student might find attending a concert preferable to obtaining a good grade on an exam. What Homans suggests is that being either deprived or satiated with a particular reward holds the explanatory key. Our student may already have four high marks for exams in the course and may feel that another high grade would not be as rewarding as this rare opportunity to attend the concert. In this case, he/she would find attending the concert more rewarding than obtaining a good grade on one exam. Perhaps if this were the first exam for that particular course, a good grade would be more desirable than attending the concert. In other words, human beings, like animals, can either be hungry for a particular reward or filled to the point of not caring for it. Deprivation–satiation has a bearing on what it is that we value at a particular time.

The Aggression–Approval Proposition:

When a person's action does not receive the reward he expected, or receives punishment he did not expect, he will be angry; he becomes more likely to perform aggressive behavior, and the results of such behavior become more valuable to him. . . . When a person's action receives reward he expected, especially a greater reward than he expected, or does not receive punishment he expected, he will be pleased; he becomes more likely to perform approving behavior, and the results of such behavior become more valuable to him. (Homans, 1974:37, 39)

In this two-fold proposition, Homans is dealing with the emotional behavior of men and women. If a person does not get what he/she expected, he/she will become angry. Let us assume that our student decided to attend the concert instead of studying for the exam but upon arriving at the concert hall, learned that his/her reserved ticket had been sold and that no other tickets were available. Obviously the student has been denied the desired reward of attending the concert. Most probably he/she will be frustrated and will take out this frustration on the person at the box office. We could take this illustration a step further to demonstrate the second part of the proposition. Perhaps the student did not really expect to get a ticket as a result of becoming angry; the anger was simply an emotional outburst. But just at that moment, the manager of the concert hall happened to be passing by and heard the student's vent of hostility. In order to quiet the student, the manager arranged for the student to be seated in a special section reserved for distinguished visitors. Obviously the student will be pleased. All other things being equal, the student feels that an outburst of anger may bring results and most likely would not hesitate to display such emotion again in similar frustrating situations in the future.

Homans emphasizes that these propositions are interconnected and must be treated as a set. At best, any one of these propositions provides only a partial explanation of human behavior. In order to explain behavior, all five propositions—success, stimulus, value, deprivation–satiation, and aggression–approval—must be considered. Although such propositions may seem obvious, Homans insists that we should not overlook the obvious in building sociological theory. For Homans it is important that these propositions be spelled out in a theory of exchange and be used in empirical research. Taking these propositions as a unit, Homans believes, will enable the sociologist to explain what structural functionalists have called "social structure."

Homans contends that our social institutions and society itself exist, in final analysis, because of the social exchange that would be analyzed with these five propositions. We could say that the government obtains its power in exchange for safeguarding the individual's well-being; a minister keeps his parish and earns a living in exchange for spending time counseling parishioners, visiting the sick, and preparing Sunday services; the educational system, complete with positions for teachers and staff, exchanges its services for student fees transformed into paychecks. Although all of the rewards we have been using as examples are material ones, Homans acknowledges that rewards may be either material or nonmaterial. A person may choose a career of teaching not simply to make a living (a more lucrative salary could be obtained elsewhere) but for the intrinsic rewards of working with young people and the satisfaction that such service brings. The humanitarian who gives up his fortune to help the poor needs no material rewards; his nonmaterial rewards may include satisfaction, the esteem of others, and a moral sense of assisting those less fortunate. For Homans, then, most institutional and noninstitutional social behavior may be explained through an application and elaboration of these five basic psychological propositions.

Exchange Theory and the Issue of Power

In simple examples of social exchange we might assume that the relationships must be symmetrical. For example, when one makes a purchase, the item bought and the money paid for it are assumed to be of equal worth. Similarly other social relations are often symmetrical, as may be evidenced in gift exchanges where the gifts are of approximate equal value, in friendship patterns between social equals, or in labor provided in exchange for a just wage.

Obviously, however, in the real world not all relationships are symmetrical. Sociologists are well aware of a stratification system that is based upon power and authority. Homans explains the origin of power and authority in terms of the *principle of least interest*: the person who has the least interest in continuing the social situation is best able to dictate the conditions for the association. This principle results in power for one participant because "one person has a greater capacity to reward another in exchange than the other has to reward him" (Homans, 1974:74). A dating relationship may be used to illustrate the principle of least interest. It has been observed by family sociologists that the person in the couple who has the less concern about keeping the relationship viable will have more to say about the rules governing the relationship. The plain-looking girl who dates the popular football star may be submissive and admiring in a way in which the campus beauty queen would find distasteful. The football star may gain power in the relationship, dictating the frequency of dates and the nature of their joint activities, and he may even begin to dictate what his girl should do with her personal time. In this relationship the football star may attain a position of power in the relationship while his steady gains prestige from dating him. Such asymmetrical relationships are definitely a part of face-to-face associations.

In formal organizations asymmetrical relations may be perpetuated through coercive power. Coercive power represents unequal exchange, and such situations are governed by exchange propositions just as noncoercive ones are. Homans asserts that when relationships are based on fair exchange, there is no need for coercion. But even when power is coercive, exchange is in evidence. Slavery in the United States may be viewed as coercive power being wielded over slaves by their masters, yet unequal exchange was in evidence. Food, shelter, and clothing were provided in exchange for services, although such exchange was not commensurate with the services rendered.

Homans (1974:75ff.) believes that there is a tendency toward an equalization of power, making coercion an exception rather than the rule in human relations. This may be evidenced by the stratification systems in society that rank group members on the basis of income and occupation. The person accorded the higher status is the one who provides more of the good that is scarce in relation to the demand but receives more of the good that is abundant (Homans, 1974:195ff.). Frequently differentiation in status within a group is agreed upon by the members, who recognize that some have the more scarce but desired resources needed by the group. In exchange for such scarce resources, the giver is accorded higher status by the other members.

We can provide a simple illustration of this rule of status, which is based upon the economic law of supply and demand. Rock singers have been earning astronomical salaries in exchange for appearing in concerts and cutting records. According to Homans's rule, they are accorded high status because they provide a scarce commodity (entertainment and probably other laten functions as well). Rock stars are given money, which is plentiful in society (if it were not, students could not afford to purchase the records and go to the concerts that make the stars rich); the young who attend the concerts receive entertainment, which can be effectively provided by only a few supergroups. Presumably the superstars have something that the local rock band that plays for most university affairs does not have. This same principle may be applied to other, more institutional status positions in a society.

The relations and rankings of people in society should be in accord with what Homans calls *distributive justice*. In interacting in society, people expect their rewards to be proportional to their costs. If the rewards are not forthcoming in accord with distributive justice, we have a situation of injustice or discrepancies in the distribution of rewards. Homans notes that we must be aware that satisfaction with a transaction is relative; that is, we may speak of relative deprivation or of relative advantages. Whether a transaction is viewed as a just or a satisfying one depends on a person's comparison group. We could continue with our example of rock groups as an illustration. A local group is brought to the campus to play for a dance on a Friday evening; this group is paid $200. The following Friday another local group comes to campus and is paid $150. The second group uses the first group as a point of comparison and feels unjustly treated. Whether in fact they are as good as the first group is not as important as that they identify with the first group. Homans formulates the following general rule on comparison groups:

> The general rule seems to be that people are more apt to compare them-selves with others they are to some degree close or similar to than with others that are distant or dissimilar. Above all they will compare them-selves with others they are in direct and personal exchange with. (Homans, 1974:252)

Much of what Homans discusses in his work is based on studies of face-to-face interaction—interaction that may be termed *subinstitutional.* Such behavior may not be formalized, yet Homans believes that it is the matter out of which institutions are made. Homans does not devote much theoretical effort to the development of macrosociological theory, which deals with the analysis of institutions. As he did in *The Human Group,* Homans continues to assert that understanding microlevel processes within small groups will enable sociologists to better understand large-scale organizations and even civilizations. The latter, for Homans, is simply an extension of the principles discovered in the analysis of ele-mentary social behavior.

Critique of Behavioral-Exchange Theory

In terms of assumptions made about the nature of people, Homans shares much with the structural functionalists. With them, Homans pre-sents an image of people that is both rational (i.e. goal-oriented) and determined by forces outside himself. In fact, Homans himself acknowl-edges that rational or goal-oriented theory and behavioral psychological theory is largely the same because the social sciences share the same body of general propositions. Homans (1967:39) believes, however, that "ra-tional theory" is more limited than behavioral psychology:

> Though it [rational theory] recognizes the importance of perception, and assumes that a man is rational in acting in accordance with his perceptions even though in the eyes of persons better informed, his perceptions may be incorrect, it simply takes the perceptions as given and does not tie them back, as behavioral psychology does, to past experience. In the same way, it takes a person's values as given and does not tie them back to deprivation and to the process by which new values are learned.

According to Homans (1967:103), although persons act rationally, they
do so under the "illusion of choice": "I speak of illusion because I my-
self believe that what each of us does is absolutely determined." Homans
acknowledges that we will always have the illusion of free will because
it allows people the conviction that they can change their condition. In
reality, however, men and women are subject to the same rigid and determined laws that govern the world of natural science.

Homans (1961:79–80) says that his model of the human being is a
new "economic man" who uses his resources to advantage. Unlike the
old economic man, who was "antisocial and materialistic, interested only
in money and material goods and ready to sacrifice even his old mother
to get them," the new economic man may have any values he wishes,
from altruism to hedonism. As long as he/she does not squander his/her
resources in order to achieve what he/she values, the behavior is economic: "Indeed if he has learned to find reward in *not* husbanding his
resources, if he values *not* taking any thought for the morrow, and acts
accordingly, his behavior is still economic. In fact, the new economic
man is plain man" (Homans, 1961:79).

Homans's image of people is not, as might be expected, without criticism. It is based upon a rather narrow Skinnerian "behaviorist psychology" that recognizes little in the nature of humans that is different from
the nature of animals. As Peter Ekeh (1974:120) observes in his analysis
of Homans's image of humans:

> The painful contradiction in Homans' social exchange theory is that he
> believes that he is dealing with a psychology, behavioral psychology, that
> studies men as men, as members of the human species, and yet it is a
> psychology that takes its principles from animal behavior. Even more
> glaring is the fact that Homans misses what is perhaps most essential in
> man: unlike animals men's actions are not *necessarily* tied to their past
> but men can act now in spite of their past provided their calculations of
> future possibilities are in their favor.

Other critics have also been disturbed with Homans's "economic
man"—particularly with its assumption that all social interaction is "fair"
or in accord with the principle of distributive justice. (For further discussion see Zeitlin, 1973; Singlemann, 1972; and Turk and Simpson, 1971).
Such critics assert that a view of the world as a system tending toward
equal exchange is not a realistic one. It would appear from these critics
that Homans's treatment of power and social justice is inadequate. Can
slavery, substandard wages, or warfare really be reduced to principles of
exchange? Many commentators on sociological theory think not.

It is out of this rational and determined image of person that Homans's view of society developed. It differs from the traditional functionalist position on two interrelated points: (1) the essence of society and (2) the issue of functional needs or prerequisites. For Homans (1971:378), society does not have an existence apart from men and women in the process of social exchange: "The institutions, organizations, and societies that sociologists study can be analyzed without residue, into the actions of men." It is this position, as we have seen, that has led to the charge of psychological reductionism. Also in disagreement with structural functionalists, Homans (1970:370) refuses to admit that social groups or systems have needs: "People, not societies have needs. This is perfectly obvious, and to assume anything else is to lead oneself directly away from telling the truth about human affairs." For Homans, the behavior of individuals rather than of abstract groups must remain the unit of sociological analysis.

Much of Homans's view of theory is in line with that of other naturalistic sociologists. Homans remains committed to the importance of defining concepts, of constructing propositional statements from these concepts, and of interrelating propositions. Moreover Homans believes in the unity of science, remaining open to the idea that the natural sciences may well provide the ultimate explanatory principles of social reality. His own work demonstrates his attempt to combine economics and sociology, with behavioral psychology providing the basis for explanation. The goal of naturalistic theory is thus to explain, not simply to describe, phenomena. Homans believes that the unifying explanatory principle of the behavioral sciences is found in Skinnerian psychology:

> I believe that this body of propositions—though it is the academic property of one of the social sciences, psychology—provides for all of them at present the most general propositions used in explanation. Not only in their subject matter, human behavior, but in their general statements about human behavior, the social sciences are one science (Homans, 1967:43).

Other naturalistic sociologists are not willing to reduce sociology to psychological explanations. This psychological reductionism is a source of discomfort to sociologists who assert that social phenomena are emergent and have properties of their own. These properties cannot be reduced to psychological explanations. (Peter Blau, who will be discussed in the following chapter, is one exchange theorist who is critical of Homans's failure to acknowledge the principle of emergence of social structures.) The particular fault of Homans's reductionist position is that taken to its logical conclusion, psychological reductionism could render sociology obsolete. Thus, although an exchange of information between sociology and psychology is highly desirable for a full understanding of people in society, reducing sociology to psychological principles does not seem to be in the interest of either discipline.

Summary

As we saw in Chapter 2, structural functionalism stressed the priority of the social structure as the unit of analysis in sociology. As a result, the importance of the individual actor was downplayed in favor of structural analysis. Homans produced analysis on this level in his classic functionalist formulation, *The Human Group,* in which the *product,* or human interaction, was the subject of study rather than the *process* through which the structure was formed.

Homans eventually became disenchanted with the simple descriptive powers offered by functionalism and was drawn to behavioristic psychological theory, which he believes has explanatory power. His work now attempts to bring the individual into sociological analysis and uses behavior to explain social structure. Although Homans uses behavioral propositions to supplement his earlier functionalist concepts, he goes further than Merton (who has not attempted to develop propositional theory) in formulating propositions and attempting to interrelate them within a single theory of social exchange.

For Homans, the goal of human behavior is an economic one of maximizing profits or rewards. All social phenomena, including coercive power, stratification, authority, and other inequalities may be analyzed in terms of exchange. This principle of exchange, observes Homans, provides explanatory powers lacking in traditional functionalist theory.

Although Homans's attempts have been well received in sociology, his work has also been criticized. The major criticism include the assertions that exchange theory does not deal with the complexity of human behavior, that it fails to deal adequately with the emergent nature of social groups, and that it suffers from psychological reductionism.

Although Homans asserts that exchange theory may be used to explain behavior on both an institutional and a subinstitutional level, his theory is basically subinstitutional and microscopic. Peter M. Blau, the exchange theorist whose work is the subject of the following chapter, extends Homans's principles to account for the emergence of larger social structures.

References

ARENSBERG, C. M., and D. MACGREGOR
  1942 "Determination of Morale in an Industrial Company." *Applied Anthropology* (1):12–34.
EKEH, PETER P.
  1974 *Social Exchange Theory: The Two Traditions.* Cambridge, Mass.: Harvard University Press.
EMERSON, RICHARD M.
  1972 "A Psychological Basis for Social Exchange." Pp. 38–57 in Joseph Berger, Morris Zelditch, Jr., and Bo Anderson (Eds.), *Sociological Theories in Progress,* Vol. 2. Boston: Houghton Mifflin Company.
FIRTH, RAYMOND
  1936 *We The Tikopia.* London: George Allen and Unwin, Ltd.
GOULDNER, ALVIN W.
  1960 "The Norm of Reciprocity: A Preliminary Statement." *American Sociological Review* 25 (April):161–178.
HATCH, D. L.
  1948 "Changes in the Structure and Function of a Rural New England Community Since 1900." Ph.D. thesis, Harvard University.
HEATH, ANTHONY
  1976 *Rational Choice and Social Exchange.* London: Cambridge University Press.
HOMANS, GEORGE C.
  1950 *The Human Group.* New York: Harcourt, Brace & World, Inc.
  1958 "Social Behavior as Exchange." *The American Journal of Sociology* 62 (May):595–606.
  1961 *Social Behavior: Its Elementary Forms.* New York: Harcourt, Brace & World, Inc.
  1962 *Sentiments and Activities.* Glencoe, Ill.: The Free Press of Glencoe.
  1964 "Bringing Men Back In." *American Sociological Review* 29 (December):809–818.
  1967 *The Nature of Social Science.* New York: Harcourt, Brace & World, Inc.
  1969 "A Life of Synthesis." Pp. 13–43 in Irving Louis Horowitz (Ed.), *Sociological Self-Images.* Beverly Hills, Calif.: Sage Publications.
  1971 "Commentary." Pp. 363–379 in H. Turk and R. L. Simpson (Eds.), *Institutions and Social Exchange: The Sociologies of Talcott Parsons and George C. Homans.* New York: The Bobbs-Merrill Company, Inc.
  1974 *Social Behavior: Its Elementary Forms* (rev. ed.). New York: Harcourt Brace Jovanovich, Inc.
MERTON, ROBERT K.
  1950 "Introduction." Pp. xvii–xviii in George Homans, *The Human Group.* New York: Harcourt, Brace & World, Inc.
ROETHLISBERGER, F. J., and W. J. DICKSON
  1939 *Management and the Worker.* Cambridge, Mass.: Harvard University Press.

SINGLEMANN, PETER
    1972 "Exchange as Symbolic Interaction: Convergence Between Two Theoretical Perspectives." *American Sociological Review* 37 (August): 414–424.
THIBAUT, J. W., and H. H. KELLEY
    1959 *The Social Psychology of Groups.* New York: John Wiley & Sons, Inc.
TURK, HERMAN, and RICHARD L. SIMPSON (Eds.)
    1971 *Institutions and Social Exchange.* Indianapolis: The Bobbs-Merrill Company, Inc.
WHYTE, WILLIAM FOOTE
    1943 *Street Corner Society.* Chicago: Chicago University Press.
WRONG, DENNIS
    1961 "The Oversocialized Conception of Man in Modern Sociology." *American Sociological Review* 26 (April):183–193.
ZEITLIN, IRVING M.
    1973 *Rethinking Sociology: A Critique of Contemporary Theory.* New York: Appleton-Century-Crofts.

4

Exchange Structuralism: Beyond Behavioral-Exchange Theory

Two dangers must be avoided in such derivation of more complex from simpler social processes, and in the study of social structure generally—the Scylla of abstract conceptions too remote from observable empirical reality and the Charybdis of reductionism that ignores emergent social and structural properties. (Blau, 1964:2–3)

Although exchange theory has clearly emerged as a distinct perspective within sociology and social psychology, it is not, as we have noted in the last chapter, without internal divergences. As Emerson (1976:335) discusses in his review article on the development and growth of social-exchange theory, there still is much diversity and controversy within the perspective. These controversial differences among major branches of exchange theory are as important as their similarities.

The two best-known sociological contributions to exchange theory have been made by George C. Homans (Chapter 3) and Peter M. Blau (whose theory is the subject of this chapter). Although Blau appears to accept much of Homans's behavioral psychology as the basis for his work, closer examination makes it apparent that differences between Blau and Homans are perhaps greater than surface similarities. Homans's theory, as we have seen, tends toward psychological reductionism, with his insistence that explaining individual behavior also explains all group behavior. Blau, as noted in the quotation at the head of this chapter, warns sociologists against the danger of a reductionism "that ignores emergent social and structural properties." Blau's emphasis on emergence, or the properties of the group that may not be reduced to an individually-oriented psychology, has led Ekeh (1974) to describe Blau's work as a "collectivist structuralist thesis" that may be contrasted with the "individualistic behaviorist theory" of Homans.

Although Blau praises Homans's microtheoretical efforts, he is critical of Homans's reductionist tendencies and asserts that one cannot generalize from a study of the microsocial world to the macro- or large-scale complex organizations. He identifies *microstructures* as being composed of interacting individuals, whereas *macrostructures* consist of interrelated groups. Although micro- and macrostructures have some similarities, there are fundamental differences. For example, Blau (1964:31) observes that small groups may be able to maintain social control through social appeal and personal obligations but that entire countries cannot. Formalized procedures and coercive powers are needed for such highly complex organizational associations. Thus, although accepting the importance of the exchange process, Blau is also interested in better understanding the functioning of complex organizations.

Blau is also aware that reductionism in sociology prevents sociologists from dealing adequately with such important emergent phenomena as power and stratification. He disagrees with Homans's assertion that such topics may be understood through the behavioral psychological principle of exchange. On the other hand, many theorists who have dealt with such topics have fallen victim to the "Scylla of abstract conceptions too remote from observable empirical reality." These macrotheorists, while concentrating on topics neglected by reductionists, have strayed from the empirical social world that remains close to microsociologists. What Blau does in his theory is to utilize the concept of exchange from microsociology and to combine it with the concept of power that has been the subject of macrotheoretical efforts. The fruit of this attempt is found in Blau's classic theoretical work, *Exchange and Power in Social Life*.

Exchange and Power in Social Life _____

Blau begins his thesis by accepting the primitive psychological principle of social exchange advanced by psychologist B. F. Skinner and further discussed by social-exchange theorist George C. Homans. These principles include the phenomena of individuals' attraction to each other and their desire for various kinds of rewards. This desire for social rewards is a "given" in Blau's theory that accounts for the origin of social structures. In answer to the question "What attracts individuals to the association?" Blau's response is "individuals are attracted to exchange by expectations of intrinsic and/or extrinsic rewards" (Blau, 1964:312).

Blau acknowledges that not all human behavior is guided by considerations of social exchange, although he contends that much of it is. He identifies two conditions that must be met for behavior to lead to social exchange: (1) the behavior "must be oriented toward ends that can only be achieved through interaction with other persons," and (2) the behavior "must seek to adopt means to further the achievement of these ends" (Blau, 1964:5). These desired ends may be *extrinsic rewards* (such as money, goods, or services), or *intrinsic rewards* (including love, honor, duty, or pursuit of beauty). Human behavior, guided by principles of social exchange, underlies the formation of social structures and social institutions.

Up to this point, Homans's and Blau's theories converge, but Blau's concerns go beyond Homans's microtheoretical emphases. Blau and Homans would concur that individuals within small groups are attracted to association with each other because of their desire for various kinds of rewards. But although exchange may be the guiding principle within small groups, the functioning of large organizations cannot be reduced to this psychological thesis. Blau moves away from Homans with his interest in large organizations and his insistence on the principle of emergence. Blau's main theoretical concern is "with the changes in social processes that occur as one moves from simpler to more complex social structures and with the new social forces that emerge in the latter" (Blau, 1964:31).

This interest may be demonstrated in the development of stratification systems in more complex groups as compared with relations in simpler groups. Although the desire for rewards is what initially attracts individuals into association with each other, the seeds for emergent phenomena are being sown. One such emergent structural trait is a simple stratification system. In the initial stages of group formation, individuals attempt to demonstrate their worth to the group. With members making contributions of differential value to the group, differentiation in status begins to develop. For example, not everyone is either able or willing to take on the responsibilities of group leadership. If members are committed to the goals of the group and are receiving rewards from it, some will step back and allow others to assume these positions. The leaders obtain deference, power, and/or material rewards in exchange for their contributions. As differentiation occurs, however, it intensifies the need for social integration of these unequal statuses. This need for cohesion is met when most group members "withdraw from the competition for status and establish mutual ties of fellowship." Such cohesion is necessary and strengthens the group as it pursues its goals. Although this process may serve to explain the development of the system, once stratification is established, it may, as we shall see, be perpetuated through power relations rather than through social exchange.

Blau acknowledges that not all social transactions are symmetrical and based on equal social exchange. Clearly, interpersonal relations may be either reciprocal or unilateral. Where there is symmetry, with both or all members receiving rewards in proportion to their investments, we may speak of an *exchange relationship*. With regard to stratification, we may speak of exchange so long as the relationship is beneficial to both high- and low-ranking members. In reality, however, such symmetrical relations may give way to coercive power, with low-ranking members receiving few rewards. A coercive power relationship is one in which there is an unequal exchange that is maintained through negative sanctions. Coercive power thus represents an emergent phenomenon that is not adequately explained through the psychological-exchange process.

Just as there is a shift from reliance primarily on social exchange to power relations within groups, there is a corresponding change in the sanctioning methods employed by groups. Although the desire for social approval is a reward that continues to be important in all societies, it is less of a pervasive source of restraining behavior in complex groups. Blau observes that in complex societies, deviants of all sorts may find subgroups of their own to avoid the impact of community disapproval. As Blau (1964:114) notes, "Impersonal restraints are, therefore, of special importance in modern societies, and a basic source of impersonal restraint is power." It is toward this macrosociological concern of *power*, rather than the microsociological phenomenon of exchange, that Blau directs most of his theoretical efforts.

THE DIFFERENTIATION OF POWER

Blau (1964:117) defines power in the Weberian sense as "the ability of persons or groups to impose their will on others despite resistance through deterrence either in the forms of withholding regularly supplied rewards or in the form of punishment, inasmuch as the former as well as the latter constitute, in effect a negative sanction." Power is thus viewed simply as control through negative sanctions, with physical coercion—or its threat—being the polar case of power.

Blau (1964:118) cites Richard Emerson's schema for examining "power-dependence" relations as a basis for analyzing the imbalance of power within and among groups. Individuals who need a service another has to offer have the following alternatives:

1. They can supply him/her with a service that he/she wants badly enough to induce him/her to offer his/her service in return, though only if they have the resources required for doing so; this will lead to reciprocal exchanges.
2. They may obtain the needed service elsewhere (assuming that there are alternative suppliers), which will lead to reciprocal exchanges, albeit in different partnerships.
3. They can coerce him/her to furnish the service (assuming they are capable of so doing). If such coercion occurs, those who are able to secure the service establish domination over the supplier.
4. They may learn to resign themselves to do without the service or to find some substitute for it.

There are numerous examples of each alternative, but we will use the hypothetical one of an individual consumer's struggle with rising utility costs. For years Consumer Jones has been engaged in what he considered to be a reciprocal exchange with his utility company; he received home energy in return for paying his bill. Rising prices, however, caused him to reevaluate this exchange and to conclude that it was not a fair one. He considered his options. If there were another supplier in his area who competed with his present one, Jones could turn to that supplier to negotiate a more equal and reciprocal exchange. If no such supplier exists, Consumer Jones is clearly in a dependent position and is likely to be coerced into paying the high bills or to face the cutoff of his energy supply. The only way to avoid being dependent on the power company (in the event of no alternate supplier) would be to do without the service entirely or to find a substitute for it. The latter could be illustrated by the man who built an underground home and used logs from his property for the little fuel that was required to heat it.

These four alternatives indicate conditions of social dependence for those needing a particular service. If the persons who desire the service are not able to meet with any of the alternatives (and thus demonstrate their independence of the supplier), they have no choice but to comply with the supplier's wishes "since he can make continued supply of the needed service contingent on their compliance" (Blau, 1964:118). This dependence upon the supplier puts the supplier in a position of power. In order for the supplier to maintain this power position, he/she must remain indifferent to the benefits offered in exchange for his/her services, and he/she must block the alternative suppliers of this service (Blau, 1964:121). Thus differentiation of power is seen to be a result of scarce goods. The outcome of this struggle is a system of stratification or ranking of persons on the basis of power.

Although the ability to coerce or force people to obey commands may be the final form of power, such power is fraught with problems. Because the use of coercive power engenders resistance and sometimes active opposition, the resultant power conflicts are best kept at a minimum in society. For the society to function smoothly, it is important that subordinates perform daily duties and comply willingly with directives from those in positions of power. Thus it is wise for those in power to play down their coercive potential, if at all possible. Consumer Jones's utility company would do well to minimize its power potential and attempt to convince him and other consumers (perhaps through advertising) that energy is still a good buy!

LEGITIMATION OF POWER WITHIN GROUPS

Blau observes (1964:200), "Only legitimate power commands willing compliance." Another term for legitimate power is *authority*. The group voluntarily accepts legitimate power or authority, thus making it binding on group members. For example, the executive office of the American government has had (and used) the *power* to spy on American citizens through the use of the CIA. It did not, however, have the *authority* to engage in such actions. Had President Ford insisted on continuing such activities once they came to light and had he defended the practice, opposition surely would have mounted. Yet the American people do accept the power of a president to veto legislation passed by Congress, to appoint a cabinet of advisers, and to fill vacancies in the Supreme Court. Such exercise of power is provided by the Constitution and is deemed to be legitimate power or authority.

Authority rests on the common norms or rules of prescribed behavior in a collectivity. These norms constrain the individual members to conform to the orders of a superior. Such norms are internalized by group members and are enforced by them. Citizens recognize the right of Congress to make laws, union members accept the right of leaders to negotiate contracts, and students concede the right of instructors to give grades. People are socialized into existing norms governing the behavior of subordinates and superordinates. Blau (1964:211) observes, "The normative standards underlying institutionalized authority do not emerge in the process of social interaction between superior and subordinates and among subordinates but rather in the process of socialization to which each of them is separately exposed in a common culture." In other words, we learn to accept the authority structure as we are socialized into our culture.

Exercising power and/or authority, however, is not without difficulties. Blau identifies a "dilemma of leadership," which requires possessing both power over others and the legitimate approval of that power. The dilemma exists in that the process of gaining power and the process of winning approval are in conflict. A person may gain his or her position of leadership at the expense of creating resentment among subordinates, thus costing him or her social approval. On the other hand, if a person is overly concerned with social approval, he or she will have problems in being an effective leader because this overconcern induces the leader to be governed by what followers like rather than by what most furthers the achievement of their common goals. Individuals who aspire to become leaders tend to resolve this dilemma by mobilizing their power first and then using it in ways that win them the approval of their followers.

Power that is exercised with moderation and that confers sufficient benefits in return for submission is the ideal. Such power elicits social approval that legitimates the authority of its commands. If power is exploitative and oppressive, it provokes disapproval and even retaliation. As the members of an oppressed group convey their feelings of outrage and hostility to one another, a consensus emerges. This group may then develop an ideology in opposition to the original group.

Whether the power tends to be legitimated or opposed also depends, in part, upon whether the standards or values governing the social relations in a group are *particular* or *universal*. Blau (1964:313) defines these two types of values as follows:

> Particularistic standards refer to status attributes that are valued only by the ingroup, such as religious or political beliefs, whereas universalistic standards refer to attributes that are generally valued, by those who do not have them as well as by those who do, such as wealth or competence.

Thus, in our own society, the universalistic standard *wealth* is desired by the poor as well as the rich. Health, beauty, and success are also universally desirable. On the other hand, being of Baptist religious persuasion would not be desired by Jews or Catholics. Democrats do not desire Republican values. Such groups have values and norms that are particularistic and are desired only by individual groups.

Although in-groups may share values and norms, particularistic norms may conflict between groups. Thus a group may agree on a particularistic goal, but this goal may be in opposition to the goals of other subgroups. An illustration from the contemporary scene might serve to clarify this principle. Until January 1973 abortion upon request was illegal in most states of the United States. This illegality may have been viewed as a universal value upheld by the law. Forces were at work, however, to change this legal situation, two important ones being the women's movement and concern about overpopulation in a world of dwindling resources. With the Supreme Court's ruling that laws prohibiting abortion in early stages of pregnancy were unconstitutional, the stage was set for a continued battle between two groups with opposing value systems: those who favored the liberalization of abortion laws, such as Planned Parenthood and the National Organization for Women (NOW), and those who are opposed to abortion, such as Birthright and Right to Life. The opposition continues, as an amendment to the Constitution is proposed to halt legal abortions. There is no way that the values of these two collectivities can be reconciled through the exchange process. Power, not reciprocal exchange, will dictate which stance on abortion will become the universalistic value and which one will become the particularistic one.

This example of in-groups (such as Birthright and NOW) also illustrates the emergence principle, which is central to Blau's theory. Group membership hinges on commonly agreed-upon values and norms. Although exchange serves as the basis for elementary personal interaction, *commonly accepted social values serve as the media of social transactions for social groups and organizations.* This principle allows a structure to function without direct social contact among individual members and over long periods of time. In the case of personal friendships, it is easier to analyze the direct exchange process of both intrinsic and extrinsic rewards. Shared social values are a key to understanding both exchange and power in large collectivities.

Blau (1964:280) identifies four types of mediating values, all of which we have considered in this section:

1. Particularistic values serve as media of social solidarity or cohesion. They help to create a common unity that substitutes for personal feelings of attraction. They simultaneously produce divisions, however, between subgroups contained within the larger collectivity. This may be illustrated by countless examples, including groups who actively work for gun control legislation versus the National Rifle Association, members of feminist organizations versus non-feminists, Republicans versus Democrats.

2. Universalistic standards of social contributions and achievements give rise to stratification systems. Status here becomes a reward that makes indirect transactions possible. The status that high government office has given to its occupants may serve as an illustration and an explanation of why men and women would give up lucrative businesses or law practices to earn less money as a Senator, a Supreme Court Justice, or a President. The universalistic standards of service to country provide status for these individuals.

3. Legitimating values, as we have seen, act as the medium for the exercise of authority and the organization of social endeavors on a large scale in the pursuit of collective objectives. Power must be legitimated and viewed as legitimate by members of the group. It must be accepted as necessary for the attainment of group goals.
4. Opposition ideals are media of reorganization and change, since they inspire support for opposition movements and legitimate their leadership. An example might be provided by talk of establishment of a "third party" by those who are dissatisfied with the activities of both Republican and Democratic party leaders.

Blau believes that the complex patterns of social life that are mediated by common values become institutionalized. Such institutions may be perpetuated for generations if three conditions are met: (1) the organizing principles must become part of formalized procedures (e.g., a constitution or other documents), so that they are independent of those people who carry them out at any one time; (2) the social values that legitimate the institutional form must be transmitted to succeeding generations through the socialization process; (3) the dominant groups in the community must be identified with these values and must lend power to support the institutions that express them. An anti-Communist America was not likely to permit the existence of an American Communist Party any more than an antireligious Soviet Union or People's Republic of China would permit the untroubled existence of these nations' established religions. Even once an institution has met the first two conditions, support must generally be lent by the dominant groups if the institution is to continue indefinitely.

To summarize Blau's discussion on the emergence of social groups, we may observe the following main ideas. First, in elementary exchange relationships, people are attracted to each other through mutual needs and satisfactions. There is the assumption that people who give rewards do so as payment for value received. Second, such exchange easily develops into a competitive relationship in which each person demonstrates the rewards that he/she has to offer in order to impress the other and to bargain for better rewards. Third, this competition generates the beginnings of a stratification system in which individuals become differentiated on the basis of the scarce resources they possess. Here we see the roots of the emergent concept of power. Fourth, power may be legitimate (authority) or coercive. Authority is based on legitimating values that enable emergent groups and organizations to function without relying on intimate, face-to-face contacts. Group members recognize the validity of group needs and goals as well as individual-level exchanges. Use of coercive power, on the other hand, is fraught with problems, particularly with the development of opposition values.

Although Blau is heavily influenced by both functionalism and exchange theory, his theory does not fall prey to their fascination with the status quo. Blau, as we shall see in the next section, makes social change an integral part of his theory.

Dialectical Forces of Social Change

In spite of strong structural functional overtones, Blau's theory demonstrates his awareness of the dynamic processes in operation that comprise the structure. Within the social structure, there are "perennial adjustments and counter-adjustments [that] find expression in a dialectical pattern of social exchange" (Blau, 1964:314). These dialectical forces are examined in terms of (1) dilemmas; (2) differentiation; (3) dynamics; and (4) the dialectical process. Unlike much functionalist theory, which has neglected or understated the importance of the dynamic processes in society, Blau incorporates a theory of social change into his model.

DILEMMAS

The pure model of social exchange in Blau's theory would be one of *reciprocal* exchange of *extrinsic* rewards. The dimensions of reciprocity and extrinsic benefit may both be modified in reality, yielding relationships that may be unilaterally based on power or based on the intrinsic reward of love, satisfaction, and so on. Blau thus asserts that exchange may deviate from this pure model and may be viewed as a mixed game, in which the partners have both common and conflicting interests.

In addition to this first dilemma of a "mixed game," there are three others that may serve to effect social change. First, although both partners have a common interest in maintaining the relationship, there is a dilemma as to how much to offer before the rewards become deflated in value. Although there is a desire to keep the relationship going (which requires an exchange of rewards), there is at the same time the dilemma that giving a reward too easily or too frequently deflates its worth. For example, the affection of a man who is slow to give it or the approval from a woman who seldom gives it is highly valued. Another dilemma exists because social actions have multiple consequences. The action necessary to attain one goal may impede the attainment of another. The dilemma of leadership discussed earlier in this chapter, where social approval and exercising power rights are in conflict, represents such a problem.

Blau (1964:320) asserts that dilemmas of individuals in unstructured situations may give rise to differentiation in status. This may resolve some of the dilemma, but such differentiation simultaneously produces new dialectical forces of change.

DIFFERENTIATION

As we have seen, exchange theorists assert that competition for scarce resources leads to a differential allocation of these resources. These are made "in accordance with the valued contributions the various members of the collectivity are expected to make" (Blau, 1964:321). Differentials with respect to access to scarce resources are followed by an allocation of leadership based on the privileged position that this respect provides. Leaders are then able to make task assignments furthering the process of differentiation through a division of labor. The emergent leaders are thus able to act on the basis of authority and/or power.

DYNAMICS

The differentiated social structure is not a static one. As we have seen, the dynamics of organized social life has its source in opposition forces. Dominant power of individuals may be exercised moderately and justly, making it profitable for others to remain under their protecting influence. Power, however, may also lead to exploitation. When people are subjected to unfair, exploitative power, the condition may give rise to an opposition that challenges dominant power. It is here that we see the seeds for conflict developing, as legitimating values may be confronted with opposition ideals.

DIALECTIC

Within social life, there are many contradictory forces. This is what is known as a *dialectic*. Reciprocity is a stablizing force in the social structure, but paradoxically, "reciprocity on one level entails imbalances on others" (Blau, 1964:336). Social forces thus could be said to have contradictory implications. This process may be illustrated by attempts to right the wrongs committed against minority groups in our own society. If a member of a minority group (such as blacks or women) is given preferential treatment in job hiring and promotions, this may cause serious opposition to develop among those majority group members who are competing for this same scarce resource. At the same time, continued exclusion of blacks and women from segments of the labor force has led to opposition from collectivities representing minority-group interests.

Blau acknowledges that social change is slow because of the resistance of vested interests and powers, traditional values, established organizations, and long-standing institutions. Forces of stability and resistance to social change are strong. Yet, as new needs and new problems arise, these dialectical forces of social change are at work, enabling structural reorganization to occur.

Critique of Blau's Theory

Blau's theory of social exchange, as we have seen, in many ways builds on that of Homans. Yet, in spite of the similarities on the topic of personal-exchange relations within small groups, there is a major difference in their respective assumptions about society. As Ekeh (1974:180) observes:

> Both [Blau and Homans] agree that complex social structures may be derived from basic social exchange processes. But Homans says decidedly that in the realm of functioning, these derived social structures have no autonomous laws of their own. On the other hand Blau terms them emergent, suggesting and saying thereby that once they emerge from the basic social exchange processes, they attain an autonomy of their own with their own laws of operation independent of the primitive processes from which they emerge.

Thus, although building on Homans's psychologically based exchange theory, Blau is reluctant to accept Homans's insistence that all social processes can be reduced to underlying psychological phenomena (Blau, 1964:193). There seems to be no resolution of the differences regarding this issue of emergence and psychological reductionism. As Homans (1971:376) clearly states:

> The question is rather on how the emergence is to be explained. Blau seems to think that an emergent phenomenon, by the very fact that it is emergent, requires new propositions for its explanation, but that is certainly not generally so. I believe that the process of emergence, and the nature of properties that emerge in social interaction, are to be explained by the same general propositions that explain nonsocial behavior.

Clearly the difference between Homans and Blau on the reality of social structures is one of differing assumptions. Neither has proved his position. Blau's acceptance of distinct emergent properties of social structures avoids psychological reductionism and allows sociology a distinct subject matter. There is no doubt that Blau's position is more in line with sociological thinking and more acceptable to most sociologists than is Homans's psychological reductionism.

Blau's image of people is one that coincides with that of other structural functionalists and differs somewhat from the image of people presented by Homans. Blau goes further than Homans to strengthen the economic basis of social-exchange behavior and seems to ignore Homans's overwhelming emphasis on operant behavioral psychology. As Ekeh (1974:169–170) has demonstrated, man's primary motives for Blau are economic ones (the profit or gain of calculated action), and he implies the use of a human model rather than one based on animal behavior.

Blau's image of people is probably closer to that of Parsons or Merton than to that of exchange theorist Homans. Although Blau sees economic motives in the traditional terms of profit or gain, Homans implies that all rational action is by definition "economic" and that the economic model is appropriate for all behavior. Blau, in accord with Parsons and Merton, believe that men and women rationally seek goals but that these goals are limited by constraints in the social structure. As we have seen, power is a phenomenon for special consideration that may not be reduced to a pure exchange model. *People are free to choose goals, but only among structurally determined alternatives.*

Blau's conception of society, as we have already suggested, also shares much with classic structural functionalism. Blau (1975:221) defines his idea of social structure as follows:

> My concept of social structure starts with simple and concrete definitions of the component parts and their relations. The parts are groups or classes of people, such as men and women, ethnic groups, or socioeconomic strata; they are the positions of people in different groups and strata. The connections among as well as within parts are the social relations of people in different groups and strata. The connections among as well as within parts are the social relations of people that find expression in their social interaction and communication.

Although Blau's conception of social structure is not unlike that of structural functionalism, there is one noteworthy difference. In structural functionalism, the existence of structure is a "given," without much theoretical attention being given to its development. In Blau's theory, we see the social structure as a phenomenon that is *emergent out of the processes of social exchange.*

Blau's theory, although sociologically improved over Homans's reductionism, is not without criticism. One of the biggest weaknesses of

Blau's theory is the major premise upon which it rests, namely, that much human behavior is guided by exchange. (For further discussion, see Bierstedt, 1965; Simpson, 1972.) The exchange process is a "given" that is not fully supported, demonstrated, or explained. If one is willing to accept the premise of the importance of exchange in social relations, one can follow Blau's theoretical development. If not, the exchange premise makes it impossible to accept the theoretical edifice.

It has been noted that Blau's theory is more complete from a sociological standpoint than is Homans's, in that Blau attempts to analyze the differences between and among collectivities. Although this attempt is laudable, the results of his theory fall short of the goal. Eisenstadt (1965) criticizes Blau for not fully analyzing the differences between interpersonal exchange and institutional behavior and organization. As we have seen, Blau identifies some of the major differences, but he does not analyze them in any depth.

Blau's work, despite such deficiencies, is a semiclassic in sociological theory. It goes beyond traditional functionalism in its recognition of power and exploitation as societal phenomena. Furthermore it does not suffer from the limitations of a static functionalist theory. Blau attempts to heighten his reader's awareness of the dynamic aspects of building and maintaining a social structure. Moreover Blau's analysis is neither simply micro nor simply macro in perspective. Blau is concerned with both the micro- and the macrosocial levels, and he attempts to illustrate how at least some basic principles are applicable to both. These strengths of his theoretical model undoubtedly outweigh the weaknesses.

Summary

Building on the principle of reciprocity as a basis for socialization, Blau analyzes the structure and dynamics of collectivities. Keeping both micro- and macrosociological levels before his readers, Blau emphasizes the differences between social behavior in small intimate groups as well as within complex organizations. Blau contends that the prototype of exchange is the *reciprocal exchange of extrinsic benefits*. Either of the dimensions of this prototype—the reciprocity or the reward—may be altered in actual relationships. Moreover the reciprocity may be absent or incomplete, as in the case of power relations based on unilateral services

For Blau, exchange is at the base of most social relations, but there are major differences between exchange as found in intimate relations and exchange as observed in complex social organizations. Some of these differences are as follows:

1. In face-to-face associations, the transactions are direct; in large collectivities, social values play a major role in mediating complex structures.
2. Complex structures are partially institutionalized; "these persisting institutional elements exert traditional constraints on other elements of community life" (Blau, 1964:282). Face-to-face associations do not possess such enduring constraining power.
3. Face-to-face associations are made up of individuals; components of large social structures are also social structures.

Although Blau's theory of social exchange and power is quite compatible with structural functionalism, it does devote more attention than classic functionalism to the phenomenon of social change. Blau identifies four components or dimensions of social change: dilemmas, differentiation, dynamics, and the dialectical process. Structural reorganization is always a possibility, as the forces for social change confront the forces of stability.

Blau has taken exchange theory out of the realm of psychological reductionism and into a sociological realm that may be used as a basis for a discussion of exchange and power within large complex organizations. His theory clearly rests, however, on the premise that much human behavior is guided by exchange. For those who reject this premise, Blau's exchange theory may be a magnificent edifice but lacking in solid foundations.

References

BIERSTEDT, ROBERT
  1965 "Critique of Blau's Exchange and Power in Social Life." *American Sociological Review* 30 (October):789–790.
BLAU, PETER M.
  1964 *Exchange and Power in Social Life.* Chicago: John Wiley & Sons, Inc.
  1975 "Parameters of Social Structure." Pp. 220–253 in Peter M. Blau (Ed.), *Approaches to the Study of Social Structure.* New York: The Free Press.
EISENSTADT, S. N.
  1965 "Critique of Blau's Exchange and Power in Social Life." *American Journal of Sociology* 71 (November):333.

EKEH, PETER P.
  1974 *Social Exchange Theory: The Two Traditions.* Cambridge, Mass.:
       Harvard University Press.
EMERSON, RICHARD M.
  1976 "Social Exchange Theory." Pp. 335–362 in Alex Inkeles (Ed.),
       Annual Review of Sociology, Vol. 2. Palo Alto, Calif.: Annual Reviews,
       Inc.
HOMANS, GEORGE
  1971 "Commentary." Pp. 363–379 in H. Turk and R. L. Simpson (Eds.),
       Institutions and Social Exchange. New York: The Bobbs-Merrill Com-
       pany, Inc.
SIMPSON, RICHARD L.
  1972 *Theories of Social Exchange.* New York: General Learning Press.
ZEITLIN, IRVING
  1973 *Rethinking Sociology: A Critique of Contemporary Theory.* New York:
       Appleton-Century-Crofts.

5

Conflict Structuralism I: Maintaining the Structure Through Conflict

> If we are not to give in to a social psychologism that would disregard an outside reality which sets bounds to the strivings and desires of individual actors and retreat into prepotent concerns with individual recognitions, perceptions, and subjective impressions, we have to return to the heritage of Marx, Simmel, and Durkheim, which is teaching us that individual striving is not sufficient to free us from the grip of societal constraints.
>
> . . .
>
> Nevertheless, I would like to show that structural analysis, like love, crucial though it is, is not enough. Exclusive concern with structural factors could lead, intentionally or unwittingly, to a neglect of social process. Structural factors, I would like to show at the hands of a few concrete examples, do not operate directly upon social behavior but are mediated through processes of social interaction among which social conflict is a major, though by no means the only one. (Coser, 1975a:210–211)

For over twenty years, Lewis A. Coser has remained committed to the prevailing model in sociology, which has emphasized social structure. At the same time he has pointed out its frequent neglect of the study of social conflict. Unlike some sociologists, who asserted the existence of two distinct perspectives—structural functionalist theory *versus* conflict theory—Coser expresses his commitment to the feasibility of combining the two approaches. Coser acknowledges that some structural arrangements are the result of agreement and consensus, a process emphasized by the structural functionalists, but he also points to another process through which the social group may be established or maintained, namely, social conflict.

Coser (1956:16–19), in discussing early American theorists, observes their cognizance of the existence of conflict—an awareness that was reflected in their spirit of societal reform. For example, Albion Small and George E. Vincent, the well-known authors of the first textbook of American sociology, reflected sociology's reform orientation when they noted, "Sociology was born of the modern ardor to improve society" (cited in Coser, 1956:17). Given this reform orientation, conflict was seen as being a basic form of human interaction and one that could have positive as well as negative implications.

Contemporary sociologists, however, have often neglected the analysis of social conflict, implicitly viewing it as pathological or destructive to the social group. Coser chooses to demonstrate the potentially positive contributions that conflict makes in both the establishment and the maintenance of the structure. He does this by building upon classic sociological statements dealing with social conflict, and particularly through a reliance on the turn-of-the-century German sociologist, Georg Simmel.

Like Simmel, Coser does not attempt to produce a comprehensive theory that would encompass all social phenomena. Simmel, being convinced that any attempt to produce a holistic social theory was premature, never produced a macrosociological treatise of the magnitude of Émile Durkheim, Max Weber, or Karl Marx. Instead Simmel advocated that sociology work to refine and develop *forms* or sociological concepts into which the *contents* of the empirical world could be put. In developing the distinction between form and content, Simmel was comparing sociology to geometry, with geometry studying physical forms while sociology studies social forms. A triangle, a square, and a circle are all examples of geometric forms. The contents—including the shape, color, size, material, and so on—of each form may vary, but the basic form can still be identified. Conflict was one such sociological form that Simmel discussed. Conflict is a form of interaction, with its place, time, intensity, and so on being subject to variation just as the content of a triangle may vary. Coser took Simmel's discussion of conflict, developed propositions from Simmel's writings, and expanded on Simmel to illustrate the conditions under which conflict contributes positively to the social structure and under which it operates negatively to weaken the fabric of society.

Group-Binding and -Maintaining Functions of Social Conflict _____

Conflict is a social process that may be instrumental in the formation, unification, and maintenance of a social structure. It enables the establishment and preservation of boundary lines between and among groups. Conflict with other groups may contribute to the reaffirmation of the identity of a group, preserving it from incorporation into the surrounding social world.

All of these positive functions of conflict (i.e., benefits from a conflict situation that strengthen the structure) may be found in illustrations where a group is in conflict with an out-group. On the international scene, we may observe how conflict, be it in the form of military action or at the treaty table, does set national geographic boundaries. At a more local level, new groups may emerge and develop structural identity because of conflict. The potential establishment of the schismatic traditionalist church (which maintains pre Vatican Council II practices of Catholicism) and the Anglo-Catholic church (which broke from the Episcopal church over the issue of the ordination of women) are other examples of the creation of new structures through conflict.

Ongoing conflict with out-groups, moreover, may reaffirm the identity of members of the group. The wars over the years have intensified the in-group identification of an Arab or an Israeli in the Middle East or a Protestant or a Catholic in Northern Ireland. Religious groups, ethnic groups, and political groups have often prospered in the face of persecution, as conflict performs the positive function of sharpening in-group identity.

SAFETY-VALVE INSTITUTIONS

One specific mechanism that may be employed to maintain a group through potential social conflict is the safety-valve institution. Through a safety valve, which allows the steam of hostilities to escape without blowing apart the whole structure, conflict helps to "clear the air" in a troubled group. Coser (1956:41) observes that such a safety valve serves "as an outlet for the release of hostilities" and that without such an outlet, relations between the antagonists would be severed.

Safety-valve institutions or practices thus allow for the expression of dissatisfaction with the structure. A student council or a faculty well-being committee might serve as a safety valve in a university, providing a means through which students and faculty may express grievances. A personnel director in a company bureaucracy may serve a similar function. The Better Business Bureau is a safety-valve organization that mitigates conflicts between business and consumer. These institutions all enable steam from a conflict situation to be released without destroying the university, the company, or the economic system.

Safety-valve institutions, while serving the positive function of regulating conflict, also involve costs. Because safety valves are not designed or intended to produce major structural changes, the basic problem may go unresolved. For example, neither student councils nor most faculty groups are in the position to make policy decisions for the university. They exist only with the approval of the university and are, at least in part, regulated and controlled by the larger structure. Similarly a company's personnel director does not really represent the interests of the workers, nor does the Better Business Bureau have the consumer's needs as its main reason for existence. All serve as mechanisms for regulating the potential conflict and indirectly for preventing conflict groups to develop (e.g., faculty or labor unions) that might engender changes through conflict. As Coser (1956:48) observes:

> Through these safety valves, hostility is prevented from turning against its original object. But such displacements also involve costs both for the social system and for the individual: reduced pressure for modifying the system to meet changing conditions, as well as dammed-up tension in the individual, creating potentialities for disruptive explosion.

REALISTIC AND NONREALISTIC CONFLICT

In discussing conflict situations, Coser distinguishes between realistic and nonrealistic conflict. *Realistic conflicts* are those "which arise from frustration of specific demands within the relationship and from estimates of gains of the participants, and which are directed at the presumed frustrating object." Workers striking against management may be an example of realistic conflict insofar as management holds the keys to salary increases and other labor benefits. *Nonrealistic conflicts*, on the other hand, are those that are "not occasioned by the rival ends of the antagonists, but by the need for tension release of at least one of them" (Coser, 1956:49). Vengeance taken in witchcraft is frequently a form of nonrealistic conflict in nonliterate societies, as is scapegoating in highly literate countries. In intergroup relations, *scapegoating* is used to describe the situation where a person may not vent his or her prejudice against the real problem group and thereby uses a substitute group as the object of prejudice. Many hardworking middle- and working-class individuals express prejudice against the "bums on welfare" for misusing hard-earned tax dollars.

The fact of the matter is, however, that much more of the tax dollar goes to the rich in the form of subsidies or indirectly through tax deductions than to the poor in the form of welfare assistance. Being unable to conflict with the politicians, who may be drawing farm subsidies, or with the oil companies, who may be granted huge oil depreciation allowances, a middle-class American may use welfare recipients as the objects of wrath against our system of taxation. Nonrealistic conflicts are thus the result of deprivations and frustrations or, as we have seen in this example, of a displacement of an originally realistic antagonism that was not allowed expression.

Granted, there may be elements of both realistic and nonrealistic conflict present in a situation. Specifically, realistic conflicts may be accompanied by emotionally distorted sentiments because tension release is disallowed in other conflict situations. For example, a strike against an employer may take on hostile traits not only because of the strain in employer–employee relations but also possibly because of an inability to resolve hostile feelings against other authority figures. Thus it is possible for aggressive energies to accumulate in other interaction processes prior to the release of tension in the conflict situation (Coser, 1956:57).

HOSTILITY IN CLOSE SOCIAL RELATIONSHIPS

Coser observes that it is possible to engage in realistic conflict without becoming hostile or aggressive. An illustration might be provided by two old law-school friends who find themselves representing adversary clients in a court of law. Each lawyer scrupulously and aggressively defends his/her client's interests during the court hearing, but after leaving the courtroom, the two may forget their differences and casually go out together for a drink to discuss old times. Examples where conflict is not accompanied by hostile feelings are usually relationships that are partial or segmented, rather than those that involve the whole personality of the participants.

When conflict develops within close social relationships, however, detachment is more difficult to maintain. Coser (1956:62) observes:

> The closer the relationship, the greater the affective investment, the greater also the tendency to suppress rather than express hostile feelings. Whereas in secondary relationships, such as with business partners, feelings of hostility can be expressed with relative freedom, this is not always the case in primary relationships where total involvement of the participants makes acting out of such feelings a danger to the relationship.

Paradoxically the closer the relationship, the more difficult it is to express hostile feelings. Yet the longer these feelings are suppressed, the more important is their expression to the maintenance of the relationship. Because total personalities are likely to be involved in close relationships, conflict, when it does break out, is more likely to be intense.

Thus, according to Coser's propositions, all things being equal, the conflict between two strangers would be less intense than conflict between a husband and a wife. Persons in such close relationships, moreover, may attempt to suppress hostile feelings to avoid conflict, but such suppression may cause the accumulation of hostilities, leading to an explosion if conflict should develop. For example, husband and wife may greatly disagree on the appropriate use of the family's income. Because in past discussions both have felt that their differences are irreconcilable but both are otherwise satisfied with the marriage, the couple are reluctant to conflict over the issue. The silence, however, does nothing to resolve the differences, and one day conflict will inevitably break out. When it does, the real issue of finances may be discussed, but extraneous elements may also emerge. The last visit of the husband's mother, the window that their young son accidentally broke, and the style of furniture selected by the wife may all drift into the argument. Such realistic issues may, moreover, be buoyed by nonrealistic issues, including frustration with an employer for refusing to give a substantial wage increase, annoyance with the repair person who overcharged for a service call, and the fact that a relative recently requested a monetary loan.

In spite of the severity of problems when conflict breaks out in close relationships, Coser insists that the absence of conflict cannot be taken as an index of the strength and stability of such a relationship. Expressed conflict, on the contrary, may be a sign of a viable relationship, whereas the absence of conflict may simply spell the suppression of problems that signal real trouble ahead.

The Issue of the Functionality of Conflict

As we have seen, conflict may be positively functional to the extent that it promotes the group and negatively functional to the extent that it works against the structure. Coser (1956:72) cites Simmel's observation that conflict may be positive in that it eases tensions within a group by establishing unity and balance. He provides indication from observations of the Jewish community that increased conflict within the group may be related to increased interaction with and integration into the general community. Because homogeneity may be necessary for the survival of an isolated group and means an absence of internal conflict, it may also imply a lack of integration of that group with the larger society. Jews confined to European ghettos may have experienced less in-group conflict, but the conflict among Jews of differing perspectives in American society reflects their integration.

Coser asserts that what is important in determining whether conflict is functional or dysfunctional is the *type of issue* that is the subject of the conflict. Conflict is positively functional if it does not question the basis of the relationship and negatively functional if it attacks a core value. For example, if one person enters a marriage because he/she desires to parent and the other member of the couple desires to remain childless, this conflict over whether or not to have children involves the basic consensual agreement about the very purpose of the relationship. Coser observes (1956:73), "One may expect that this type of conflict will presumably have more profound impact on the relationship than a conflict over particular plans to spend a vacation or to allocate the family budget." When conflict develops over peripheral issues, it may be instrumental in advancing the struture in the ways already described. When it develops over a core value, however, conflict may threaten the very existence of the social group.

Coser continues by observing that loosely structured and open societies institute safeguards against the type of conflict that would endanger basic group consensus through attack on its core values by allowing conflict over nonessential issues. Such conflicts between and among various antagonistic groups cancel each other out and actually serve to "sew the social system together." In conflicting over more peripheral values, opposing groups may never touch an area that would cause disintegration along one primary line of cleavage. The United States represents such an open, loosely structured society where conflicts over issues ranging from abortion to nuclear energy to taxation abound. The issues are not core values, and such conflict does not threaten the social structure. It may in fact promote structural solidarity in that groups may take different positions on different issues, disagreeing on any single point of cleavage.

·　In-group conflict in both large and small structures may be an indicator of a healthy, viable relationship. Coser strongly disagrees with those sociologists who have always viewed conflict in only a negative light. Disagreement between husband and wife, employer and employee, nurse and doctor is a normal occurrence that may, in fact, enhance the structure created by the relationship. In fact, societies and groups that allow conflict are the ones that are least likely to be seriously threatened by eruptions that would tear apart the social structure. In such situations, conflict does not ordinarily develop around core values and may help to strengthen the structure. In totalitarian groups, conflict is suppressed, and when it does develop, it may tear apart the group. Thus Coser (1956:85) strongly denies that the absence of conflict can be used as an indicator of the "strength and stability of a relationship."

Conditions Affecting Conflict with Out-Groups and Group Structure _____

As we have already seen, Coser demonstrates that conflict with outside groups may help to establish structural boundaries. But conflict with out-groups may also increase integration within the groups. Coser (1956:92–93) feels that "the degree of group consensus prior to the outbreak of the conflict" is the most important correlative as to whether conflict does in fact increase group cohesion. Coser further observes:

> If a group is lacking in basic consensus, outside threat leads not to increased cohesion, but to general apathy, and the group is consequently threatened with disintegration. Research on the impact of the depression on the family has shown, for example, that families lacking internal solidarity before the depression responded apathetically and were broken, whereas solidary families were actually strengthened. (Coser, 1956:93)

When a small, tightly knit group is struggling with an outside enemy, it is unlikely to be able to tolerate much internal dissension. This type of group works to maintain group uniformity and reacts to departures from it. Such a group may be illustrated by a religious sect that works either to convert the dissenter or to force him/her from its ranks. Coser (1956: 103–104), still building on the writings of Simmel, reformulates the latter's proposition as follows:

> Groups engaged in continued struggle with the outside tend to be intolerant within. They are unlikely to tolerate more than limited departures from the group unity. Such groups tend to assume a sect-like character: they select mmbership in terms of special characteristics and so tend to be limited in size, and they lay claim to the total personality involvement of their members.

Coser observes that the social cohesion in such sectlike groups depends upon the total sharing of all aspects of group life. The only way such a group can solve the problem of dissent is through the dissenter's voluntary or forced withdrawal from the group. Groups of the "church type," on the other hand, are not involved in continuous struggle with the outside and tend to make no special claims on the total personalities of their members. Such groups are likely to allow areas of "tolerated conflict" to exist, and they exhibit an ability to modify and change.

The tightly knit, sectlike group may be dependent on outside enemies for group survival. Its conflict with other groups may have a realistic base, but frequently (as we have already seen with other emotionally close relations) this conflict is based on nonrealistic issues. As Coser (1956:105) expresses it: "Just as such a conflict is governed not by the desire to obtain results, but by a need to release tension in order to maintain the structure of the personality, so the group's search for enemies is aimed not at obtaining results for its members, but merely at maintaining its own structure as a going concern." Thus a sectlike group that is intolerant of internal expression of conflict may have to manufacture enemies, even if none exist, to drain off any feelings of hostility and anger, preventing a member's wrath from being vented on any issue internal to the group.

Coser cites examples of this phenomenon from historical accounts of the development and rise of labor unions. Similar examples, however, could be found in nations at war, in the rise of a religious sect, or among extreme political groups in a nation. Whereas internal controversy cannot be tolerated, for example, among a sectlike religious group such as the Children of God, the struggle of such a group with nonbelievers possibly strengthens its ability to attract and maintain converts. If the struggles that have brought such a group to the attention of the news media were suddenly to cease, Coser would suggest that new enemies might be sought to strengthen further the group's growth and increasing cohesion. Such a group not only achieves a structural identity through its opposition with the out-groups but also experiences increased integration and cohesion in its struggle.

Continuing with the example of the Children of God, we can see an illustration of still another proposition dealing with ideology and conflict. Members of a religious sect such as the Children of God are often described as fanatics, as being brainwashed, and in other such terms. Some would be more willing to suffer death than to give up their beliefs. Similar examples may be cited from the lives of early Christians, the early Mormons, the Communists, or any of a number of advocates of causes of "freedom" in various nations and with varying persuasions. Coser (1956:118) explains such a commitment through the following proposition:

> Conflicts in which the participants feel that they are merely the representatives of collectivities and groups, fighting not for self but only for the ideals of the group they represent, are likely to be more radical and merciless than those that are fought for personal reasons.

Elimination of the personal element tends to make conflict sharper, in the absence of modifying elements which personal factors would normally introduce. The modern Marxian labor movement exemplifies the radicalizing effects of objectification of conflict. Strict ideological alignments are more likely to occur in rigid than in flexible adjustive structures.

In summary, conflict with out-groups may increase the internal cohesion of a group *if* there is basic consensus on core values already existing within a group. In loosely knit or churchlike structures, as long as the outside threat is perceived to be a concern to the group, other differences within the group may be tolerated without their posing a serious threat to group stability. In tightly knit or sectlike groups, however, internal conflict is more likely to be disallowed expression. The focus of conflict for such groups tends to be with out-groups. In fact, Coser suggests that rigidly organized struggle groups may actually search for enemies in order to facilitate unity and cohesion. Such groups may perceive an outside threat that does not actually exist; yet such imaginary threats have the same group-integrating potential as realistic threats.

Without question, the functionalism of the 1950s, with its focus on social integration, had neglected the issue of conflict in society. This approach tended to view conflict as disruptive and dissociating. Coser, while remaining firmly committed to the structural functionalist tradition, demonstrated that conflict may be a means of balancing power and interest groups in such a way as to maintain society as an ongoing concern. Coser (1956:157) concludes his discussion of the relationship between social conflict and social structure with the following summary:

> Our discussion of the distinction between types of conflict and between types of social structures, leads us to conclude that conflict tends to be dysfunctional for a social structure in which there is no or insufficient toleration and institutionalization of conflict. The intensity of a conflict which threatens to "tear apart," which attacks the consensual bases of a social system, is related to the rigidity of the structure. What threatens the equilibrium of such a structure is not conflict as such, but the rigidity itself which permits hostilities to accumulate and to be channeled along one major line of cleavage once they break out in conflict.

Critique of Conflict Structuralism _____

Although Coser is sometimes placed in a paradigm different from that of other structural functionalists, careful reading of his work will indicate that he has always remained committed to this mainline theoretical position.[1] That Coser's contributions to theory remain firmly in the functionalist tradition, although not in the extreme naturalistic model, may be demonstrated in the underlying assumptions about people and society implicitly contained in his sociological theory.

Coser (1967:9) makes it quite clear that he regards conflict theory as a partial theory rather than as an approach that can explain all social reality. He concurs with functionalist Robin Williams's statement: "Actual societies are held together by consensus, by interdependence, by sociability and by coercion. . . . The real job is to show how actual social structures and processes operating in these ways can be predicted and explained" (cited in Coser, 1967:9). The vision Coser has for sociological theory is a unified one including partial theories of conflict as well as consensus. Such partial theories perform the task of "sensitizing the students to one or another set of data relevant to full theoretical explanation" (Coser, 1967:9). He compares sociological theory to that of other social sciences and makes the following observation:

> In the last analysis there can be only one overall sociological theory even though it consists of sets of partial theories of the middle range considered important for the illumination of that particular social dimension. Just as sophisticated political theory has long abandoned the fruitless discussion as to whether consent or coercion is the "real basis" of government; just as psychology has long abandoned the vain quest of deciding whether nature or nurture is the main determinant of personality; so sociology should be mature enough to leave aside such fruitless lines of inquiry. A mature political theory is aware that consent and coercion are at the basis of the political order; a mature psychology is aware of the indissoluble and intricate interplay of nature and nurture in the determination of psychological phenomena. It would be a regressive step indeed were sociology to revert at this stage to such primitive and fruitless dichotomizing. (Coser, 1967:9–10)

In the tradition of Durkheim, who stressed that sociology must use social facts to explain other social facts, Coser argues for the need of a

---

[1] In his book on sociological theory Turner (1974), for example, lists Coser as a contributor to conflict theory. Collins (1975) in his comprehensive treatment of conflict sociology, however, does not cite Coser, nor does he list Coser among the references used for his work. Similarly Zeitlin (1973) asserts that Coser does not depart significantly from functionalism. If there is a conflict paradigm in sociology, the author concurs with those who assert that Coser is not representative of it. In fact, in a personal conversation with Professor Coser during which the author asked him what sociological contribution he wished to be remembered for, Coser good-naturedly replied, "Well, *not* for my contribution to conflict theory." Coser's contribution has been to bring conflict as a social process into structural analysis.

sociological theory that will use objective indicators to explain objective social reality. (Consider Coser's quote at the beginning of this chapter.) Thus Coser's model of people is clearly out of the social psychological realm and squarely in the more traditional sociological camp. Men and women are not free spirits doing whatever they wish but are constrained by the social situations in which they find themselves. Reality for Coser is not the subjective reality of Charles Horton Cooley or George Herbert Mead, but rather the objective reality of Durkheim and the functionalists. Persons are thereby constrained by forces of the social structure that limit freedom and creativity. It is the task of sociology to discern these social constraints. For example, Coser himself has done a sociological analysis of the evolution of the Western intellectual class. In introducing this work he observes, "Just as animal species grow only in environments conducive to their growth, so human types develop only if they encounter favorable institutional settings" (1970:3). Although intellectuals, Coser feels, help to establish cultural norms and values, they can do so only in favorable climate. "Actors and settings" must both be present for knowledge to develop. This same emphasis is in evidence in Coser's excellent treatment of classic scholars in *Masters of Sociological Thought* (1977). Using a sociology-of-knowledge framework that links thought to both the larger cultural and the more personal milieu, Coser demonstrates how the theorist's work is related to the historical context and to personal life history.

Clearly the social structure exists on its own and operates as a constraint for Coser as it does for structural functionalists. Coser (1975a:215) expresses it as follows: "The sociology of conflict must search for the structurally rooted interests and values that lead men to engage in conflicts with each other, if it is not to dissolve into psychological disquisitions about innate aggressiveness, original sin, or plain human cussedness." What Coser has contributed to the functionalist orientation is his description of how social structures may be the product of social conflict and how they may be maintained by such conflict. His propositions largely revolve around the intensity of and the functions of social conflict for social institutions.

Although Coser is committed to a unified scientific theory of society, he tempers any move toward extreme naturalism or extreme determinism in human action. This approach may be demonstrated by his methodological orientation, which freely uses history as a source of data to support his theoretical contentions. (Functionalism has often been accused of being ahistorical if not antihistorical, a charge that cannot be leveled against Coser.) In fact, Coser may be placed more toward the humanistic end of our naturalistic–humanistic continuum, discussed in Chapter 1. He seems far more concerned with sociology's "creative ability" and "innovative effervescence" than he is with the question of "How scientific is sociology?" Undoubtedly Coser views sociology as a science, but it is a young discipline that should not prematurely seek the rigorous method of science at the expense of substantive issues. In his (1975b:671–700) presidential address to members of the American Sociological Association, Coser was critical both of the extreme subjective emphasis in some theoretical endeavors, as represented by an approach known as *ethnomethodology* (discussed in Chapter 12), and of the extremely precise measuring attempts of some mathematical theory, as represented by *path analysis* (discussed in Chapter 9). He asserted that both approaches share "a hypertrophy of method at the expense of substantive theory" (Coser, 1975:698). He expressed his concern about the state of contemporary sociology in the following statement:

> In both cases [path analysis and ethnomethodology], I submit, preoccupation with method largely has led to neglect of significance and substance. And yet, our discipline will be judged in the last analysis on the basis of the substantive enlightment which it is able to supply about the social structures in which we are enmeshed and which largely condition the course of our lives. If we neglect that major task, if we refuse the challenge to answer these questions, we shall forfeit our birthright and degenerate into congeries of rival sects and specialized researchers who will learn more and more about less and less. (Coser, 1975:698)

Coser's own work suffers from a lack of methodological rigor, as do many of the works that bear the label *theory* in sociology. His concepts are often intuitively pleasing but impossible to operationalize for precise testing. (Take for example the concept of *core value* discussed earlier. How can one determine whether an issue is a core value until after the fact, that is, after an attack upon it destroys the structure. There are traces of tautology or circular reasoning in this concept and others that are essential to Coser's theory.) Yet as many theorists have argued, it is more important to address relevant theoretical issues in a less-than-precise manner than to study trivia with a great deal of sophistication.

Summary

Coser developed his conflict perspective from the work of German sociologist Georg Simmel. Based on Simmel's treatise of conflict as a form of association, Coser laid out propositions for testing the functionality of conflict for the social group. Like Simmel's theoretical attempts, Coser's too represents an effort to construct a partial rather than a total theory of society.

With much functionalist analysis implying that conflict is dysfunctional for a group, Coser sought to spell out conditions under which conflict contributes positively to the maintenance of the social structure. Conflict as a social process may be the mechanism through which groups are formed and group boundaries are established. Conflict may, moreover, bind group members together through a reaffirmation of group identity. Whether conflict is a source of group cohesion or group dissolution is dependent upon the origin of the tension, the issue of the conflict, the manner in which the tension is handled, and, most important, the type of structure in which the conflict develops. Coser distinguishes between in-group and out-group conflict, between core values and more peripheral issues, between conflict that produces structural change versus conflict channeled into safety-valve institutions, and between conflict in loosely knit versus tightly knit structures. He also differentiates realistic conflict from its nonrealistic counterpart. All of these points are factors in determining the function of conflict as a social process.

Coser's work on conflict can best be described as *conflict functionalism*. Without abandoning the concepts and many of the assumptions of structural functionalism, he attempts to add the dynamic dimension of conflict to this theory. For Coser the integration perspective and conflict perspectives are not rival explanatory schemes. As he has observed, both are "partial theories sensitizing the observer to one or another set of data and events relative to a full theoretical explanation. . . . [Thus] conflict and order, disruption and integration are fundamental social processes which, though in different proportions and admixtures, are part of any conceivable social system" (1972:2–3).

References

COLLINS, RANDAL
   1975 *Conflict Sociology*. New York: Academic Press, Inc.
COSER, LEWIS A.
   1956 *The Functions of Social Conflict*. New York: The Free Press.
   1967 *Continuities in the Study of Social Conflict*. New York: The Free Press.
   1970 *Men of Ideas: A Sociologist's View*. New York: The Free Press.
   1972 "Introduction to Issue." *The Journal of Social Issues* 28:1–10.
   1975a "Structure and Conflict." Pp. 210–219 in Peter M. Blau (Ed.), *Approaches to the Study of Social Structure*. New York: The Free Press.
   1975b "Two Methods in Search of a Substance." *American Sociological Review* 40:691–700.
   1977 *Masters of Sociological Thought*, 2nd ed. New York: Harcourt Brace Jovanovich, Inc.

TURNER, JONATHAN H.
   1974 *The Structure of Sociological Theory.* Homewood, Ill.: The Dorsey
        Press, Inc.
ZEITLIN, IRVING M.
   1973 *Rethinking Sociology.* New York: Appleton-Century-Crofts.

6

Conflict Structuralism II: A Proposed Explanation of Social Structure

> The intent of a sociological theory of conflict is to overcome the predominantly arbitrary nature of unexplained historical events by deriving these events from social structural elements—in other words, to explain certain processes by prognostic connections. Certainly it is important to describe the conflict between workers and employers purely as such; but it is more important to produce a proof that such a conflict is based on certain social structural arrangements and hence is bound to arise wherever such structural arrangements are given. Thus it is the task of sociology to derive conflicts from specific social structures and not to relegate these conflicts to psychological variables ("aggressiveness") or to descriptive-historical ones (the influx of Negroes into the United States) or to chance. (Dahrendorf, 1958:172)

Lewis Coser was not alone in his dissatisfaction with the neglect of conflict in contemporary sociological theorizing. Shortly after the appearance of Coser's work (1956), the German sociologist Ralf Dahrendorf rewrote his theory of class and class conflict in English during his brief stay in the United States (1957–1958). (Dahrendorf's theory, originally published in his native tongue, was not readily accessible to American sociologists who were not fluent in German.) Like Coser, Dahrendorf is critical of traditional structural functionalism because of its inability to deal with change. Rather than using Simmel (as did Coser) as a theoretical springboard, Dahrendorf builds his theory around partial refutation, partial acceptance, and modification of the sociological theory of Karl Marx. Like Coser, Dahrendorf originally viewed conflict theory as a partial theory, contending that it was but one of the perspectives that could be used to analyze social phenomena. Dahrendorf contended that society was Janus-faced, with one face being conflict and the other being cooperation. (He later modified this position, asserting that anything that structural functionalism could analyze, conflict theory could analyze better.)

Although Dahrendorf is a leading critic of structural functionalism and a self-described "conflict theorist," serious question may be raised about how much he has departed from the functionalist school.[1] What is apparent, however, is that Dahrendorf has raised an important criticism of this once-dominant approach to sociology, namely, its failure to deal with social conflict. He insists that the process of social conflict is the key to social structure. Along with Coser, Dahrendorf has been a major theoretical voice urging that a conflict perspective be used in the attempt to better understand social phenomena.

A Reconsideration of Marxian Theory

As we have already noted, Dahrendorf bases his theory on a partial refutation, a partial acceptance, and a reformulation of the theory of Karl Marx. In an attempt at partial refutation of Marx, Dahrendorf outlines some of the changes that have occurred in industrial societies since Karl Marx's nineteenth-century society. Among them are (1) the decomposition of capital, (2) the decomposition of labor, and (3) the rise of the new middle class. We will briefly discuss each of these changes perceived by Dahrendorf.

When Marx wrote on capitalism, ownership and the control of the means *of production were vested in the same* individuals. The industrialists, or bourgeoisie, managed and owned the capitalist system, and the workers, or proletariat, were dependent upon this system for survival. What Marx did not foresee, Dahrendorf contends, is the separation of ownership and control of the means of production that has occurred in the twentieth century. The rise of corporations with shares owned by many, none of whom may have exclusive control, serves as an example

---

[1] Weingart (1969:151–165) questions whether Dahrendorf in fact has moved beyond functionalist theory. He contends that Dahrendorf's theory is beset by the same problem that Dahrendorf has imputed to functionalist theory, namely, its failure to account for the rise of conflict from the legitimated relations of the social system. We contend that Dahrendorf's theory is not a replacement for functionalism, as its creator suggests, but is complementary to integration theories of social structure.

of what Dahrendorf has called the *decomposition of capital.* In this age of specialization, it is probable that the person(s) who controls the company may not own it, just as the person(s) who owns it may not control it. Given this era of specialization and expertise, the management of a company may be hired employees just as factory workers are. Both factory workers and office personnel may own shares in the company, making them part owners. The decomposition of capital makes it difficult, according to Dahrendorf, to identify Marx's bourgeoisie, who have exclusive monopoly of both ownership and control. With the advent of the twentieth century, this ownership and control are diversified and are no longer vested in a single individual or family.

Not only has there been a decomposition of capital, Dahrendorf asserts, but there has also been a *decomposition of labor.* The proletariat is no longer a single homogeneous group. By the late nineteenth century, a clearly stratified working-class was emerging, with skilled laborers at the top of the hierarchy and unskilled workers at the bottom. The proletariat does not exist as an undifferentiated mass any more than the bourgeoisie does. Carpenters, plumbers, and truck drivers are favored with much higher wages than sanitary engineers, waitresses, and drill-press operators.

The decomposition of both capital and labor has led to swelling of the middle class that was not envisioned by Marx. This contributed to the failure of Marx's predicted materialization of a class revolution. Marx recognized the existence of a middle class in the nineteenth century, but he felt that most of this small group would join the proletariat in its struggle with the bourgeoisie when the day of revolution arrived. He did not foresee the rise of labor unions, accompanied by social mobility for the workers. As Dahrendorf (1959:61) observes, "It is quite possible that this theory [Marx's] contains an element of truth, but if it does, then the remarkable spread of social equality in the past century has rendered class struggles and revolutionary change utterly impossible." It is thus social mobility that prevents revolutions from fermenting in modern capitalist societies. If such mobility were suddenly to come to a halt, Dahrendorf would predict a breakdown of the societal structure through revolutionary activity.

According to Dahrendorf, the major theoretical reason that a Marxian revolution is unlikely is that conflict tends to be regulated through institutionalization. This regulation or institutionalization is evidenced in the rise of labor unions, which have facilitated social mobility and which regulate conflict between workers and management. Through the institutionalization of conflict, every society has the ability to cope with new problems that arise within it. The institutionalization of class conflict, asserts Dahrendorf (1959:65), began with a recognition of both labor and management as legitimate interest groups: "Organization presupposes the legitimacy of conflict groups, and it thereby removes the permanent and incalculable threat of guerrilla warfare. At the same time, it makes systematic regulation of conflicts possible. Organization is institutionalization."

In noting these historical changes since the time of Marx, Dahrendorf, feels that he has refuted some aspects of Marxian theory. But refutation, for Dahrendorf, is not enough: "Refutation of old theories makes sense only if it becomes a point of departure for the development of new theories" (Dahrendorf, 1959:73). Dahrendorf then takes it upon himself to formulate a conflict theory that takes into account the historical developments he has discussed.

Toward a Sociological Theory of Conflict in Industrial Society

In developing a sociological critique of Karl Marx's theory, Dahrendorf sustains some Marxian assertions while rejecting others. Because of societal changes, such as those discussed in the previous section, the revolution prophesied by Marx failed to occur in industrialized countries. Moreover it is clear that social classes are no longer based solely on the ownership of the means of production, as Marx suggested. Yet Dahrendorf accepts the idea of class conflict as being one form of conflict and as being one agent of social change. He proceeds to modify Marx's theory of class conflict to include more recent developments.

Dahrendorf proposes that there is a new basis for class, replacing Marx's conception of ownership of the means of production as underlying class distinctions. Authority relations of subordination and superordination, says Dahrendorf, provide the materials from which classes emerge. There is a dichotomy between those who are dominated and those who are subjected. In other words, some participate in the authority structure of the group and others do not; some have authority and others are without it. Dahrendorf (1959:173) acknowledges the difference between those who have a little authority and those who have a great deal of authority. The difference in the degree of domination may be, and often is, very great. Basically, however, there remains a two-class system (within a specified association) that is, those who participate in the authority structure through domination and those who do not through subjection. The class struggle that Dahrendorf discusses is thus one over *authority* rather than one over *ownership of the means of production*. Who owns the means of production is not, in modern industrialized society, as important as who wields the legitimate control.

Quasi Groups and Interest Groups

Dahrendorf contends that in every association characterized by conflict there is a tension between those who share in the authority of the structure and those who are subjects of the structure. As Dahrendorf (1959:176) expresses it:

> Empirically, group conflict is probably most easily accessible to analysis if it be understood as a conflict about the legitimacy of relations of authority. In every association, the interests of the ruling group are the values that constitute the ideology of the legitimacy of its rule, whereas the interests of the subjected group constitute a threat to this ideology and the social relations it covers.

The *interests* that Dahrendorf refers to may be either *manifest* (or recognized) or *latent* (that is, potential interests). Latent interests are "undercurrents of behavior" that are predetermined for a person by virtue of occupying a particular role but that remain unconscious. These are "psychological formulations," which are not properly sociological subject matter until they become conscious goals. Thus persons may be members of a class lacking authority, but as a group they may not recognize their plight. This has been the case for many minority groups whose consciousness became heightened during the 1960s, groups including blacks, women, native Americans, and Chicanos. As latent or unrecognized interests became manifest in the form of conscious goals (e.g., equal pay, equal opportunity for employment), organizations develop that Dahrendorf refers to as *manifest groups*. For example, prior to the 1960s, women were by and large a quasi group, being denied authority in most of the social structures in which they participated. With the advent of the mid-1960s, the latent interests of women became conscious or manifest, and women's liberation groups developed. Thus the conflict between men in positions of authority and women in positions of subjugation is regulated or mitigated through structural organization. The age-old potential conflict between the sexes is now being regulated through the institutionalization of such conflict. It is futile, says Dahrendorf, to try to suppress or to obliterate conflict. In modern societies, conflict must be regulated through institutionalization once opposing interests are recognized.

Conflict Groups, Group Conflicts, and Social Change

According to Dahrendorf's formulation (1959:206), class conflict must be understood as "conflict groups arising out of the authority structure of imperatively coordinated associations." These conflict groups, once they are established as interest groups rather than quasi groups, engage in conflicts that do bring about changes in the social structure. The conflict between labor and management, for example, which was the prime topic of concern for Marx, became institutionalized through labor unions. The unions, in turn, successfully engaged in conflict that brought about changes in both the legal sphere and the economic arena and concrete alterations in the society stratification system. The rise of the new middle class described earlier in this chapter was in fact a structural change brought about through the institutionalization of class conflict.

Dahrendorf emphasizes that his conflict theory is a pluralistic one in contrast to Marx's simple two-class model. Marx used the whole society as the unit of analysis, with persons either controlling the means of production through ownership or in not sharing in such ownership. People were either *have's* or *have-not's*. In replacing property relations with authority relations as the center of the class theory, Dahrendorf (1959:213) observes that this two-class model applies not to total societies but only to specific associations within societies:

> If, in a given society, there are fifty associations, we should expect to find a hundred classes, or conflict groups in the sense of the present study. Apart from these, there may be an undetermined number of conflict groups and conflicts arising from antagonisms other than those based on the authority structure of associations.

Dahrendorf acknowledges that this extreme scattering of conflict groups and conflicts is rarely the case in real life. Usually different conflicts are superimposed on given historical societies, so in actuality conflict fronts are reduced to a few dominant ones. This phenomenon implies that the authority figures of one institution (such as the church) need not participate in the authority of another institution (such as the state). If such dissociation occurs in most institutions, the intensity of conflict is contained. In other words, if there is a strong association in which subordinate members of one group are repeatedly the subordinate members of other groups, any eruption of conflict would be more intense. Dahrendorf (1959:215) expresses it in the following propositionlike statement: "When conflict groups encounter each other in several associations and in several clashes, the energies expended in all of them will be combined and one overriding conflict of interests will emerge." In the example we have given of women as a quasi group become manifest, we can observe that women were part of the subjected segment of most groups. Legally a woman was subject to her husband, in offices she was repeatedly bypassed for promotions into positions of authority, and even in voluntary organizations she frequently was excluded from the authority structure because of her sex. This same repeated exclusion from the authority structure could be observed in the history of minority-group relations, labor relations, and relations among nations.

Dahrendorf contends that property, economic status, and social status, although not determinants of class as he uses the term, do influence the intensity of conflict. He proposes the following proposition: "the lower the correlation is between authority position and other aspects of socioeconomic status, the less intense are class conflicts likely to be, and vice versa" (1959:218). In other words, groups of people enjoying relatively high economic status are less likely to engage in intense conflict over the authority structure than are those who are deprived of both socioeconomic status and authority.

Conflict for Dahrendorf, as for Coser, cannot be obliterated from society. It is functional for the development and change of societal structures. What is essential is that conflict be regulated through effective institutionalization rather than attempts being made to suppress it.

Critical Evaluation of Dahrendorf's Theory

In many ways, Dahrendorf's conflict theory resembles that of Lewis Coser. In his best-known work, *Class and Class Conflict in Industrial Society* (1959), he proposes (like Coser) that conflict theory is only a partial theory.[2] For both Coser and Dahrendorf, conflict is a phenomenon that must be considered in the analysis of social structure.[3] The similarities between these two theorists and between Dahrendorf and the structural functionalists can further be observed in the assumptions they make about the nature of people, the nature of society, and the importance of sociological theory.

Dahrendorf has provided an explicit discussion of the model of human beings that is considered by him the essence of sociological analysis.

---

[2] Dahrendorf (1968:129–150) changes this position in a later essay where he argues for the superiority of the constraint position. There is no problem that can be described in equilibrium terms that cannot be described at least as well in constraint terms. Dahrendorf contends that the constraint approach is more general and more plausible and "generally more informative about the problems of social and political life" and should replace functionalism.

[3] Turner (1974:121–147) has demonstrated the compatability and complementarity of Coser's and Dahrendorf's theories in attempting to synthesize the two works. He specifically looks at the issues of causes of conflict, intensity and violence of conflict, duration of conflict, and outcomes of conflict. Turner observes that the two theories are "divergent" but "highly complementary."

He observes that all the people discussed by social science are artificial abstract creatures. Such models are useful to a pursuit of scientific analysis. For example, economics describes *homo oeconomicus*, which represents "the perfectly informed, thoroughly rational person." Yet this model has proved useful in discussions of the consumer, who carefully weighs utility and cost before making a purchase. Another model of human beings is provided by psychology as "the person who, even if he/she always does good, wants to do evil." Such a person is kept in check by his/her superego, which controls evil impulses. Sociology provides yet another model, *homo sociologicus*, which treats the intersection of people with society. As with *homo oeconomicus* and the psychological person, *homo sociologicus* is an abstracted type that allows one to pursue scientific discussion and analysis. It represents only an incomplete view of the person.

Dahrendorf (1968:19–87) asserts that *role* is the key concept in the understanding of the sociological person. Each person occupies many social positions and each position must be acted out. Dahrendorf (1968:58) observes that every role leaves its players free, to some extent, by not pronouncing on certain matters. Society helps to shape the person's behavior, but the person is partially free to help shape society. For example, the role of father implies that the man takes an interest in and partial responsibility for meeting the emotional needs of his children. Exactly how these needs are met, however, varies from family to family without rigid prescriptions or proscriptions from society. A degree of freedom and flexibility may be observed in the enactment of all of our roles. Dahrendorf (1968:44) comments on the need for balance between the image of a free and a role-determined person: "The problem of man's freedom as a social being is a problem of the balance between role-determined behavior and autonomy, and in this respect at least the analysis of *homo sociologicus* seems to confirm the dialectical paradox of freedom and necessity."

There is thus a paradox between the two images of the person: the *moral image*, which views a person as an integral, unique, and free creature, and the *scientific image*, which describes a person as a differentiated, exemplary, aggregate of predetermined roles. We have already seen that functionalism and other naturalistic theories have tended toward the scientific image. Humanistic or interpretative theories, on the other hand, have tended toward the moral image. Although acknowledging the existence of a moral image, Dahrendorf views *homo sociologicus* as a representative of the scientific image. For Dahrendorf (1968:81), "the two characters of man are an expression of essentially different possibilities of knowledge." Dahrendorf (1968:101) observes that sociological theory says nothing about people's moral quality. He (1968:90–91) emphasizes that "*Man behaves in accordance with his roles.* Thus man basically figures in sociological analyses only to the extent that he complies with all the expectations associated with his social positions." It is important, therefore, not to reify *homo sociologicus* and to keep in mind that this model is necessarily a partial portrait of the real human being.

Dahrendorf's basic image of society is also consistent with that of structural functionalism in that society has a true reality. Dahrendorf (1968:51) makes it clear that for him society is more than "all of the people in a given society." Yet unlike most structural functionalists, Dahrendorf views coercion and conflict as central to an understanding of society's structure. He observes that most people in any given society play no part whatever, direct or indirect, in formulating role expectations. It is the task of sociology as the study of society to identify those agencies responsible for social rules and to describe them with operational precision. In our discussion of Dahrendorf's theory of class, we have seen how important authority is to social organization and how conflict over authority leads to the development of institutions in our society.

In line with structural functionalist thought, Dahrendorf views the social role as the link between the scientific image of the person and his/her social structure. He (1968:53) describes the structure of society as "a giant organization chart in which millions of positions are centered in their fields like suns with their planet systems." Such an organization chart, although quite complex, is the subject matter of sociology.

Although holding fast to a scientific model of the person and society, Dahrendorf departs from scientific sociology's emphasis on the need for a value-free sociology.[4] Because the real person is more than *homo sociologicus*—he/she is moral as well as scientific—sociologists should not be content with a value-neutral stance to the field. Dahrendorf (1968:18) asserts:

> But it seems to me more important today to warn against the radical separation of science and value judgments than to warn against their commingling. Our responsibility as sociologists does not end when we complete the process of scientific inquiry; indeed, it may begin at that very point. It requires no less than the unceasing examination of the political and moral consequences of our scholarly activity. It commits us, therefore, to professing our value convictions in our writings and in the lecture hall as well.

[4] Based on his comments on value-free sociology (presented in part in Chapter 1), Dahrendorf could have been placed in the final section of this text dealing with evaluative or applied theory. We decided against this only because there is little in Dahrendorf's theory itself to demonstrate evaluative theory. Although he acknowledges his commitment to it, his best-known work does not provide illustrations of evaluative theory to the same degree as those authors selected for Part III.

Dahrendorf emphasizes that sociologists must be sensitive to the implications of their sociology. He (1968:86) unequivocally states, "Anyone who cannot bear the melancholy insufficiency of a sociological science of man should renounce the discipline, for a dogmatic sociology is worse than no sociology at all."

In spite of his call for a relevant sociology that considers "what a modern, open civilized society might look like" (a task he sees as "the domain of theory") and his charge that it is "the sociologist's business once he is equipped with his theories to take part in the process of changing reality" (Dahrendorf, 1968:278), Dahrendorf's own major theoretical attempt remains clearly in the naturalistic, nonevaluative tradition. Although he speaks like a prophet when writing about theory, his theory is decidedly an important contribution to the priestly attempt to explain social structure.

Summary

The German sociologist Ralf Dahrendorf utilizes the Marxian conflict theory of the struggle between classes to build his theory of class and class conflict in contemporary industrial society. Class, for Dahrendorf, does not mean ownership of the means of production (as it did for Marx) but rather the possession of authority, which implies the legitimate right to dominate others. The class struggle in modern societies of both capitalistic and communistic economies, of both totalitarian and free governments, revolves around the control of authority.

Dahrendorf sees conflict groups as arising out of the common interests of individuals who are able to organize. Dahrendorf describes this process, through which quasi groups become interest groups capable of having an impact on the structure. The institutions formed as a result of these interests are vehicles through which social change occurs. Attempts should be directed toward the regulation of societal conflict through effective institutionalization rather than toward its suppression.

Dahrendorf's theory is admittedly a partial theory of society. Through it he demonstrates how organizations can and do arise out of class conflict. The partial nature of his theory may also be seen in his discussion of the nature of the human being and the nature of sociology. Sociology has for its subject matter social (as opposed to moral, psychological, economic, and so on) person. At the same time, sociologists must be cognizant of the other facets of people or risk the protrayal of an abstract person who has no relevance to the larger world.

References

DAHRENDORF, RALF
   1958 "Toward a Theory of Social Conflict." *Journal of Conflict Resolution* 2
       (June):170–183.
   1959 *Class and Class Conflict in Industrial Society.* Stanford, Calif.: Stanford
       University Press.
   1968 *Essays in the Theory of Society.* Stanford, Calif.: Stanford University
       Press.
TURNER, JONATHAN H.
   1974 *The Structure of Sociological Theory.* Homewood, Ill.: The Dorsey
       Press, Inc.
WEINGART, PETER
   1969 "Beyond Parsons: A Critique of Ralf Dahrendorf's Conflict Theory."
       Social Forces (December):151–165.

7

Conflict and Structure in an Evolutionary Perspective

One of the more surprising developments in the social sciences in recent years has been the rebirth of interest in evolutionary theory. . . . The reason for this renewal of interest is not hard to find. Despite the abundance of theories in contemporary social science, none of the others takes seriously the need for *making sense of the basic patterns of history.* (Lenski, 1975:135)

A number of writers on contemporary theory have advocated a synthesis of the conflict and structuralist perspectives in preference to two distinct theories (see for example, van den Berghe, 1963, and Zeitlin, 1973). In Chapter 5 we saw how Lewis Coser attempted to bring the attention of functionalists to the social process of conflict and to incorporate it into functionalist analysis. Although admittedly a partial theory, Coser's effort did sensitize many functionalists to their neglect of the positive functions of social conflict. Yet, for the most part, as we attempted to demonstrate, Coser's theory rests firmly in the functionalist tradition, sharing most of functionalism's assumptions about the nature of people and society. Although an improvement over a more static, ahistorical functionalist analysis, it still fails to deal adequately with long-term historical trends and the relation of coercive power to them.

Gerhard E. Lenski has developed a theory that purports to be a synthesis rather than a simple juxtaposition of conflict theory with functionalist analysis. Although his theory deals specifically with social stratification, it does represent an attempt to collapse 10,000 years of man's history into a sociological model. Lenski's integration of functionalist and conflict assumptions occurs, as implied within the quote at the beginning of this chapter, within an evolutionary framework. It is evolutionary theory, according to Lenski, that can analyze structure as well as process without being limited to a narrow time span.

Lenski's theory of stratification thus attempts to synthesize functionalist and conflict endeavors to explain the existence and operation of social classes. Both functionalists and conflict theorists have developed their own respective theories on social stratification. Davis and Moore (1945) have written what has become a classic article discussing social stratification from a functionalist perspective. In this article they assert that stratification is indispensable for a society:

> As a functioning mechanism a society must somehow distribute its members in social positions and induce them to perform the duties of these positions. It must thus concern itself with motivation at two different levels: to instill in proper individuals the desire to fill certain positions, and, once in these positions, the desire to perform the duties attached to them. (Davis and Moore, 1945:243)

Davis and Moore contend that the ranking of occupations is due to a difference in the functional importance of different positions; that is, the reward offered to fulfill the position must be sufficient to induce people to accept hard-to-fill jobs that are essential to a society. Social inequality is a device, therefore, that ensures that the most important positions are conscientiously filled by the most qualified persons. Interrelated with this determinant is the fact that some positions require skills, talents, and training that make recruits scarce in number. Davis and Moore (1945: 243) note: "Modern medicine, for example, is within the mental capacity of most individuals, but a medical education is so burdensome and expensive that virtually none would undertake it if the position of the M.D. did not carry a reward commensurate with the sacrifice."

Although Davis and Moore's argument is an early functionalist attempt and has served as a point of departure for other later theories of stratification, it is clearly based only on an integration and consensus model. (Consider the similarities between Davis and Moore's line of theoretical reasoning and Blau's exchange structuralism discussed in Chapter 4.) It is implied that social classes are necessary to the functioning of a society, that these classes operate together to ensure that the society's needs are met, and that the system is at least tacitly agreed upon by members of the society. This stratification system is thus a reward (or punishment, as the case may be) for services rendered to the smooth functioning of society. Such a model, however, represents only a partial view of stratification.

The functionalist model of stratification has often been contrasted with the conflict model, which emphasizes force and coercion rather than consensual agreement. The basis for many conflict theorists' models of stratification may be found in the works of Karl Marx. For Marx, the basis for social classes is in the exploitation of one class by another rather than in consensus. In terms of capitalist society, Marx argued that the owners of the means of production represented the upper class that was oppressing and forcibly controlling the lower class of workers. This two-class model, according to Marx, is repeatedly seen in history, whether it be in the relations of master–slave, of lord–serf, or of bourgeoisie–proletariat. For Marx, it is the conflict that propels change, and only conflict can move the social order from a system of class oppression to a classless society.

These two approaches to stratification—functionalism and conflict theory—rest upon two different traditions based on differing assumptions about the nature of people and the nature of society. Functionalism is based upon a conservative tradition that views stratification as being essential to meeting the needs of society as a whole. Conflict theory, on the other hand, questions the existence of such "societal needs." It is more concerned with the needs, desires, and interests of individuals and their subgroups (rather than of larger societies) in their struggle for valued goods and services that are in short supply. Such differences reflect opposing assumptions about the nature of people. Lenski observes that functionalists stress the social nature of human beings; that is, individuals are unable to survive without living in groups with others. At the same time, however, they "have been distrustful of man's basic nature and have emphasized the need for restraining social institutions" (Lenski, 1966:22). Conflict theorists, on the other hand, are more optimistic about the goodness of man and are more distrustful of social institutions that thwart this nature. Stemming from these opposing views of people, functionalists and conflict theorists also have differing views of society. Functionalists are more prone to view society as a perfect and complete system, whereas conflict theorists are more likely to view society as a battleground in which various struggles occur.

Lenski is skeptical of all such categorical dichotomies in sociological theory that view people as either "good" or "bad" and society as either a "system" or a "nonsystem." Rather than creating categorical concepts that reflect either–or dichotomies, sociologists should attempt to construct variable concepts that reflect the degree to which a particular phenomenon is present. For example, it is not a matter of whether or not society is a perfect system but rather the degree to which systemic features exist. Similarly it is not a matter of whether people need total constraint or no constraint but the degree to which constraint does exist. In avoiding categorical conceptual distinctions, Lenski suggests that both functionalist and conflict theories provide propositions from which a single theory of

stratification may be derived. It is to this task of synthesizing conservative and radical positions that Lenski directs his efforts in studying power
and privilege in society.

The Structure and Dynamics of Distributive Systems

Using selected assumptions from both the more conservative structural functionalist tradition and the more radical conflict approach to
human nature, Lenski advances two laws of distribution of goods and
services. These postulates, which flow from Lenski's assumptions, may be
summarized as follows: (1) people are social beings who are required to
live in society; (2) human beings usually place their own or their group's
best interests before the interests of others (although they may seek to
hide this fact from themselves and others); (3) human beings have an
insatiable appetite for the goods and services available in a society; and
(4) individuals are unequally endowed with an ability to engage in the
struggle for these scarce goods and services (Lenski, 1966:30–32). If these
postulates about man's social, yet self-seeking, nature are correct, then
Lenski argues that two propositions follow: (1) "men will share the
product of their labors to the extent required to insure the survival and
continued productivity of others whose actions are necessary or beneficial to themselves" and (2) "power will determine the distribution of
nearly all of the surplus possessed by a society" (Lenski, 1966:44).
(Lenski admittedly allows little room for altruism in human activity; he
believes that almost all actions are based on self-interests.)

Using these assumptions and postulates, Lenski continues to build a
theoretical edifice that he tests in his treatise through data from history.
Lenski recognizes that there are vast differences among stratification systems despite the universality of human nature. He asserts that the different forms of distribution of goods and services are related to the level
of technological development in the society. In less developed societies,
goods and services are distributed on the basis of individual need. In more
advanced societies, power is the force behind the distributive system.
Lenski (1966:46) predicts:

> in the simplest societies, or those which are technologically most primitive,
> the goods and services available will be distributed wholly, or largely,
> on the basis of need. . . . With technological advance, an increasing pro-
> portion of the goods and services available to a society will be distributed
> on the basis of power.

Thus Lenski hypothesizes that power and need are the two principles that govern stratification systems. The more complex the society, the more important power becomes in the allocation of available resources.

Lenski then proceeds to discuss the phenomenon of power in more technologically advanced societies. Although the use of force or coercion is the "most effective instrument for seizing power in society" and "remains the foundation of any system of inequity" (Lenski, 1966:51), force is not the most effective means of retaining a power position once it has been secured. At this point, the importance of creating and maintaining an institutional or structural base of operation becomes apparent. The new rule must be legitimated, transforming the rule of might into the rule of right. What this implies is that force must be replaced by institutionalized power that is both socially acceptable and much less personal.

Lenski (1966:59) observes that a reading of history makes it apparent that there is a circulation of political power between periods of coercive rule, or "the rule of might," and periods of institutional rule, or "the rule of right." The rule of might is characterized by a forcible seizure of power by a new elite, which involves an initial phase of violence. During this phase, the organized resistance is either destroyed or suppressed. The second phase is one in which the regime strives to reduce its dependence on naked force and to increase its legitimate authority. The trend at this time is toward constitutionalism, or the rule of right. Unless there is a steady succession of challenges against the reigning power elite, the long-term trend involves a reduction in the active role of force and coercion and an increase in the role of persuasion and incentive. At some time, this constitutional rule of right is again challenged by force and the cycle begins again.

Lenski admits that the duration, the economic situation, and the ideological nature of the political cycles vary greatly and cautions that the differences between political cycles should not be minimized At the same time, however, there is a natural tendency for those who seize power by force to strive to rule by constitutional means, so far as circumstances permit. Yet in the end, every regime is destroyed by force or threat of it. This is the basic theme on which there are a thousand variations (Lenski, 1966:61).

The Structure of the Stratification System

Interconnected with the dynamics or process of the stratification system just described are the structural aspects of the system. Here Lenski is concerned with three units that comprise the system: individuals, classes, and class systems. Individuals make up classes and represent the basic level of analysis. Classes in turn combine to form class systems. Individuals, classes, and class systems all exist in relation to each other and in relation to the competition for scarce resources.

Lenski (1966:74–75) defines *class* as "an aggregation of persons in a society who stand in a similar position with respect to force or some specific form of institutionalized power, privilege or prestige." In his work, however, Lenski focuses on the power class, which he feels determines the distribution of privilege and prestige in societies with any significant surplus of goods. Class, for Lenski, is *power class*. Although this power class may vary from that of industrial leaders to members of a military junta to organized factory workers, each group of persons occupies a similar position with respect to the classic Weberian definition of power as the probability of persons or groups carrying out their will even when opposed by others. Classes are defined in terms of the degree of power they possess in controlling scarce resources.

In complex industrial societies, a single individual may be a member of any number of classes. Class membership must be seen as a multidimensional phenomenon. Lenski (1966:75–76) illustrates this with a single individual who:

> may be a member of the middle class with respect to property holdings, a member of the working class by virtue of his job in a factory, and a member of the Negro "caste." Each of the major roles he occupies, as well as his status in the property hierarchy, influences his chances of obtaining the things he seeks in life, and thus each places him in a specific class. Since these resources are so imperfectly correlated, he cannot be located in any single class. In this connection, it may be appropriate to note that this tendency seems to become progressively more pronounced as one moves from technologically primitive to technologically advanced societies. In other words, *the necessity of multidimensional analyses seems greatest in modern industrial societies.*

It is thus important to note that class is a more complex phenomenon in modern industrial society, where individuals are simultaneously members of a number of classes, each with varying power potential.

Moreover each class contains variations, and different degrees of affluence exist among, for example, factory workers or blacks, yet both groups may be seen as classes with respect to power. (It may help to recall how frequently a political candidate may demonstrate his/her awareness of broad class distinctions when seeking the "black vote" or "labor's vote.") Despite various rankings *within* as well as among classes, members of a particular class stand in a similar position with regard to interests and in opposition to classes who do not share these interests.

Classes, as described above, in turn form class systems. Lenski (1966:80) defines a *class system* as "a hierarchy of classes ranked in terms of some single criterion." Thus all members of a society are ranked within any single class system. In a hypothetical society, for example, the *political class system* may consist of 10 per cent elites or leaders, 20 per cent bureaucrats, 50 per cent apoliticals, and 20 per cent enemies of the regime. In this same fictional society, the *property class system* may be ranked from 10 per cent wealthy, to 25 per cent middle class, to 45 per cent poor, to 20 per cent impoverished. The *occupational class system* may be ranked from the large landowners to independent farmers, officials, and merchants, to peasants and artisans, and finally to beggars and the unemployed. Lenski thus attempts to demonstrate that the structure of distributive systems is such that there may be competition for scarce resources not only between individuals and classes but also among class systems. Lenski cites the illustration of efforts to equalize educational opportunities, which would increase the importance of the educational class system while decreasing the importance of the racial and sexual class systems. The move has been to force employers to use educational qualifications in hiring more than racial or sexual class-system membership. Another illustration of the struggle between class systems may be seen in totalitarian countries, where political class-system membership is increased at the expense of other systems, particularly the property class system. Prestige and privilege are given to high-status party members rather than, as in capitalist systems, to those who own the most property.

Lenski's picture of the stratification system as being comprised structurally of individuals, classes, and class systems is complex and reflects the diversity of industrial society. He views it as "a system of wheels within wheels" with an obvious structural functionalist image of interconnectedness and interdependence. At the same time, he recognizes the dynamic fact of stratification in life—namely, antagonism and hostility—which he relates to the structural features of a society.

Lenski (1966:85) logically deduces some propositions that may be tested based on the postulates he advances on both the structure and the dynamics of distributive systems. Among these propositions are the following:

1. ". . . the degree of inequality in distributive systems will vary directly with the size of a society's surplus."
2. ". . . vertical mobility rates . . . will tend to vary directly with the rate of technological and social change."

3. ". . . the degree of class hostility will tend to vary inversely with the rate of upward mobility."

Using both anthropological and historical monographs as well as sociological studies, Lenski then proceeds to examine his postulates and their derived propositions in light of various societal types. The societal types that Lenski selected for study in his work are hunting-and-gathering societies, simple horticultural societies, agrarian societies, and industrial societies.

Inducing Evidence for the Stratification Thesis _____

Hunting-and-gathering societies are those in which "techniques of food production are primitive and inefficient (in the sense of product value per unit of energy expended)," and where "other elements of technology are also primitive" (Lenski, 1966:96). People in hunting-and-gathering societies live close to subsistence, living life on a day-to-day basis. Variance among hunting-and-gathering societies is frequently a direct result of differences in physical environment. Lenski observes that a key to discussing the stratification system in such societies is "the absence of any appreciable economic surplus" (1966:102), and observers have noticed a "close approximation to equality in the distribution of goods" (Lenski, 1966:103). In hunting-and-gathering societies, the scarce supply of economic goods does not permit stratification to develop along these lines. The distribution of prestige, however, is a very different matter from the distribution of goods. As Lenski (1966:104) notes, "Here there is no problem of short supply, and inequality does not threaten the group's chances of survival. As a consequence, the unequal distribution of honor tends to be the rule rather than the exception in hunting and gathering societies." Based on available anthropological data, Lenski (1966:109) demonstrates through the use of inductive logic that "in primitive hunting and gathering societies, power, privilege, and prestige are largely a function of personal skills and ability. Inheritance only provides opportunity; to be of value to the individual, confirming actions based on personal qualities are required." Partly because of the stress on personal ability, the rates of both intergenerational and intragenerational mobility are very high in such societies.

In summary, because hunting-and-gathering societies have little surplus of goods and resources, the stratification system is not contingent on such a surplus. The survival of the group requires cooperation in allocating what is available, meeting minimal survival needs for individuals in the society. Still there is a stratification system in operation—one that is based on prestige and honor.

Simple horticultural societies represent the next step in the evolutionary development of distributive systems. These are "societies built upon the foundation of a gardening economy . . . which rely on the digging stick" (Lenski, 1966:118) as the primary tool. *Advanced horticultural societies* are also built upon gardening but use the hoe and practice other advanced techniques, such as terracing, irrigation, and fertilization. In comparing simple and advanced horticultural societies, Lenski observes an outstanding feature. There is a striking development of systems of inequality built into many more of the advanced horticultural societies as compared with their simple horticultural counterparts. Based on this observation, Lenski (1966:160) advances the following principle: "among societies at an advanced horticultural level of development, the separation of the political and kinship systems and the resulting development of the state are necessary preconditions for the development of marked social inequality." He adds further that "institutions of government provide the key to the solution of the major questions concerning distribution and stratification in societies at this level" (Lenski, 1966:160). As advanced horticultural societies develop, there is an emergence of heredity as a basis for class.

In summary, simple horticultural societies are much like hunting-and-gathering societies in their absence of a surplus that would enable the development of more defined social classes. With improvement in gardening techniques comes some surplus in advanced horticultural societies and the development of a separate political system. Here we see the beginnings of a class system based upon birth rather than primarily upon achieved contributions to the group.

Agrarian societies mark another important stage in human history, made possible through the invention of the plow and the harnessing of animal energy. Lenski (1966:193) also points out that the advances in productive technology "were matched by advances in military technology" and techniques of waging war became more and more efficient. Here we see the emergence of a military class that takes its position alongside the political class. Other classes are also added to the hierarchy in agrarian societies, including foreign ethnics (from wars waged), merchants (because of the improvement in transportation of goods), and urban dwellers, including the governing class, who are able to live off the surplus produced by the agrarian peasants. This societal type is characterized by a rigidly stratified society with much reliance upon heredity as a basis for class.

Industrial societies represent the next stage in the evolutionary development of the stratification system. These differ greatly from the agrarian societies in some very important ways. Lenski (1966:298) notes, "The raw materials used are far more diversified, the sources of energy quite different, and the tools far more complex and efficient." There is both a great increase in consumption of goods and a great increase in their production. Lenski proposes that partly because of the great ability to produce, making desired goods less scarce, inequities in advanced industrial societies may be showing signs of abating. He observes (1966: 308), "the appearance of mature industrial societies marks the first significant reversal of the age-old evolutionary trend toward ever increasing inequality." The relationship of inequality to the social structure appears to be a curvilinear one that increases in advanced horticultural and agrarian societies and shows some decrease in highly developed industrial societies. At the same time, however, Lenski leans toward the conservative position that given the nature of man, inequalities will always exist in societies. Lenski utilizes sociological studies that have been done on the stratification systems in industrial societies to document this thesis of the movement, in both ideology and practice, toward a less rigidly stratified society.

After analyzing in great detail the similarities and differences among the societies in his typology, Lenski revisits the general theory of stratification that he had logically deduced in the first part of his work. He concludes that the general theory he presented at the outset is a valid one:

> The most basic characteristics of distributive systems do appear to be shaped by the interaction of those *constant elements* in the human situation which we identified earlier and the *variable element of technology.* As hypothesized, the influence of these factors appears to be mediated by a series of social organizational factors whose variation is greatly influenced by prior variations in technology. (Lenski, 1969:435)

Lenski's propositions, as we have seen, are directly dependent on his assumptions about people and society. These assumed traits are constants that have not changed during human history. Lenski observes that he has taken a basically conservative view of human nature, seeing people as being largely self-seeking. He feels that he leans toward the radical tradition, however, in his view of society, seeing societies as very imperfect systems. With regard to the question of the "degree to which systems of inequality are maintained by coercion," Lenski's answer is that it depends upon the degree of technology. The theory tends in the conservative direction in analyzing societies with little or no economic surplus. In societies in which the surplus is more substantial, the radical position of coercion's role in maintaining the stratification system is emphasized (Lenski, 1966:441). Thus Lenski asserts that his theory can be said to be neither conservative nor radical, functionalist nor conflict-oriented, but an integration of two opposing theoretical perspectives, relying on an evolutionary framework in tracing the development of technology.

Critique of Lenski's Evolutionary Synthesis

As we have already seen, Lenski admittedly accepts a view of people as self-seeking. This assumption is central to the theory developed and is a model of humans that is consistent with that advanced by functionalism. This may be demonstrated by Davis and Moore's theory of stratification presented at the beginning of this chapter. People's egoistic, self-seeking nature is controlled by the institutional structure of the society. Lenski (1966:26) supports this assertion by pointing out that research reveals the human infant as an extremely self-centered creature who is motivated entirely by a desire to satisfy his/her own needs and desires. As children become socialized into the world of other people, they learn the norms of the group. Lenski (1966:27) notes, however, that "adherence to the rules can be accounted for merely as a form of *enlightened self-interest.*" Lenski acknowledges that altruistic action is possible but believes that it is extremely infrequent at the level of major social decisions. We could infer that Lenski's human being is rarely free and voluntary but rather is usually determined by his/her innately self-seeking nature, which is somewhat curbed by the norms of the social structure.

Lenski's theory of society tends more toward the conflict perspective than does his image of people. He is hesitant to accept the notion of even an abstract perfect system. As Lenski (1966:34) expresses it, "if there is no such thing as a perfect social system we should stop spinning theories which postulate their existence and direct our energies toward the building of theories which explicitly assume that all human organizations are *imperfect systems.*" Moreover he contends that both cooperation and conflict are part of this imperfect system—that both of these processes are normal features of human life. As we have seen in Lenski's own theory of stratification, the predominance of conflict or consensus is contingent upon the period and the type of rule. Rules of might are tension- and coercion-filled, whereas rules of right are based on a normative, consensual order.

Yet both cooperation and conflict are continuously present in both types of rule.

Lenski's approach to the study of stratification is to utilize history to uncover the patterns that may be found among the specifics of historical facts. He asserts (1975:141) that an evolutionary model is appropriate and that the societies themselves (rather than abstracted elements) must be analyzed:

> In the hope of understanding societies better, we shifted the focus of our attention from societies themselves to their constitutent elements— to institutions, communities, associations, roles and individuals—and we became so fascinated with all of the substantive questions raised by these lesser entities and the methodological problems involved in their study that we often forgot the larger questions that gave rise to sociology in the first place.

Focus on the elements rather than the whole reduced sociology to a study of specific social facts at a specific time without regard for the broader issues and the long time span of human history. It is this ahistorical and partial view that also contributed to the rift between radical and conservative theory, conflict and functionalist orientations. Lenski calls for an evolutionary model that allows the social scientist to see the extent to which both positions and their respective assumptions reflect the social world.

The evolutionary model allows social scientists to trace development and change within social structures. It also permits them to identify the determinants of the structures they purport to study. Lenski (1975:147) identifies what he believes to be the chief determinants of the social structure for the duration of human history:

1. Man's genetic heritage (that is, the tools and behavioral tendencies with which he was involved by the process of organic evolution).
2. The technologies he slowly fashioned to enhance this heritage.
3. The environmental barriers to human activity and technological development, specifically environments that impeded the flow of information from other societies.
4. The deadly competition between societies striving to maintain their territorial resource bases.

Lenski contends that even our present technological societies are influenced by such determinants. Although he observes that ideology and knowledge may come to play a more important role in shaping the social structure than they have in the past, he is cautious about overemphasizing such a possibility. For him it is primarily the development and change in the technological base that have caused changes in the social structure. Only an interdisciplinary study of "the totality of human social structure" will be able to demonstrate the interaction of genetic, environmental, and technological factors in society.

Summary

Lenski's theory of stratification purports to be an attempt to synthesize conflict theory and functionalism into a single unified theory within an evolutionary framework. From radical conflict theory, Lenski derives his postulates on the nature of society, the use of coercion in stratification systems, and the degree to which societal conflict generates inequality. From conservative functionalism, Lenski takes his views on human nature and the inevitability of inequality. Lenski attempts to combine aspects of the radical and conservative positions on how rights and privileges are acquired and the role of the state in the stratification system.

Power and Privilege (Lenski, 1966) is a study of the distributive system of total societies in which Lenski attempts to answer the question: Who gets what and why? The answer proposes a curvilinear relationship between technology and its resulting social structure and the rigidity of the stratification system within it. Primitive societies reveal little economic stratification because of a lack of surplus, but they do have an open system based on personal prestige. In such societies, conflict and coercion are minimal. As societies develop a higher level of technology and a more complex structure, a surplus of economic goods becomes available for the winners of the competitive struggle. Conflict and coercion, both within and among such societies, play an important role in the stratification system. The inequalities in highly developed technological societies, however, show some signs of abating as an increased surplus of goods is available. Although Lenski does not feel that given human nature, complete equality can ever be achieved, highly complex industrialized societies are less rigidly stratified than agrarian societies.

References

DAVIS, KINGSLEY, and WILBERT E. MOORE
   1945 "Some Principles of Stratification." *American Sociological Review* 10:242–249.

LENSKI, GERHARD E.

    1966 *Power and Privilege: A Theory of Social Stratification.* New York: McGraw-Hill Book Company.

    1975 "Social Structure in Evolutionary Perspective." Pp. 135–153 in Peter M. Blau (Ed.), *Approaches to the Study of Social Structure.* New York: The Free Press.

VAN DEN BERGHE, PIERRE L.

    1963 "Dialectic and Functionalism: Toward a Theoretical Synthesis." *American Sociological Review* 28 (October):695–705.

ZEITLIN, IRVING M.

    1973 *Rethinking Sociology.* New York: Appleton-Century-Crofts.

8

General Systems Theory: A Move Toward a Unified Theory of Behavioral Science

Socio-cultural evolution, like organic evolution, has proceeded by differentiation from simple to progressively more complex forms. Contrary to early conceptions in the field, it has not proceeded in a single definable line, but at every level has included a variety of different forms and types. Nevertheless, longer perspectives make it evident that forms apparently equal in given stages have not been equal in terms of their potentialities for contributing to further evolutionary developments. Still, the variability of human patterns of acting is one of the facts about the human condition. (Parsons, 1977:24)

All of the theorists discussed in the previous chapters have admittedly developed only partial theories of society in contrast to the grand theoretical tradition of most of the classic writers. This may be evidenced by the ahistorical character of much structural functionalist analysis, a deficiency Lenski and to a lesser extent Coser attempted to remedy with their own partial theories. (Remember, Lenski's work deals only with stratification, and Coser is analyzing conflict as only one form of association.) Classical sociology, on the other hand, has dealt with total societies through a period of time, as in the following illustrations of grand theory: Auguste Comte's "law of three stages," with societies moving from the theological through the metaphysical to the positivistic period; Émile Durkheim's evolution of organic solidarity from mechanical solidarity, with the former's greater division of labor and changes in law; Vilfredo Pareto's "circulation of elite" through periods of innovative followed by more conservative rule; and Max Weber's analysis of the increasingly rational nature of modern societies.

As may be demonstrated by the quotation used to open this chapter, it is within this grand theoretical tradition that Talcott Parsons has elected to work. It has been the effort of his career to integrate the theoretical wealth of the sociological classics into a comprehensive and total theory. Parson's career, which spans nearly a helf century, can be divided into at least three stages, with the final one clearly building on the edifice of the first two. These three stages include the social-action school, traditional functionalism, and finally general or modern systems theory. We will briefly consider the first two phases, placing most of our emphasis on the third phase, which represents Parsons's most recent theoretical efforts.

Phase I: The Social-Action School _____

During his student years and his early career as a young instructor, Parsons developed an interest in the writings of four distinct social scientists: sociologist Émile Durkheim, economist Alfred Marshall, sociologist-engineer Vilfredo Pareto, and sociologist-economist Max Weber. The outcome of this interest in Durkheim, Marshall, Pareto, and Weber was a book published in 1937 entitled *The Structure of Social Action*. It represented a synthesis of the works of these four scholars about the socio-economic order and marked what Parsons (1970b:831) has termed "a major turning point in my career." This synthesis was intended, in Parsons's own statement, to present "a study of social *theory,* not *theories*" with the aim of providing "a *single* body of systematic theoretical reasoning the development of which can be traced through a critical analysis of the writings of this group [Marshall, Durkheim, Pareto and Weber]" (Parsons, 1937:v).

The focus of *The Structure of Social Action* was the concept of rational social action, a theoretical contribution of the great master Max Weber. Weber's (1947:88) classic definition of sociology makes social action central for sociologists: "Sociology is a science which attempts the interpretative understanding of social action in order thereby to arrive at a causal explanation of its course and events." This study of "social action," for Weber, meant researching the subjective meaning or motivation attached to social acts. His work on *The Protestant Ethic and the Spirit of Capitalism* (1958) is an example of such a study of social action. In it Weber discusses the relationship between a move toward a rational, this-worldly religion (Protestant Calvinism) and a rational pursuit of profit (capitalism). Other trends in this move toward rational social action may be demonstrated by the rise of bureaucratic organizations (as opposed to more personal but less goal-oriented structures) and the rise of legal-rational leaders (e.g., leaders chosen on the basis of qualifications rather than on charismatic or traditional traits). Action in contemporary societies is more prone to rationality, that is, to seeking an end or goal (e.g., organization, leadership) with the *most appropriate* means (e.g., *impersonal* organization, *qualified* leadership).

Parsons's theory of action, influenced by Durkheim, Marshall, and Pareto as well as Weber, emphasizes the situational factors contributing to individual action. It is important to note, however, that Parsons's primary concern as a macrotheorist is not with individual acts but rather with societal values and norms that guide and regulate human conduct. Objective conditions (structural features) combine with collective commitment to a value for the development of a particular form of social action. For example, Protestantism could not have contributed to the rise of capitalism either if people were not committed to the religious tenets or if all Protestants had been exterminated. The structure as well as the social action must be simultaneously the concern of social scientists for Parsons.

Because of its development of structural concerns, *The Structure of Social Action* may (perhaps only in retrospect) be seen as a step toward Parsons's development of structural functional theory. Weber's concept of "rational action" continues as the core idea in Parsonian theory, but in the second phase, we see more emphasis on a description of the structure. Phase II is dominated by Durkheim's functional and organismic perspective (viewing society as analogous to a living organism made up of interdependent parts) and Pareto's concept of system (which sees society as a whole in balance or equilibrium). It was Pareto and Durkheim who provided the sociological concepts used to build Parsons's macrofunctional theory of society.

Phase II: Macrofunctionalism [1]

Although he retained the concept of social action as basic to his theory, Parsons's intellectual pursuits gradually shifted away from an emphasis on social action toward an emphasis on the structure and functioning of societies. The structure was conceptualized in terms of a system with interpenetrating and interdependent parts. In spite of his continuing

---

[1] Much of this section has been adapted from Martindale's (1960:484–490) discussion of the works of Talcott Parsons.

intellectual affair with Weber, the influence of Durkheim's and Pareto's writings were on the ascent. In the 1940s, Parsons began to stress the importance of functionalism as a sociological theory, as is demonstrated in his 1947 presidential address to the American Sociological Society on "The Position of Sociological Theory" (Parsons, 1949:Ch. 1). Parsons's first full-scale systematic venture into functionalist theory construction was *The Social System,* published ·in 1951. The book rests as securely on Pareto's development of "social system" as Parsons's earlier work relied on Weber's conceptualization of "social action." Although Parsons retained the concept of "social action," it became simply an element out of which social systems were constructed.

The social system was viewed by Parsons as one of three ways in which social action is organized. Two other interrelated action systems also existed: the cultural system of shared values and symbols and the personality system of individual actors. Parsons was primarily concerned in his 1951 treatise with the social system. If a social system is total, it is a society. If it is a partial system, it may be represented by any number of much smaller systems, for example, the family, the educational system, and religious institutions.

We can link the individual with the social system and analyze it through the concept of the *status role.* A *status* is a position in the social system, such as teacher, mother, or president, and the *role* (used in the functionalist sense) is the expected behavior or normative behavior attached to the status of teacher, mother, or president. In other words, the individual occupies a place (status) in the social system and acts out this status (role) in accord with the norms or rules set down by the system. These roles are reciprocal in that they involve mutual expectations. Thus the status of being a "husband," brings with it a normative role (e.g., being a good provider), but this role is not a solitary one. Rather the role of "husband" is reciprocal in that it involves an interdependence with the role of "wife."

The social system, according to Parsons, tends toward *equilibrium* or stability. In other words, order is the norm of the system. When any disorder or aberration from the norm does occur, the system adjusts and attempts to return to normalcy. This concept of the equilibrium of systems is one that Parsons owes to the sociologist-engineer Vilfredo Pareto.

If Parsons's conception of society as a system in equilibrium can be traced to Pareto, his view of the state of integration of the system is a debt owed to Durkheim. In his essay "Durkheim's Contribution to the Theory of Integration of Social Systems," Parsons (1960a:4) observes:

> It can be said, I think, that it was the problem of the integration of the social system, what holds societies together, which was the most persistent

preoccupation of Durkheim's career. In the situation of the time, one could not have chosen a more strategic focus for contributing to sociological theory.

It was also during this period that Parsons developed his famous "pattern variables" as a means of categorizing action or for "classifying types of roles in social systems" (Parsons, 1960b:193). This fivefold scheme was viewed as "the main theoretical framework for the analysis of social systems" (Parsons, 1970b:844) and was derived from Toennies's classic dichotomy of *Gemeinschaft* and *Gesellschaft*. The pattern variables may be identified as follows:

1. *Affectivity versus affective neutrality.* This simply means that the person acting in a relationship works toward the gratification of affective or emotional needs *or* that he/she is affectively neutral. Seeking to gratify these needs is appropriate to a husband–wife relationship, for example, but not expected in a salesclerk–customer relationship. The husband–wife relationship is deemed to be an affective one; the clerk–customer transaction is an affectively neutral one.

2. *Self-orientation versus collective orientation.* In a self-oriented relationship, the person pursues his/her own private interests; in a collective orientation, the interests of a group predominate. For example, a person trying to "make a deal" on the purchase of a new car is interested in the outcome for himself/herself rather than in the economic well-being of the auto dealer or the larger community. This same individual might be a strong advocate of wage–price controls, feeling that such controls are good for the economic collectivity and only of indirect benefit to him/her personally.

3. *Universalism versus particularism.* In a universalistic relationship, the actor relates to another person according to criteria applicable to all; in a particularistic relationship, select standards are employed. The government that supposedly hires persons on the basis of job qualifications, including passing a civil service exam, would be an example of a universalistic relationship. It theoretically hires persons on the basis of standards applicable to persons regardless of sex, race, ethnicity, and so on. To exclude a person because of membership in a particular racial, ethnic, or sexual group would be particularistic.

4. *Quality versus performance.* *Quality variable* refers to ascribed status or membership in a group based on birth. *Performance* means achievement or what a person accomplishes. An example of a quality relationship would be for a wealthy young person to develop friendships only with other wealthy young persons; a performance relationship might be a friendship based on mutual likes and dislikes, regardless of differences in age or social class.

5. *Specificity versus diffuseness.* In a specific relationship, the person relates to another only in terms of the segmented or limited situation at hand. A clerk and customer provide an illustration of a very limited relationship based on a sale–purchase. A family relationship, on the other hand, is an example of a diffuse relationship, where the whole person (rather than a limited status) is involved in the interaction process.

These pattern variables may be combined, Parsons asserts, to account for any action in a social system. The relationship may be characterized by affectivity and quality, such as in a parent–child relationship, which is ascribed and satisfies affective needs. Or a relationship may be less intimate, as that between a cab driver and a passenger, where we see an illustration of a specific and effectively neutral contact.[2] These pattern variables are viewed by Parsons as the cornerstone upon which his theory of action builds into complex social systems.

Parsonian theory during the first two phases admittedly dealt more with static description of the social structure than with the dynamic issue of social change. It was Parsons's (1970b) contention that the components of the system must be described *before* theorists can progress to the discussion of social change. Continuing in the grand theoretical tradition that he began nearly forty years earlier, Parsons attempts to infuse the breath of change into his previously static model.

Phase III: General Systems Theory _____

The theory of Talcott Parsons may be viewed as one in transition from traditional functionalism toward a general systems model. Before progressing with our discussion of Parsonian theory, we should give some attention to the interdisciplinary general or modern systems theory of which Parsonian theory is the best sociological example.

GENERAL SYSTEMS THEORY: TOWARD A UNIFIED THEORY OF SCIENCE

General or modern systems theory did not originate in the social sciences, nor is it a new development. For approximately forty years, bi-

---

[2] Some of the pattern variables have undergone modifications since Parsons first introduced them. For example, in response to a critique by Robert Dubin, Parsons dropped "self-orientation/collective orientation" and elaborated on other aspects of pattern variables. These have been related to the question of system goals and the means of achieving them (the instrumental–consummatory axis) and to the question of the relationship of the system to its environment (the internal–external axis) discussed later in this chapter. For further discussion see Parsons (1960b).

ologist and natural scientist Ludwig von Bertalanffy had been writing and promulgating its development. It was not until 1955, however, that Bertalanffy called for a new discipline to carry on his work. He asserted that there existed models, principles, and laws that apply to generalized systems, irrespective of their particular kind. In view of this Bertalanffy argued:

> It seems legitimate to ask for a theory, not of systems of a more or less special kind, but of universal principles applying to systems in general. In this way we postulate a new discipline called *General Systems Theory.* Its subject matter is the formulation and derivation of these principles which are valid for "systems" in general. (Bertalanffy, 1955:32)

Bertalanffy observes that because of increased specialization in all scientific endeavors, communication among and sometimes within disciplines is becoming increasingly difficult. Yet in spite of the relative isolation of the different fields of science, some common concepts and principles may be emerging. Bertalanffy asserts that the potentially most fruitful similarities revolve around the concept *system.* This concept has appeared in physics and biology, chemistry and economics, psychology and sociology.

Bertalanffy (1955:35) warns that his theory is "not a search for vague and superficial analogies." He does identify (1955:38) five major aims of general systems theory to positively indicate its intent:

1. There is a general tendency toward integration in the various sciences, natural and social.
2. Such integration seems to be centered in a general theory of systems.
3. Such theory may be an important means for aiming at exact theory in nonphysical fields of science.
4. Developing unifying principles running "vertically" through the universe of the individual sciences, this theory brings us nearer to the goal of the unity of science.
5. This can lead to a much-needed integration in scientific education.

Bertalanffy deplores the emphasis that has been given to physical reductionism by those who want a unified theory of science. Proponents of "physical reductionism" stress the need to reduce other disciplines (sociology included) to the laws of physics.[3] Bertalanffy feels that this approach is a disservice to science, for there must be an exchange of information (rather than a one-way flow of information) among the fields.

---

[3] We have already discussed another type of reductionism, psychological reductionism, in our discussion of George C. Homans (see Chapter 3). For an illustration of a defense of physical reductionism in sociology see Catton (1966).

An excessive reliance upon physics may be misleading. Bertalanffy (1955: 49) states, "We cannot reduce the biological, behavioral, and social levels to the lowest level, that of constructs and the laws of physics. We can, however, find constructs and possibly laws within the individual levels." Discovering the themes of knowledge running through all scientific disciplines and promoting communication among fields is one of Bertalanffy's goals. Through a synthesis of such knowledge a major step may be taken toward the unification of science.

General systems theory has found advocates in nearly all of the natural and social sciences.[4] Of the best-known social theorists, Talcott Parsons's recent works are generally cited as the best sociological example of what Bertalanffy was advocating. Parsons's theory, as we shall see, is not narrowly confined to sociology but traces its roots to a theory of all living systems. We have already noted that his first major work was a purported synthesis of four major writers on society. Parsons continues his affinity for synthesis and integration of diverse ideas in the tradition called for by Bertalanffy.

The work of Talcott Parsons represents an unrelenting attempt at theory construction for a period of approximately forty years. The best we can hope to do is to scratch the surface of Parsonian theory and present a skeletal framework to enable the interested student to proceed further on his/her own. We will consider each of the following three issues: (1) Parsons's conception of grand theory, as illustrated by his theory of action; (2) the position of society in this action theory; and (3) the infusion of change into the model.

PARSONS'S CONCEPTION OF GRAND THEORY

Parsons's intellectual pursuits have included a study of biology, economics, and sociology, as well as Freudian psychology.[5] These eclectic interests are well represented in his complex sociological theory. As we have already suggested, sociological theory does not stand alone for Parsons; it is intimately intertwined with other behavioral sciences, including economics and political science, and aspects of biology, anthropology, and psychology.

Parsons conceives of a unity of these behavioral sciences. All of them involve a study of living systems. He realizes that nonliving systems (for example, physical-chemical ones) share some properties of living systems, but he chooses not to develop their differences and similarities. Rather

---

[4] For an edited collection of papers by general systems theorists from various disciplines, see Buckley (1968).

[5] For a personal account of major sources of influence, see Parsons (1970b).

he proceeds with an analysis of living systems and argues "that the concept of function is central to the understanding of all living systems" (1970c:29). The concept of a *living system* is derived from biology; and like Durkheim before him, Parsons sees an analogy between society and the living organism. Parsons's development attempts to demonstrate (1) that living systems exist within and react toward an environment and (2) that this living system "maintains a pattern of organization and functioning which is both different from and in some respects *more stable* than its environment" (Parsons, 1970:30–32). He emphasizes that living systems are *open systems;* that is, they experience interchange with their environments.

To summarize what we have written thus far about Parsons's grand theory, we may observe the following points: (1) Parsons is a systems theorist; (2) he attempts to pull together materials from all disciplines studying living systems, including biology, psychology, anthropology, and economics; (3) society, the subject matter of sociology, is but one of a number of living systems; (4) although societies have boundaries of their own, they are interdependent with other living systems. With regard to the last point, there are conceptual boundaries to a system (implying a need for "mediation of internal combinations" or interrelationship of parts), but because these systems are open systems, there is also a need for "external relations with the environment." In other words, there are two dimensions in the analysis of living systems: one is the interrelation of parts making up the system, and the second involves the exchange of the system with its environment. For example, we could conceptualize a family system in terms of the component statuses of husband, wife, children, but our discussion should also include how the family interrelates with other partial social systems. Similarly we may talk about the larger societal system, made up of its institutional parts, but it too is an open system with reciprocal influences on other systems, including the biological and psychological ones.

Functional Imperatives or Prerequisites. The common traits that run through all living systems are four functional imperatives or functional prerequisites. Parsons asserts that there are certain functions or needs that must be met for *any living system* to survive. These functional imperatives include two sets of concerns: (1) they deal with the need of the internal system or the need of the system in dealing with the environment (internal–external axis), and (2) they deal with the meeting of the *end* or goal and the *means* necessary to attain the end (instrumental–consummatory axis). Based on these premises, Parsons deductively creates four functional imperatives. These four primary functions, which are *imputed to all living systems,* are latent pattern-maintenance (L), integration (I), goal attainment (G), and adaptation (A). *Pattern maintenance* refers to the problem of how to ensure a continuity of action in the system according to some order or norm. *Integration* deals with the Durkheimian issue of coordinating and fitting the parts of the system into a functioning whole. The question of meeting the ends of the system and the establishment of priorities among these goals is dealt with in the prerequisite of *goal attainment. Adaptation* refers to the ability of the system to secure what it needs from its environment and to distribute these resources through the entire system. These four commonalities are found in all living systems, whether they be biological, social, or psychological. Parsons (1970c:35) emphasizes that "the four-function scheme is grounded in the essential nature of living systems at all levels of organization and evolutionary development, from the unicellular organism to the highest human civilization."

The two axes upon which the functional imperatives are based are illustrated in Figure 2. In it we see the interrelationship of the functional imperatives through the cybernetic process [6] (designated by the arrows) of Parsons's open-system model. This scheme of four functional imperatives is used throughout Parsonian theory and will be illustrated as we proceed with a description of the interrelated structure of systems.

In Parsons's formulation of grand theory, living systems are the first-level system. The *system of action* that accounts for all meaningful human behavior is a subclass of living systems. Therefore the four functional

[6] *Cybernetics* was originally applied in the natural science fields of genetics, engineering, and mathematics; only during the 1960s did this concept become significant for sociological theory. Theodorson and Theodorson (1969:101) define *cybernetics* as "the study of communication among men, animals, and machines, with particular emphasis on the *feedback* of information and the function of feedback in the process of control." The arrows in Figure 2 designate the feedback process among the functional prerequisites.

By *feedback* a cybernetic theorist means "a process by which knowledge of the results of past performance (by an individual, a group, or a machine) leads to modification of future performance, thereby keeping performance effectively directed toward the attainment of a goal" (Theodorson and Theodorson, 1969:155). The important points to remember about feedback are that (1) past performance has bearing on subsequent action and (2) performance is directed toward the attainment of a goal. An automobile (as does any machine) provides any number of illustrations of feedback mechanisms, including its air injection system. An air injection system, one of the antipollutant devices, contains a belt-driven air pump that supplies air to an injection manifold. Injection of air causes combustion of any unburned hydrocarbons in the exhaust manifold rather than allowing them to escape into the atmosphere. The burning of these hydrocarbons could cause backfiring from an overly rich mixture. To prevent this, the air injection system has an antibackfire valve to control the flow of air from the pump. Thus the performance of the air pump and the injection manifold is related to the antibackfire valve. They work together in a dynamic way to minimize the emission of pollutants into the air.

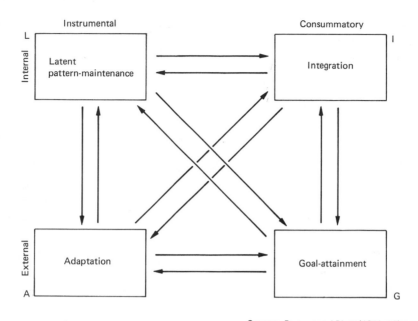

Source: Parsons and Platt (1972: 12)

FIGURE 2

imperatives dealing with the relation of the system to its environment and
the means through which this is accomplished must be met. Building on
the idea he advanced in *The Social System* (1951) of three interdependent systems (the cultural, the social, and the personality), Parsons adds
a fourth system, the behavioral organism. In this way, Parsons is able to
treat each of these systems as fulfilling a functional imperative of the
action system, which, as we have already noted, is but a subclass of living systems. The social system is a source of integration; the personality
system meets the need of goal attainment; the cultural system maintains
the pattern of the system; the behavioral organic system meets the adaptive need. Jackson Toby (1977:4) discusses Parsons's functional imperatives with regard to the action system as follows:

> On what he [Parsons] calls the level of the "general theory of action,"
> he means that behavior tends to have four distinct, symbolically organized emphases: (1) a search for psychic satisfactions, (2) an interest in
> decoding symbolic meanings, (3) a need to adapt to the physical-organic
> environment, and (4) an attempt to relate to other members of the human
> species.

In turn, each of these subsystems must have the four functional
imperatives fulfilled within them to be classified as a system. Parsons

(1970c:44) emphasizes the interdependence of each of these systems when he observes: "Concretely, every empirical system is all of them at once; thus, there is no concrete human individual who is not an organism, a personality, a member of a social system, and a participant in the cultural system." Different disciplines have as their subject matter a particular system for concentration. Anthropology, with its study of culture, contributes much to the understanding of the imperative of pattern maintenance. Psychology studies the personality and the corresponding imperative of goal attainment. The behavioral organism and its process of adaptation is researched by branches of biology. It is the task of sociology to study the social system and the functional imperative of integration.

THE POSITION OF SOCIETY IN THE GENERAL SYSTEM OF ACTION [7]

As we have seen, the social system is viewed by Parsons as but one component of the more general system of action. The four subsystems of the action system each meet one of the functional prerequisites. The cultural system is responsible for latent pattern-maintenance (L) as well as creative pattern-change. The personality system meets the prerequisite of goal attainment (G) in that it implements the cultural principles by offering reward or punishment to induce desired behavior. The behavioral organism

> is conceived as the adaptive subsystem, the locus of the primary human facilities which underlie the other systems. It embodies a set of conditions to which action must adapt and comprise the primary mechanism of interrelation with the physical environment, especially through the input and processing of information in the central nervous system and through motor activity in coping with exigencies of the physical environment. (Parsons, 1971:5)

The social system is responsible for the integration of the subsystems into a unified system of action.

As is illustrated in Figure 3, Parsons's logic dictates that in each of the four subsystems of action (cultural, social, personality, and behavioral-organic) the functional imperatives of LIGA must be met. This is true for the social system as it is for other systems. Within the social system, latent pattern-maintenance is accomplished through the fiduciary

---

[7] Parsons's theory of society has been developed largely from two of his works: *Societies: Evolutionary and Comparative Perspectives* (1966) and the companion volume, *The System of Modern Societies* (1971).

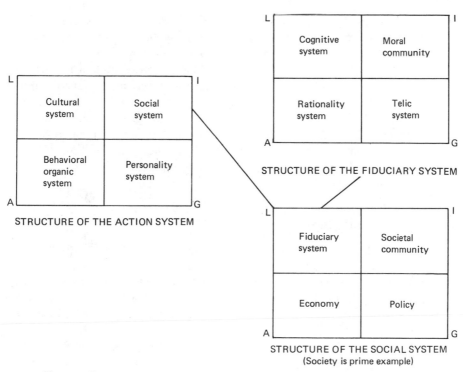

FIGURE 3

subsystem,[8] a system closely linked to the cultural system. The prerequisite of integration is met through the societal community, adaptation through the economic system, and goal attainment through the polity.

Society, the subject matter of macrosociology, is but one example of a social system, albeit a most important one for analysis: "We define society as a type of social system characterized by the highest level of self-sufficiency relative to its environments, including other social systems" (Parsons, 1971:8). Most social systems—schools, churches, families, businesses—are but subsystems of a society. These subsystems interrelate to comprise this most self-sufficient of the social systems (and the one that has the most control over its environment), that is, society.

In summary, it is apparent that Parsons's grand theoretical scheme goes beyond any of the more partial theories of contemporary sociology in several ways. First, it is interdisciplinary, requiring a knowledge of at least biology, psychology, economics, and political science for an

---

[8] The term *fiduciary* refers to the trusteeship roles that bearers and transmitters of the cultural tradition play with regard to the rest of society.

understanding of how society as an open system operates. Second, it purports to incorporate a more limited social psychological theory (micro-theory) of action within its macrosociological design. Parsons terms his theory "action theory," which analyzes "the structure and processes by which human beings form meaningful intentions and implement them in concrete situations" (Parsons, 1977:249). Third, any of the more limited concerns of sociological theory—stratification, social exchange, political power, and so on—can and does find a place in Parsons's complexly structural theory, with systems interrelating with other systems through the meeting of the functional imperatives or prerequisites.

THE INFUSION OF CHANGE INTO A TRADITIONAL FUNCTIONAL MODEL

Although Parsons's early theory was an attempt at creating a macro-theory of society, pieces of the puzzle were lacking, causing his theory to be less integrated than the creator desired. New links and new elements were discovered by Parsons over the years, such as the addition of a fourth subsystem of the action system, the behavioral-organic, which we noted earlier.

Another modification was a shift from Parsons's development of equilibrium (emphasizing stability of systems) to the concept of homeostasis or dynamic equilibrium and finally to the cybernetic model of general systems theory (Parsons, 1970b:849–850). Parsons observes (1) that cybernetics could better explain control in society; (2) that it bypassed the argument of what *determines* what by recognizing that combinations of factors work together through a *feedback* process; and (3) that it helped to open new possibilities for dealing with the vexing problems of stability and change in systems. Parsons accepted cybernetics and evolution as viable means of infusing change into his structural model.

Within a cybernetic model, Parsons advances an evolutionary theory to account for the movement of societies from primitive to modern, with there being four main processes of structural change: differentiation, adaptive upgrading, inclusion, and value generalization (Parsons, 1971: 26–28).

Differentiation (which bears a strong resemblance to Durkheim's increasing division of labor in modern society) is defined as "the process by which a unit or subsystem having a well-defined place in the society divides into units that differ in *both* structure and functional significance for the wider system" (Parsons, 1977:250–251). This process is interconnected with the second process of adaptive upgrading in the evolutionary process: "If differentiation is to give rise to a more evolved system, each newly differentiated substructure must have enhanced adaptive capacity for performing its primary function as compared to the performance of that function in the previous, less specialized structure" (Parsons, 1977:251). In other words, the newly evolved differentiated structures must be able to do a better job of meeting the system's needs than did the undifferentiated parent subsystem.

Adaptive upgrading is defined as "the process by which a wider range of resources is made available to social units so that their functioning is freed from some of the ascriptive restrictions imposed on less evolved units" (Parsons, 1977:249). The example given by Parsons is the ability of modern factories to produce a greater variety of goods more economically than could peasant households. The differentiation process is represented by the development of factory structures. Adaptive upgrading may be seen in the fact that factories do not rely on members of one family (family membership being an ascribed status) but draw from a much larger pool of potential workers (based on who can perform the task or achieved status).

Both differentiation and adaptive upgrading create problems in the integration of the parts of the system. Adaptive upgrading allows greater freedom from all-encompassing restrictions to members of the system (people have some choice in the jobs they take) and requires much more generalized commitments from a worker than did the peasant household. The peasant household required a more total commitment to the family, which also served as the base of the economic operation. The problem of integrating the differentiated factory and family systems is solved through *inclusion,* the third process of structural change, and through *value generalizations,* the fourth process, which legitimates the new developments. In other words, new norms or rules had to develop to govern both the family and the factory to ensure integration of the two differentiated structures. One such norm might be the right of young people to select their own spouse and to choose a place of residence apart from their respective families. Another norm allows for the child, rather than the parent, to determine the line of work he/she will enter and where this job will be pursued. These norms and numerous other ones regulating activity in both the family and the work world must be legitimized or given a "seal of approval" in the society. This has occurred in part through *value generalization,* or "the couching of a value pattern at a higher level of generality than in a less evolved situation in order to make it relevant to a broader range of exigencies" (Parsons, 1977:251). One such value generalization in modern society has been the rise of individualistic philosophies concerned primarily with individual (as opposed to collective) rights. It is thus the right of the individual to select his/her own spouse, line of work, level of education, and so on rather than the right of the family to limit individual freedom and options.

The drift of Parsons's evolutionary theory of society is toward an increased ability of systems to control their environment. Through both a theoretical analysis of the functional prerequisites of societies and an examination of archaeological, anthropological, and historical evidence, Parsons identifies some of the major breakthroughs in evolutionary development that make this control possible. One is the emergence of a stratification system that recognizes inequalities, allowing competent leaders to emerge who are in the best position to control the environment. Another is the breakthrough of "explicit cultural legitimation," which allows the cultural systems to legitimate variance in authority and prestige. Still another is a generalized legal system governed by universalistic norms, that is, norms applicable to the society as a whole. The direction of the evolutionary process is away from ascription and particularism toward achievement and universalism (see the earlier discussion of pattern variables).

Although Parsons's priority is admittedly a study of the structure of action systems, in his recent writings there is more evidence of his concern with process. This is evidenced by evolutionary theory and his use of the cybernetic model described in this section. We see in his recent work not only an attempt to create a single unified theory of social action applicable to the twentieth century but also an attempt to discuss long-range trends in the development of systems through the use of archaeological and historical data.

Critique of Parsonian Theory

It is impossible to overestimate the immense impact that Talcott Parsons has had on the development of American sociology. As Gouldner (1970:168), himself an outspoken critic of Parsonian theory, has stated:

> Intellectually viable or not and socially "relevant" or not, it is Parsons who, more than any other contemporary social theorist, has influenced and captured the attention of academic sociologists, and not only in the United States but throughout the world. It is Parsons who has provided the focus of theoretical discussion for three decades now, for those opposing him no less than for his adherents.

To the extent that there has been a central theorist in contemporary sociology, this theorist has been Talcott Parsons.

Parsons's image of people, society, and theory are within the naturalistic camp of mainline sociology, as may be demonstrated by his assumptions about people. Parsons's image of the person clearly tends toward the deterministic end of the theoretical continuum.[9] Men and women are purposive (rational) in their actions, but their actions are controlled by the internalization of social norms. Like that of Merton (see Chapter 2), Parsons's view of choice in action is one of structurally created choices. This may be illustrated by the pattern variables and their attempt to categorize action. It may be said that Parsons's image of the human being is one of a self-seeking creature who is capable of decision making in satisfying his/her needs but who is also constrained by norms and situational conditions.

In general, however, it is not the person that is the focal point in Parsonian theory; rather it is the action of systems. Parsons's social system, the subject matter of sociology, correlates with his complex structurally determined image of people. All systems are open systems, that is, subject to influence by and capable of influencing other systems. The reality of the system takes preeminence over individuals. In other words, the social structure has an existence of its own and is not simply a group of individuals in interaction. As Mullins (1973:58) observes:

> Parsons, who was simply not interested in the activities of individuals, chose to investigate the sets of rules and norms that ordered society. He assumed (1) the existence of a set of values that stretched across American society and (2) the operation of these values in a set of norms about how social life was lived.

A primary criticism of the manner in which Parsons treats society is the conservative bias inherent in structural functionalism and its inability to deal adequately with revolutionary or rapid social change. (This bias has been briefly discussed in the chapter on structural functionalism.) Wrong (1959:378) astutely observes, "The trouble with Parsonian theory is that in trying to explain conformity and social stability . . . he manages to make their opposites appear even more problematical. That violence, revolution, and historical change occur at all becomes incomprehensible." Although Parsons has attempted to shift toward a revision of his functionalist model through general systems theory, his revisions can still account for only slow changes within the system, still failing to account adequately for violence and revolution.

Nor does Parsons's use of evolutionary theory within this cybernetic model satisfy his critics. Evolutionary theory has already gone through

---

[9] Scott (1963:716–735) contends that early Parsonian "action theory" was more voluntaristic than Parsons's later functional theory. I would agree with Turner (1974), Toby (1977), and others who contend that Parsons's image of people has been consistently deterministic.

one round of sociology, reaching an apex in the writings of the nineteenth-century British classical sociologist Herbert Spencer (see Chapter 2 for a brief discussion of Spencer's contribution to functionalism). Although Parsons's version attempts to steer clear of the romantic overtones of the inevitability of progress of much nineteenth-century evolutionary thought, it fails, as did its predecessor, to *explain* the process of change. In other words, Parsons describes the move toward modern society, but he fails to contribute substantively with a detailed explanation of *how* a society moves from one stage to another. For many, Parsons's evolutionary scheme is simply old wine in a new bottle.

The nature of Parsonian theory has also been severely criticized even by sociologists who are committed to naturalistic theory (as well as, as may be expected, by those who are more humanistic in orientation). Parsons's commitment to grand theoretical issues, to the chagrin of many naturalistic sociologists, fails to provide empirically testable propositions. Robert K. Merton, one of Parsons's most distinguished students, questions whether grand theory can be operationalized and researched. For this reason, Merton views Parsons's theory as a general theoretical orientation rather than a genuine sociological theory (Merton, 1968:54). How does a sociologist begin to study a self-sufficient social system, intimately linked with a cultural system, a personality system, and a behavioral system? Where would a researcher begin to test the four functional prerequisites that Parsons deems necessary for any action system? It would be difficult to demonstrate empirically that Parsons is either correct or incorrect in his assertions.

Although Merton questions the grandiose nature of Parsonian theory, Zetterberg (1965:21–29) asserts that although Parsons's theory provides definitions and concepts, it is not genuinely theoretical. Zetterberg would prefer to refer to Parsons's works as a "general taxonomy of the social sciences." This taxonomy provides concept and definition after concept and definition; and although it is a scheme for classification and description, it is not theoretical. According to Zetterberg (1965:28), "Theories summarize and inspire, not descriptive studies, but *verificational studies* —studies construed to test specific hypotheses." Both Merton and Zetterberg are in agreement that Parsonian theory, as it now stands, has failed to advance empirically testable propositions.

Turner (1974:51–54) further comments on the problem of the testability of Parsons's theory, observing that "it often appears that Parsons abandons the action scheme when addressing empirical events." Given Parsons's own commitment to the need to empirically test propositional statements that are logically deduced, Turner asserts that Parsons's action theory "remains an interesting, and perhaps even inspirational, conglomerate of suggestive concepts," but it fails the test for theory and theory building that Parsons has set for the field.

Parsons's commitment has been to a naturalistic sociology that is integrated with other scientific endeavors. He realizes that the task he has set for himself is monumental and that he has not "solved . . . all problems." He does claim, however, that "the problems I had been concerned with were theoretically important ones" (Parsons, 1971:38). There can be no doubt that Parsons has been an important, if not the most important, figure in the shaping of American sociology.

Summary

Parsons's writings represent an unrelenting effort to produce a unified social theory, from his early days as a social-action theorist to his major contributions to functionalism to his present work as a general systems theorist. Given the interdisciplinary nature of his theory, Parsons is a voice heard not only in sociology but in other behavioral sciences as well.

Parsons's theory provides that all living systems must have met the four functional imperatives of pattern maintenance, integration, goal attainment, and adaptation. One subclass of living systems is the action system, including the behavioral subsystem, the psychological subsystem, the cultural subsystem, and the social subsystem. The most self-sufficient of the social systems is society, which serves to integrate the action system. The fiduciary system, the societal community, the polity, and the economy are identified as the functional imperatives of society.

Although Parsons asserts that an analysis of social structure must precede social change, he acknowledges that society is dynamic rather than static. Parsons's cybernetic model identifies four interrelated evolutionary processes of change: differentiation, adaptive upgrading, inclusion, and value generalization. Each of these processes produces feedback in the other processes and in the social structure.

Parsons's theory has undergone continual revisions for nearly four decades. A major thrust has been a movement away from functionalism toward general systems theory, complete with its evolutionary provisions for social change. At the same time, however, Parsons's work is continuous and cumulative. Social action (developed in Phase I) and structural functionalism (developed in Phase II) remain, although subject to modification, intact within the evolutionary and cybernetic model of his most recent works.

References

BERTALANFFY, LUDWIG VON

1955 "General System Theory." *Main Currents of Modern Thought* 11 (March):75–83.

1962 "General System Theory:.A Critical Review." *General Systems* (7): 1–20.

1968 *General System Theory.* New York: George Braziller, Inc.

BUCKLEY, WALTER (Ed.)

1968 *Modern Systems Research for the Behavioral Scientist: A Sourcebook.* Chicago: Aldine Publishing Company.

CATTON, WILLIAM R. JR.

1966 *From Animistic to Naturalistic Sociology.* New York: McGraw-Hill Book Company.

DUBIN, ROBERT

1960 "Parsons' Actor: Continuities in Social Theory." *American Sociological Review* 25 (August):457–466.

GOULDNER, ALVIN W.

1970 *The Coming Crisis of Western Sociology.* New York: Basic Books, Inc.

MARTINDALE, DON

1960 *The Nature and Types of Sociological Theory.* Boston: Houghton Mifflin Company.

MERTON, ROBERT K.

1968 *On Theoretical Sociology.* New York: The Free Press.

MULLINS, NICHOLAS C.

1973 *Theories and Theory Groups in Contemporary Sociology.* New York: Harper & Row, Publishers.

PARSONS, TALCOTT

1937 *The Structure of Social Action.* New York: McGraw-Hill Book Company.

1949 *Essays in Sociological Theory.* New York: The Free Press.

1951 *The Social Systems.* New York: The Free Press.

1960a "Durkheim's Contribution to the Theory of Integration of Social Systems." Pp. 3–34 in *Sociological Theory and Modern Society.* New York: The Free Press.

1960b "Pattern Variables Revisited: A Response to Robert Dubin." *American Sociological Review* 25 (August):467–483.

1966 *Societies: Evolutionary and Comparative Perspectives.* Englewood Cliffs, N.J.: Prentice-Hall, Inc.

1970a "Commentary." Pp. 380–399 in Herman Turk and Richard L. Simpson (Eds.), *Institutions and Social Exchange: The Sociologies of Talcott Parsons and George C. Homans.* New York: The Bobbs-Merrill Company, Inc.

1970b "On Building Social System Theory: A Personal History." *Daedalus* 99 (Fall):826–881.

1970c "Some Problems of General Theory in Sociology." Pp. 27–68 in John C. McKinney and Edward A. Tiryakian (Eds.), *Sociology: Perspectives and Developments.* New York: Appleton-Century-Crofts.

1971 *The System of Modern Societies.* Englewood Cliffs, N.J.: Prentice-Hall, Inc.

1977 *The Evolution of Societies.* Englewood Cliffs, N.J.: Prentice-Hall, Inc.

PARSONS, TALCOTT and GERALD M. PLATT

1972 *The American University.* Cambridge, Mass.: Harvard University Press.

SCOTT, JOHN FINLEY

1963 "The Changing Foundations of the Parsonian Action Scheme." *American Sociological Review* 28 (October):716–735.

THEODORSON, G. A., and A. G. THEODORSON

1969 *A Modern Dictionary of Sociology.* New York: Thomas Y. Crowell Company.

TOBY, JACKSON

1977 "Parsons' Theory of Societal Evolution." Pp. 1–23 in Talcott Parsons (Ed.), *The Evolution of Societies.* Englewood Cliffs, N.J.: Prentice-Hall, Inc.

TURNER, JONATHAN H.

1974 *The Structure of Sociological Theory.* Homewood, Ill.: The Dorsey Press, Inc.

WALLACE, WALTER L.

1975 "Structure and Action in the Theories of Coleman and Parsons." Pp. 121–134 in Peter M. Blau (Ed.), *Approaches to the Study of Social Structure.* New York: The Free Press.

WEBER, MAX

1947 *The Theory of Social and Economic Organization.* New York: The Free Press.

1958 *The Protestant Ethic and the Spirit of Capitalism.* New York: Charles Scribner's Sons.

WRONG, DENNIS H.

1959 "The Failure of American Sociology." *Commentary* 28:375–380.

ZEITLIN, IRVING M.

1973 *Rethinking Sociology: A Critique of Contemporary Theory.* New York: Appleton-Century-Crofts.

ZETTERBERG, HANS L.

1965 *On Theory and Verification in Sociology.* Totowa, N.J.: The Bedminster Press.

9

The Use of Mathematics in Sociological Theory

> Sociologists have used for some time the methods of classical statistics in the interpretation of many varieties of sociological data. However, due to the lack of a procedure for incorporating statistical results into social theory, parameter estimates have seldom had a direct bearing on the evaluation and reformulation of sociological theory. . . . causal models seem to offer one promising strategy to the sociologist for increasing the interaction between theory and research. (Land, 1969:3–4)

The founding father of sociology, Auguste Comte, once asserted that mathematics is "the most powerful instrument that the human mind can employ in the investigation of the laws of natural phenomena" (Comte, 1853:32). As sociology continued its quest for naturalistic sociological theory, it is not surprising that mathematics, which has served the natural sciences so well, should be used to chart the way.

Although mathematical sociology has developed as a specialty within the larger discipline, many adherents prefer to avoid such a specialty status. Its promoters assert that it is not a "narrow area of specialization that is of interest only to a small clique of misplaced mathematicians," but rather it is "relevant to all areas of sociology" (Beauchamp, 1970:4). For this reason, one may question the usefulness of the term *mathematical sociology* with the argument that almost all sociology employs, to some degree or another, the tool of mathematics. One may take an even more serious stand against the term *mathematical theory* when discussing perspectives in sociology. Mathematics per se is a language rather than a theory. It is a language, however, that is very precise and that may further the development of sociological theory. Bartos (1967:3–4) compares the mathematical model to the organic model that was so popular in sociological theory at the turn of the century and that provided a basis for functionalism's development. As we have seen (in Chapter 2 on functionalism), this simplistic biological model became outdated and now has a more limited role within contemporary sociological theory, especially in Parsonian theory (discussed in the previous chapter). Similarly mathematics does not provide a single and unique theory for sociology but rather provides a model within which divergent theories may develop.[1]

Nor are sociologists in agreement as to what might be categorized as mathematical sociology, even if one is amenable to the term. It appears to cover two broad approaches: (1) one that may be termed an *abstract theoretical approach,* which is concerned with using mathematical knowledge with more emphasis on mathematical modeling than on concrete data or with using mathematical knowledge to play "what if" games with sociological phenomena; and (2) one that may be termed the *statistical* or *applied approach,* which observes patterns in empirical observations and attempts to construct theories from the data. The first approach may be represented by game theories as applied to sociology, and the second may be found in path analysis as developed into what has been called *new causal theory.* This chapter will present a brief discussion of game theory and will place more emphasis on new causal theory, a theory that has assumed an increasingly important place in the discipline within the last ten years.[2]

Theory of Games: Definitions and Illustrations

Game theory is an interdisciplinary arena, bound by the language of mathematics, that has interested some sociologists. Game-theoretical

[1] The organic model was used in sociology by both Herbert Spencer, the British opponent of increased governmental activities and promoter of the concept of the "survival of the fittest," and his American opponent, sociologist and social reformer Lester Frank Ward, with his call to use sociology for the improvement of society. This same model provided a base for the theoretical works of Émile Durkheim, the founding father of functionalism, who cannot be easily drawn into the Spencer–Ward theoretical debate. As we have seen, in a more limited sense, it exists in Parsonian theory, particularly in its concern with the behavioral organic system. In this sense, we speak of an organic model rather than a theory, just as it might be more appropriate to speak of mathematical models rather than of a mathematical theory (in sociology).

[2] Books on mathematical sociology vary greatly in content and emphasis. I am sure that not all mathematical sociologists would agree with my choice of these two approaches of game theory and path analysis. For an introduction to these and other "theories" dealt with by "mathematical sociologists," see Fararo (1973) or Leik and Meeker (1975).

models are not concerned with simple description of reality nor with the prediction of future events. The emphasis is on how people *should* behave *if* they were acting rationally and in accord with game strategy. In other words, it is very much of a "what if" model, employing logic and mathematical theorems, that asserts that given X and the rationality of men and women, Y events will follow.

Basically we could divide games into two major categories: zero-sum and non-zero-sum games. A zero-sum game is defined by the principle of "winner take all." Most parlor games are zero-sum games, including checkers, many card games, and tic-tac-toe. Both players know the fixed rules of the game, each has freedom of choice within the rules, and each makes his or her choice without knowing his or her opponent's choice. A good deal is known mathematically about such two-person, zero-sum games, and this knowledge forms the basis for the entire theory of games. The zero-sum model is based on potential conflict and antagonism. Both players strive for a winning status—there cannot be two winners. Moreover this model assumes limited information about what the game partner(s) is/are doing. The only shared information is the rules of the game. In real life, persons are not usually involved in such winner-take-all situations, nor are they prohibited from communicating their actions or negotiating with other players in the game of life.

This brings us to a second category of games, namely, the two-person, non-zero-sum game. Because there is no integrated theory of non-zero-sum games (as there is with zero-sum games), such games are often designated with such nicknames as "battle of the sexes" or "prisoner's dilemma" (Bartos, 1967:223). We will briefly consider the prisoner's dilemma, a most frequently cited illustration, as our example of a non-zero-sum game.

Let us suppose that two men who are suspected of commiting a crime together are arrested and placed in separate cells. Each suspect has a choice of action: he may either confess or remain silent. Because the prisoners are in separate cells, there is no way that they may confer, but both know the possible consequences of their respective decisions. Let us suppose that these consequences are as follows:

1. One suspect confesses and the other does not. This means that the one who confessed goes free because he has cooperated with the law in turning state's evidence, but his partner goes to jail for twenty years.
2. Both suspects confess, and both go to jail for five years.
3. Both suspects remain silent, and both are sent to jail for one year on the charge of carrying a concealed weapon.

A game theorist would take this dilemma and ask, What *should* a prisoner do if he were acting logically in his own self-interest. Unlike the case of zero-sum games, prisoner's dilemma offers the possibility of either cooperation (based on trust) or acting only in self-interest. If both partners were naive to game theory, both would remain silent and serve a one year's jail sentence. Of the possible outcomes, this one is the best for *both* partners when considered together, but it is not necessarily the best game strategy. Partner A could be pardoned for confessing if Partner B does not also confess. In this case, Partner A would be set free and Partner B would serve twenty years. For Partner A this would be the best strategy—*if* Partner B does not also confess. (If both A and B confessed, both would go to jail for five years.) There is clearly an element of risk involved in either confessing or not confessing.

Based on this example, we see that both players have the choice of acting either coooperatively or uncooperatively. If both A and B act cooperatively (in not confessing), this results in the best combined outcome for A and B. If A and B both act uncooperatively (in confessing), this results in the worst combined outcome (five years in prison for each). Yet in acting cooperatively, Prisoner A must depend on Prisoner B's goodwill. He may not be rational in doing so and therefore may opt to play uncooperatively.

The basic model provided by the prisoner's dilemma situation can be expanded and applied to the study of society. Davis (1970:95–96) cites five examples of possible prisoner's dilemma situations in contemporary society.

1. Two different firms sell the same product to a certain market. Neither the product's selling price nor the total combined sales of both companies vary from year to year. What does vary is the portion of the market that each firm captures, and this depends on the size of their respective advertising budgets. For the sake of simplicity, suppose each firm has only two choices: spending $6 million or $10 million.
2. There is a water shortage and citizens are urged to cut down on water consumption. If each citizen responds to these requests by considering his own self-interest, no one will conserve water. Obviously, any saving by an individual has only a negligible effect on the city's water supply, yet the inconvenience is very real. On the other hand, if everyone acts in his own self-interest, the results will be catastrophic for everyone.
3. If no one paid his taxes, the machinery of government would break down. Presumably, each person would prefer that everyone pay his taxes, including himself, to having no one pay taxes. Better yet, of course, everyone would pay taxes except the individual himself.
4. After several years of overproduction, farmers agree to limit their output voluntarily in order to keep the prices up. But no one farmer produces enough seriously to affect the price, so each starts producing what he can and selling it for what it will bring, and once again, there is overproduction.

5. Two unfriendly nations are preparing their military budgets. Each nation wants to obtain a military advantage over the other by building a more powerful army, and each spends accordingly. They wind up having the same relative strength, and a good deal poorer.

As we can see from such examples, the activity of persons in society, with its mixture of cooperation and competition, is more analogous to the prisoner's dilemma than to a parlor game. Our world is not a simple competitive one where what one person wins, the other loses. All may be losers—or all may be limited winners. Cooperation, along with competition, is a definite aspect of social life.

Although such non-zero-sum models are much more applicable to the study of society, they are much less developed than their zero-sum counterparts. Theorems have been developed for zero-sum-games, but such theorems for non-zero-sum games, especially games involving more than two persons, are less than convincing. Although the theory of games has been used to analyze human actions ranging from military strategy to economic situations to marital relations, the results, although intellectually and mathematically stimulating, have failed to yield sociological theory. Davis (1970:x) summarizes the situation as follows:

> The most satisfactory theory, at least from the point of view of the mathematician, is that of the competitive, two-person game; but in real life the purely competitive game is rare indeed. For the more common, partly competitive, partly cooperative, two-person game, in fact, no generally accepted theory exists.

Yet some sociologists continue to work the mine of game theory in hopes of discovering theoretical nuggets bringing us closer to the riches of scientific theory.

New Causal Theory

Although game theory has found its way into sociology, it has not gained the favor of the discipline that the statistically based new causal theory is enjoying. New causal theory is more than a mathematical model. It purports to be a means through which the gap between theory and research may be bridged. Rather than using hypothetical models or "if . . . then" situations, new causal theory is firmly grounded in the empirical social world. It is an extension of the use of statistical analysis, including the widely used "path analysis," to construct sociological theory.

Nicholas Mullins (1974:213–249) has traced the development of new causal theory in sociology. He contrasts the interconnection of the theory and the data of new causal theory with the more abstract, theoretical concerns of structural functionalism. Although structural functionalists have been concerned with the development of theory, the theorists usually developed models for research sociologists to test. The methodologists, on the other hand, developed techniques for those interested in such testing to use in conducting research. Mullins (1974:214) notes that this "pattern was established by Robert K. Merton and Talcott Parsons; neither man was methodologically sophisticated but both were able to find methodologically sophisticated colleagues (e.g., Paul Lazarsfeld and Samuel Stouffer, respectively) and students with whom to work." Thus was created an artificial role division between "theorists" and "methodologists." Mullins (1973:240) comments, "A person who did both theory and methodology was considered an exceptional sociologist, and there were very few exceptional sociologists."

New causal theorists are committed to the interrelationship of theory and methodology, not only in principle (as was true of many function alists), but in practice as well. They routinely use the methodologist's tools as they do their work as theorists in substantive areas of sociology. These mathematically oriented sociologists have rejected any division between theory and method and assert that theory must be built from a "methodological base." Mullins sees a close relationship between structural functionalists and these new causal theorists. He observes that the latter (who are now at the top of the profession) differ from the former primarily with respect to skills and interests. These differences, it must be emphasized, are not irreconcilable. Mullins (1974:241) predicts, "My expectation is that new causal theory's relatively few differences with standard American sociology (structural functionalism) will gradually be resolved and that the two will synthesize; the result will be a more useful sociology because new causal theory will have added the synthetic approach to the theorist's ideas and skills."

Mullins observes that new causal theorists are already in places of power and respect in sociology. Although he acknowledges that the group "has not completely taken over the discipline" (and most likely will not be able to do so), Mullins (1974:238) does "expect a flood of research, publications, and coauthorships" to continue from its members. The example that we will use for new causal theory is a co-authorship by Peter M. Blau (whose exchange functionalism we discussed in Chapter 4) and Otis Dudley Duncan. Blau and Duncan's *The American Occupational Structure* (1967) remains one of the best-known attempts to develop new causal theory.

The American Occupational Structure:
An Example of New Causal Theory

New causal theorists, as we have already noted, are committed to the intimate relationship between theory and research. Although at times their efforts have been viewed only in methodological terms, the exemplary works reveal both theoretical and methodological concerns. Blau and Duncan (1967:1) modestly state their aim in writing their book:

> The objective of this book is to present a systematic analysis of the American occupational structure, and thus of the major foundation of the stratification system of our society. Processes of social mobility from one generation to the next and from career beginnings to occupational destinations are considered to reflect the dynamics of the occupational structure. By analyzing the patterns of these occupational movements, the conditions that affect them, and some of their consequences, we attempt to explain part of the dynamics of the stratification system in the United States. The inquiry is based on a considerable amount of empirical data collected from a representative sample of over 20,000 American men between the ages of 20 and 64.

After noting that they have not taken it upon themselves to demonstrate the relevance of the findings for "social policy and action programs," the writers continue:

> Neither have we set ourselves the objective of formulating a theory of stratification on the basis of the results of our empirical investigation. This does not mean that we have restricted our responsibility to reporting "the facts" and letting them speak for themselves, or that we favor an artificial separation of scientific research and theory. On the contrary, we seek to place our research findings into a theoretical framework and suggest theoretical interpretation for them.

What Blau and Duncan stress is that theory building is a cumulative effort; and no single research endeavor, including their own, can result in a finished theoretical product. They are confident, however, that their extensive work will bring the field closer to such knowledge.

Blau and Duncan have focused their major work upon social mobility and stratification in the occupational structure, and the example we will use of a new causal theoretical model comes from their discussion of stratification. Blau and Duncan (1967:63) note that in our society, stratification or "the process by which individuals become located, or locate themselves, in positions in the hierarchy comprising the system" may be due to either ascription or achievement. In modern society, stratification involves both ascription (privileges due to birth) and personal achievement. Blau and Duncan (1967:64) contend, "The problem of the relative importance of the two principles in a given system is ultimately a quantitative one. We have pushed our ingenuity to its limit in seeking to contrive relevant quantifications." They have selected relevant quantitative variables that they believe to be sufficient to describe "major outlines of status changes."

In their basic model they have analyzed only five variables: V, or "father's educational attainment"; X, or "father's occupational status"; U, or "respondent's educational attainment"; W or "status respondent's first job"; and Y, or "status of respondent's occupation in 1962." The letters are arbitrary symbols selected to represent each of the variables in a type of shorthand process. Each of these variables has also had the responses coded numerically. For example, 0 equaled "no school," 1 equaled "elementary, one to four years," . . . 7 equaled "college, four years," and 8 equaled "college, five years or more."

Blau and Duncan (1967:164) summarize their scheme as follows:

> The governing conceptual scheme in the analysis is quite a commonplace one. We think of the individual's life cycle as a sequence in time that can be described, however partially and crudely, by a set of classificatory or quantitative measurements taken at successive stages. Ideally we should like to have under observation a cohort of births, following the individuals who make up the cohort as they pass through life. As a practical matter we resorted to retrospective questions put to a representative sample of several adjacent cohorts so as to ascertain those facts about their life histories that we assumed were both relevant to our problem and accessible by this means of observation.

The variables they selected for analysis are presented in the correlation matrix in Figure 4. What this matrix does is to present data showing the relationship between the respondent's occupational status in 1962 and his first job, education, father's occupation, and father's education. Using the same sample, the respondent's first job (which presumably came before 1962) is correlated with his education and the father's occupation and education. The respondent's education is then correlated with the father's occupational status. Finally, the father's occupational status is correlated with the father's education. With a perfect correlation or relationship between variables being equal to 1, we can observe differences in the degree of correlation. A stronger relationship (.596) is observed between variable Y (1962 occupational status) and variable U (education) than between variable Y (1962 occupational status) and V (father's education), which has a correlation of .322.

Reporting such simple correlations, although descriptive, is not in itself theoretical. In order to develop their model further, Blau and

SIMPLE CORRELATIONS FOR FIVE STATUS VARIABLES

Variable	Y	W	U	X	V
Y: 1962 occupational status	...	.541	.596	.405	.322
W: First-job status		...	.538	.417	.332
U: Education			...	.438	.453
X: Father's occupational status				...	.516
V: Father's education					...

FIGURE 4

Duncan had to make some assumptions about the causal ordering of these variables. The determinance of causality in such research is a stringent logical procedure that must "go beyond mere impressionism and vague verbal formulations." The search for causal inference coupled with the correlation of variables led the researchers to order these five variables. Based on statistical correlations provided by their data and using rules of logic, the authors constructed the model of the process of stratification that appears in Figure 5. This simple path diagram may be interpreted to mean that both the father's education and the father's occupation temporally come before—and thus "cause"—the respondent's education, his occupation, and his first job. Similarly, the respondent's education is prior to and causally related to his first job as well as his occupation in 1962.

Acceptance of the adequacy of this path diagram is contingent upon both theoretical and empirical considerations. These include, first, assumptions about causal ordering: "At a minimum, before constructing the

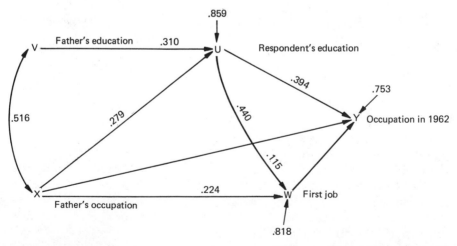

FIGURE 5

Source: Blau and Duncan (1967: 170)

diagram we must know or be willing to assume, a causal ordering of the observed variables. . . . This information is external or *a priori* with respect to the data, which merely describe associations or correlations" (Blau and Duncan, 1967:171).

Second, the causal scheme "must be complete, in the sense that all causes are accounted for." The way this is handled in the model is to treat unmeasured causes as a "residual factor, presumed to be uncorrelated with the remaining factors lying behind the variable in question." Thus in Figure 5, .818 or nearly 82 per cent of the "cause" of variable W has not been measured; in variable Y, the model fails to account for 75 per cent of the "cause"; and in variable U, the figure is 85.9 per cent. Blau and Duncan are aware that much still remains to be explained by these residual factors, which are being treated essentially as "black boxes." They comment (1967:172), "We are a long way from being able to make causal inferences with confidence and schemes of the kind presented here had best be regarded as crude first approximations to adequate causal models."

The third consideration is whether the path model is satisfactory with respect to those variables actually included in the model: "On the empirical side, a minimum test of the adequacy of the causal diagram is whether it satisfactorily accounts for the observed correlations among the measured variables" (1967:173). Blau and Duncan then test the fundamental statistical theorem involved in this path analysis and find it basically satisfactory.

Blau and Duncan welcome any modification of their model that would help to better explain the process of stratification. Rather than viewing their work as a finished theoretical product, they see it as an initial step in constructing more precise theory. This requires both the tools of logic and the skillful handling of empirical data.

Path analysis, one of several statistical techniques that may be employed to construct causal theory and the technique employed by Blau and Duncan, provides a simplified model of reality in that it uses only a limited number of variables and demonstrates their interrelationship. The Blau and Duncan model uses, as we have seen, five variables: father's education, father's occupation, respondent's education, respondent's first job, and respondent's occupation in 1962. This model admittedly does not describe the entire reality but is rather a limited view of occupational mobility. Other variables that may be relevant (e.g., birth order, IQ, mother's education, historical factors) are extraneous to this particular model. The aim is to select the most relevant variables, that is, the variables that will contribute most toward explaining the phenomenon under consideration. Other variables (such as those mentioned) are termed *exogenous variables* and are not dealt with in the model per se.

Path analysis, like all statistical techniques, requires that certain assumptions be met before the data can be used validly. Although we are unable to go into a discussion of these assumptions in this text,[3] it is important to note that the variables under consideration must be capable of being precisely measured. Income and education are unquestionably such variables. It is more difficult and subject to more controversy to attempt to use this, or other advanced statistical techniques, on less quantifiable variables, such as job satisfaction or the relationship of the father with his son. The degree to which path analysis may be employed in constructing theory—particularly theory that is any more than a limited explanation of a limited social phenomenon—remains an unanswered question.

Critique of the Use of Mathematics in Sociological Theory

In concluding each chapter, we have dealt with the image of people and society implicitly or explicitly present in the theory under consideration. These questions appear inapplicable to mathematical sociology for a reason suggested in the opening paragraphs of this chapter: there is a good deal of question as to whether or the degree to which any of the theories proposed are in fact *sociological* (as opposed to simply mathematical). In other words, there are theories of games, but they are mathematical problems rather than sociological ones. Similarly any theoretical aspect of path analysis is a statistical problem rather than a sociological one. The assumptions of concern are mathematical and statistical ones, better discussed in sociological methods and statistics classes, where the necessary mathematical background can be developed. It may be contended that mathematical sociology is simply an *application of* mathematical theorems to sociology rather than a theory in its own right.

We can infer, however, that in order to employ such a model, mathematical sociology is contingent upon a deterministic view of people. Given a knowledge of all of the variables, for example, we should be able to compute the probability that a person would be occupationally mobile. In using the tool of mathematics and statistics in studying human behavior, sociologists are often implying that persons are governed by the same type of deterministic laws that govern the natural sciences.

As we have already noted, there is no single way to employ mathe-

[3] For a brief discussion of the principles of path analysis and the assumptions it makes, see Land (1969).

matics in theory construction, making it difficult to critique the theoretical assumptions without specifically singling out individual approaches. In order to develop a general critique, we will rely on Massarik's (1965) discussion of the varying approaches to the use of mathematics in the social sciences and his treatment of the four mathematical and anti-mathematical subcultures. We will briefly consider each in an attempt to demonstrate the problems of being blindly either for or against the use of mathematics in sociology.

1. The Shadow Tribe: Form Without Substance. Earlier attempts to use mathematics in sociology included men like Stuart C. Dodd, who "spoke with verve and conviction of the need for a mathematical sociology" (Massarik, 1965:10). Although Dodd's work took on the appearance of logic and precision, it was purely descriptive and added little, if anything, to the sociologist's ability to construct better theory. Massarik (1965:10) notes, "The difficulty can be traced to the employment of shadowy systems of notation that lacked any proper mathematical significance."

Although adherents of such techniques seemed promising to some during the 1930s and the 1940s, Massarik notes (1965:11) that as time went on, "it became clear that this culture's children were doomed to be stillborn." Offshoots of such attempts may have contributed to later mathematical developments of the field, but the "shadow tribe" never developed its promise and is important to only the history of mathematical sociology.

2. The Bland Statistician: The Culture of the Formula User. Massarik (1965:12) defines this culture as one "whose lifeblood is the flow of data and whose status symbols are the performance of mathematical manipulations." Although the proper use of statistics is indispensable for the sociologist, the "bland statistician" smacks of scientism rather than true science. Massarik (1965:12) observes:

> As mathematical statisticians and methodologists create new procedures, the culture of the formula user is subject to vogues, to the ascendancy and disappearance—of fads. Various techniques tend to have their day of popularity, for instance, analysis of variance, multiple correlation, factor analysis these are examples of techniques that, while persistently useful for particular problems, were also used to excess at certain stages in the history of the behavioral sciences because they seemed to be "the thing to do."

Given the popularity of path analysis in sociology in recent years, some applications of it may be subject to this type of criticism. One could question, as has Lewis Coser (1975), whether path analysis has the potential to yield anything toward a better theoretical understanding of social phenomena.

Indiscriminate use of statistics in sociology has been encouraged by the development of computer technology. Many sociologists have not been adequately trained in the area of mathematics and statistics, which is one factor contributing to the misuse and abuse of statistics in the field. At the same time, the computer can produce piles of statistical analyses, many of which may not be suitable to the data. It is against this indiscriminate use of statistical procedures that Massark directs his second attack.

3. *The Worlds of Antimathematics.* Strong opposition has developed both within the social sciences and within the larger society to the use of mathematics in the study of people. Massarik (1965:15–16) points to several sources of such opposition. One is the fear that mathematics will tend to dehumanize; this fear is nurtured by the increased use of computer methods in business and government. The battle cry is "I don't want to be a number; I am a human being!" Massarik (1965:16) observes that such thinking in sociology is manifested by those who assert that "the essence of human behavior is too subtle, too variable, too complex— too important—to be reduced to allegedly misleading, simple, numerical terms." Other social scientists opposed to the use of mathematics in sociology have refused to learn its language and to communicate with those who are building mathematical models. Still other social scientists are ambivalent about how mathematics may be used in sociology; they may attempt to use it but are often guilty of inappropriate mathematical applications.

Opposition to the use of mathematics in sociology is more likely to come from humanistic sociologists than from naturalistic ones. As we shall see in following chapters, humanistic sociologists' assumptions about people are different from those of their naturalistic colleagues. Given basic differences in assumptions, their opposition to naturalistic theory would also include the more specific mathematical theories.

4. *The Model Builder's Culture: A World in Ascent.* In considering the "model builder," Massarik is concerned with sociologists who are fascinated with the mathematical model without regard to the real empirical world. Although model building may lead to fruitful developments in sociological theory, it also has a certain seductiveness, so that model building becomes a goal in itself rather than the means to the goal of a better understanding of human behavior. As Massarik (1965:17) notes:

The model itself becomes a soul-satisfying, plausible, and conceptually elegant end product. It may prove *logically* sound—or it may be attacked on *logical* grounds. But the temperament of the model builder may be such that he is more comfortable with the abstraction than with the hard, somewhat "dirty" data, especially whole-system, gestaltist data, naturalistically derived. The model itself has become an "autonomous motive"; and now its empirical test appears less urgent, a digression from the exciting schematic "mainstream."

A sociologist who is all involved in the mathematical theorems of game theory without regard for its utility in the social sciences might be an example of this fourth pitfall. In fact, much mathematical sociology does consist of model building without the use of data (unlike new causal theory), making it susceptible to Massarik's last criticism.

Summary

Sociology has long been plagued by a dichotomy between theory and research, a situation deplored by naturalistic and humanistic sociologists alike. Whereas humanistically oriented sociologists often attack research procedures for their preoccupation with natural science techniques, some naturalistic sociologists would like to use methodological precision for constructing theory. New causal theory has been heralded by some as an approach that utilizes the precision of statistical analysis and its resultant data as a base for the construction of theory.

In its best form, it makes use of the computer to analyze social phenomena in their complexity. It enables the sociologist to move away from simple theories that seek a single cause for a phenomenon toward more complex, multicausal models. Through techniques like path analysis, its proponents would assert, the sociologist comes closer to empirically based theory. New causal theory may fit Massarik's (1965:14) description of the appropriate use of mathematical models, where "Multiple causation and the richness of interplay among many forces will more and more be handled appropriately without doing fatal violence to the apparently limitless variety of human relationships."

Many sociologists, particularly those toward the more humanistic end of our sociological continuum, are skeptical of the usefulness of mathematics in theory construction. Although limited use of mathematics and statistics is valuable for analyzing data, they argue, it is not useful for developing theory. Those who are more optimistic about the potential of mathematics for precise theory construction point to the appropriate use of path analysis in the construction of new causal theory. Whether new causal theory does in fact have theoretical potential and represents the link between data and theory sought by the natural sociologists *or* whether it is simply a data-analyzing technique with limited, if any, theoretical value remains to be seen. To date, its theoretical fruit is decidedly immature. Only time will determine whether it will mature and ripen or whether it will die oh the vine.

References —————————————————————————————

BARTOS, OTOMAR J.
   1967 *Simple Models of Group Behavior.* New York: Columbia University Press.
BEAUCHAMP, MURRAY A.
   1970 *Elements of Mathematical Sociology.* New York: Random House, Inc.
BLAU, PETER M., and OTIS DUDLEY DUNCAN
   1967 *The American Occupational Structure.* New York: John Wiley & Sons, Inc.
COMTE, AUGUSTE
   1853 *The Positive Philosophy.* London: John Chapman.
COSER, LEWIS A.
   1975 "Two Methods in Search of a Substance." *American Sociological Review* 40:691–700.
DAVIS, MORTON D.
   1970 *Game Theory: A Nontechnical Introduction.* New York: Basic Books, Inc.
FARARO, THOMAS J.
   1973 *Mathematical Sociology: An Introduction to Fundamentals.* New York: John Wiley & Sons, Inc.
LAND, KENNETH C.
   1969 "Principles of Path Analysis." Pp. 3–37 in E. F. Borgatta and G. W. Bohrnstedt (Eds.), *Sociological Methodology 1969.* San Francisco: Jossey-Bass, Inc.
LEIK, ROBERT K., and BARBARA F. MEEKER
   1975 *Mathematical Sociology.* Englewood Cliffs, N.J.: Prentice-Hall, Inc.
MASSARIK, FRED
   1965 "Magic, Models, Man, and the Culture of Mathematics." Pp. 7–21 in F. Massarik and P. Ratoosh (Ed.), *Mathematical Explorations in Behavioral Science.* Homewood, Ill.: Richard D. Irwin, Inc.
MULLINS, NICHOLAS C.
   1973 *Theories and Theory Groups in Contemporary American Sociology.* New York: Harper & Row, Publishers.

Postscript on
Naturalistic Sociology

In the opening chapter, we noted that there are varying degrees of adherence to the ideal type of theory we termed *naturalistic*. It represents one end of the theoretical continuum that seeks theory in sociology that is akin to theory in the natural sciences. It is characterized by the assumption that the behavior of men and women is subject to fixed patterns that are empirically observable. The task of sociological theory is to discover the scientific laws that explain human behavior.

It is not uncommon for the theorists discussed in this section to be put into opposing "schools" of sociological thought. One popular artificial dichotomy is a "conflict school" versus the "order" or "functionalist school." According to this model, Lenski and Coser would represent the conflict approach, and most of the other theorists would be placed in the "order" school. We contend that creating such a division between "order" and "conflict" is not reflective of the social world, which contains both phenomena. Much of the reported difference between the so-called order school and the conflict school of sociology is a difference in emphasis. Merton, for example, does not deny social conflict but emphasizes order and harmony in his functionalist paradigm. Conversely, Coser, who is often termed a "conflict theorist," does not deny order in the social structure but simply demonstrates that conflict is a process through which the structure may develop or change. Blau clearly accepts both order and conflict in his discussion of the role of both exchange and power in social relations. In his theory of stratification, Lenski, as we have seen, attempts to synthesize the conservative order perspective with the more radical conflict approach.

What we have attempted to demonstrate in this section is that the naturalistic sociologists, be they of the "order" perspective or the "conflict" perspective, share basic assumptions about the nature of people, society, and the appropriateness of natural science theory in serving as a model for the social sciences. All of the theorists have presented a theory that presupposes that human beings are somewhat determined by their social world in the same manner that the naturalistic world is governed by fixed laws. Although people have choices, these choices are, for the most part, structurally determined. Factors in society act to constrain individuals and to determine their actions. Although the degree to which such assumptions are either expressed or held does vary, naturalistic sociologists are commited to the usefulness of acknowledging the similarities between the natural and the social sciences.

At the same time, however, there is diversity within the naturalistic framework. This includes, as we have seen, whether emphasis is placed on order or on conflict. It may also be illustrated by whether the theorist focuses on grand theory or on more limited partial theories. Differences may also be seen between the attempt to construct theory from existing data (inductive theory) as attempted by new causal theorists and theory logically constructed to provide propositions for later empirical testing (deductive theory)—and whether both approaches should be used, as Lenski has attempted doing in his analysis of the stratification system. (Each of these sources of diversity could also be found within the humanistic framework.) We contend that the major difference among naturalistic sociologists can be traced to differing opinions as to the best way of constructing theory.

  ⁕ It would be fair to contend that naturalistic theorists are committed to precision in theory construction; yet there are varying degrees of this commitment. We have seen that some naturalistic theorists emphasize the development and definition of concepts that are arranged in categories or taxonomies. These theorists are committed to the position that the conceptual level of theory construction may not be bypassed quickly. Talcott Parsons (discussed in Chapter 8) represents one such scholar who has emphasized abstract concepts and their categorization rather than propositional statements. Other naturalistic theorists quickly define their concepts and then move on to developing propositional statement. Lewis Coser (Chapter 5) is illustrative of this approach. In Coser's work, each proposition forms a base for a new chapter, but little attempt is made to interrelate these propositions systematically. Because theory is defined as a set of interconnected propositions, some theorists have not only defined concepts but developed propositions and attempted to interrelate them into a single theory. George Homans's (Chapter 3) work on exchange theory provides one such example. Still other theorists are more concerned about critiquing theories in light of the naturalistic model than about developing theories themselves. Robert Merton (Chapter 2), while giving sociology some brilliant theoretical insights, represents such a metatheoretical approach; that is, he writes about sociological theory rather than formulating a theory as a set of interrelated propositions. Each of these four emphases—concepts, propositions, interrelated propositions, and metatheories—represents a varying type of commitment to naturalistic theory.

  There is still another approach to naturalistic theory that not only uses an analogy between the natural sciences and the social sciences but is actually committed to the unity of all science. Such a position asserts that there must be a unified theory of society (rather than seemingly unrelated partial theories) and that ideally this theory is to be incorporated into a unified scientific theory. Although we are nowhere near approaching such a unified body of knowledge, scientists should keep this model in mind while working within their respective disciplines. General or modern systems theory as represented by Talcott Parsons (discussed in Chapter 8) provides an illustration of this approach. General systems theory stresses the need for a common language and a common model to facilitate the communication among the scientific specialties in order to work toward a unified natural science and social science theory.

In summary, we may say that naturalistic theory advocates that sociology fashion itself in the image of the natural sciences. In terms of the concrete application of this model, however, there are varying degrees and types of adherence to naturalistic theory. In reality, we have very little naturalistic theory in sociology if we were to apply the strict requirements set down by the philosophers of science regarding interrelated propositions and empirical testability. This is a persistent sociological dilemma—a discrepancy between the ideal theory and the theories that we find both in the history of social thought and in the works of contemporary theorists. In many ways, because of the complexity of our subject matter, our sociological products have not yet reached our scientific aspirations.

CONTRIBUTORS TO INTERPRETATIVE SOCIOLOGY

part II

10

Acting in the Play of Life: Dramaturgy As Theory

> Because the language of the theater has become deeply embedded in the sociology from which this study derives, there is value in attempting from the start to address the matter of the stage. There is value, too, because all kinds of embarrassments are to be found. All the word (*sic*) *is* like a stage, and we *do* strut and fret our hour on it, and that is all the time we have. But what's the stage like, and what are those figures that people it? (Goffman, 1974:124)

In most naturalistic sociological theories, the major emphasis has been on emergent groups or larger social structures. With the possible exception of George Homans's social behaviorism,[1] individuals in interaction are not the focal point of theoretical concern. Whether social groups are analyzed in terms of conflict, consensus, or a synthesis of the two processes, individual behavior is generally bypassed as a not-so-important cog in the structural wheel.

The individual, in naturalistic sociology, is seen as responding directly to structured social stimuli. The issue of attaching meaning or interpretations to human interaction is bypassed in favor of a deterministic image of people that better fits the naturalistic model. There is little evidence in most of these theories (with the possible exception of exchange theory) of the building process that is part of human interaction. Hu-

[1] Although Homans does favor inductive sociological theory that begins with the study of the *behavior* of individuals, we have seen that his model of people is admittedly deterministic and his model for theory is clearly naturalistic. As we shall demonstrate in this chapter, Goffman's model of people is somewhat determined and perhaps not far removed from Homans's in theory. Goffman's conception of theory and his skillful use of humanistic data sources, however, moves him away from the naturalistic and toward the humanistic end of our theoretical continuum.

manistic social psychological theories attempt to shift the emphasis from the *product* to the *dynamic process* of human participants in interaction, which ultimately creates the product. It places the emphasis on the human actors rather than on the social structure.

It is important to remember, however, that there are varying degrees to which theorists may emphasize the social structure as determining a person's actions or the actions of persons in contributing to the social structure. Functionalist thought is more characteristic of the former, and social psychological theory better represents the latter. Homans, as we have seen, began his career as a theorist in the functionalist camp and moved toward social psychological theorizing. Erving Goffman, on the other hand, is frequently classified as a theorist who is very concerned with the analysis of human interaction, but his critics view his works as placing too much emphasis on structured situations that determine human action. Goffman, like Homans, may be placed somewhere on the continuum between extreme naturalism and extreme humanism.[2]

Goffman's theory, like Homans's, takes the individual (rather than the larger structure) as the unit of analysis. Unlike Homans, however, Goffman does not use another scientific theory (as Homans utilized behavioral psychology and economics) to develop his sociological model. As may be gleaned from the introductory quotation for this chapter, Goffman uses the analogy of drama and the theater to describe the actions of people. It is for this reason that Goffman has been labeled a *dramaturgist*, employing the language and imagery of a theater stage. Goffman's 1959 work, entitled *The Presentation of Self in Everyday Life*, provides the basis for his theory on the individual acting in the social world, a framework that he continued to utilize in a series of later works.

The Presentation of Self in Everyday Life

Rather than focusing on the social structure, Goffman is interested primarily in face-to-face interaction or co-presence. *Face-to-face interaction* is defined by Goffman (1959:15) as "the reciprocal influence of in-

---

[2] Although Goffman was trained in sociology during the height of functionalism's influence, he represents a significant departure from functionalism in his emphasis on the individual as well as in his choice of techniques to gather data in support of his theoretical assertions. It is not without significance that Goffman is an educational product of the University of Chicago, which parented much social psychological theory in the United States. Homans, on the other hand, was trained at Harvard, the cradle of American functionalism.

dividuals upon one another's actions when in one another's immediate physical presence." Usually there is an occasion of activity made up of a series of individual acts. The total activity of a given participant in a social situation is termed a *performance*, with the other persons involved in the situation being either observers or co-participants. Actors are those who play a *routine*. Goffman (1959:16) defines a *routine* as "the pre-established pattern of action which is unfolded during a performance and which may be presented or played through on other occasions."

In discussing performances, Goffman observes that the individual may put on a show for others, but the performer's own impression of this performance varies. A person may be sincerely convinced about the act he/she is staging, or he/she may be cynical about his/her performance. For example, a physician may be cautious or even doubtful about his/her ability to cure a particular illness. In interacting with the anxious patient, however, the physician may put on a performance, assuring the patient that "everything will be all right." In the course of daily interaction, the performer is usually taken with his/her act, and the audience accepts the performance. When a physician prescribes a particular drug to reduce a sinus infection, for example, he/she believes that this action will help to alleviate the suffering of the patient, and the patient usually trusts this diagnosis and the prescribed remedy.

According to Goffman, there are two regions of this performance: the *front region* and the *backstage*. The *front* is "that part of the individual's performance which regularly functions in a general and fixed fashion to define the situation for those who observe the performance" (Goffman, 1959:22). This includes a *setting* and a *personal front*, which can be further subdivided into an *appearance* and a *manner*. Using the example of a physician, his/her daily routine occurs in the setting of a properly equipped office. *Appearance* has been defined (Goffman, 1959:24) as "those stimuli which function at the time to tell us of the performer's social statuses." A white coat and a stethoscope around the neck may serve as such stimuli to distinguish the physician from other office employees. *Manner* refers "to those stimuli which function at the time to warn us of the interaction role the performer will expect to play in the oncoming situation" (Goffman, 1959:24). For example, we would expect the physician to be self-assured, unemotional, and calm during his/her dealing with the patient, helping to set the tone of a professional relationship between physician and patient.

Goffman (1959:48) suggests that during a routine a person presents an idealized version of himself/herself: "a performer tends to conceal or underplay those activities, facts and motives which are incompatible with an idealized version of himself and his products." Although an individual has numerous routines, he/she tends to act as if the one at hand is the most important. Thus the physician may be a loving wife and mother, a champion tennis player, and an amateur poet, but her routine as physician underplays the other roles when she is at the office. Similarly, on the tennis court her routine as a champion player takes precedence over her role as a physician. Another part of the "idealized" version of the self entails the performers' tendency to "foster the impression that their current performance of their routine and their relationship to their current audience have something special and unique about them" (Goffman, 1959:48). No patient wants to be treated like the commodity he/she is, the physician must attempt to stress the uniqueness of the patient–physician relationship without stepping outside of appropriate professional behavior.

In addition to this front region in which performances are given, there is also a backstage. The identification of this back region is contingent upon the audience under consideration. The physician's private office may become a brief haven where he can take off his white coat, put his feet on the desk, and joke with his nurse during a brief break in appointments. Although his nurse observes him in this back region, patients may not. A few minutes later, his same office may become a consultation room and thus a front region.

Routines are often not enacted alone. Goffman (1959:79) uses the term *team* to designate "any set of individuals who co-operate in staging a single routine." Such a team might be a physician and his/her receptionist or a president and his/her board of advisers. Goffman (1959:82–83) observes some basic elements of team performance:

> First, it would seem that while a team-performance is in progress, any member of the team has the power to give the show away or to disrupt it by inappropriate conduct. Each teammate is forced to rely on the good conduct and behavior of his fellows, and they, in turn, are forced to rely on him. . . .
>
> Secondly, it is apparent that if members of a team must co-operate to maintain a given definition of the situation before their audience, they will hardly be in a position to maintain that particular impression before one another. . . . Teammates, then, in proportion to the frequency with which they act as a team and the number of matters that fall within impressioned protectiveness, tend to be bound by rights of what might be called "familiarity."

Goffman (1959:86) contends that public disagreement "among members of the team not only incapacitates them for united action but also embarrasses the reality sponsored by the team." Team members must be able to be trusted during the routine; therefore they must be chosen carefully. A nurse who gossips about a patient to another patient, an attorney who advises a client of a partner's inadequacy, or a White House aide who accuses a president of a crime are all examples of disruptions of team routines.

Teams then stage a routine for the benefit of an audience. Goffman (1959:105) refers to a team as a "kind of secret society" that is not all that it may appear to be on the surface. Goffman continues:

> Since we all participate on teams we must all carry within ourselves something of the sweet guilt of conspirators. And since each team is engaged in maintaining the stability of some definitions of the situation, concealing or playing down certain facts in order to do this, we can expect the performer to live out his conspiratorial career in some furtiveness.

A performer must successfully play a character. In time of crisis or disruption, he/she must possess certain attributes "to save the show." There are three categories of attributes and practices identified by Goffman (1959:212) that are used to prevent embarrassment to performers:

1. The defensive measures used by performers to save their own show;
2. The protective measures used by audience and outsiders to assist the performers in saving the performers' show;
3. The measures the performers must take in order to make it possible for the audience and outsiders to employ protective measures on the performers' behalf.

The defensive measures include dramaturgical loyalty (almost a moral obligation to keep mum about their operation), dramaturgical discipline (including sticking to one's own part and not getting carried away by one's own show), and dramaturgical circumspection (determining in advance the best method to stage the show). Goffman asserts that loyalty, discipline, and circumspection are three essential attributes if the team is to perform in safety.

One of the most important protective practices is tact. Both performers and audience ensure that the back region is not easily accessible. Goffman (1959:229) notes, "Individuals voluntarily stay away from regions into which they have not been invited." When interaction must proceed in the presence of outsiders (as when two groups sit next to each other in two restaurant booths), tact requires that persons mind their own performance.

If "the audience contributes in a significant way to the maintenance of a show by exercising tact or protective practices on behalf of the performers," the performer must act in such a manner as to make such tact possible. Thus we have "tact regarding tact" (Goffman, 1959:234). Goffman cites the example of a secretary who tactfully tells a visitor that her boss is not in. It would be wise for the visitor to step back from the inter-office telephone so that he cannot hear what the secretary is being told by the man who is presumably not there to speak to her.

In *The Presentation of Self*, Goffman treats social establishments as closed systems; that is, he is concerned only with the particular perfor-mance at hand without regard to the importance of other institutions to this performance. Goffman (1959:240) observes that there are various perspectives through which an establishment may be viewed. These in-clude perspectives that are technical (analyzing the institution in terms of its efficiency), political (in terms of demands), structural (in terms of status), cultural (in terms of an institution's moral values), and drama-turgical (according to the analysis described in the last few pages). Dramaturgy treats the self as a determined product of the social situation in much the same way as a character on stage is a product of a prewritten script detailing his/her lines and activities. The character exists within the closed system of the theater stage, without regard to the larger world outside the theater. *The primary task of this actor is to manage the im-pression that he/she gives during the performance.*

Viewing the self as a product of a closed system continues in Goff-man's empirical study of a mental hospital. Dramaturgy becomes the de-scriptive framework in which Goffman presents his findings on the "social world of a hospital inmate, as this world is subjectively experienced by him" (1961a:ix).

Asylums: *An Empirical Dramaturgical Analysis of a Total Institution*

The Presentation of Self, although citing examples from everyday life, does not blend empirical research with theory. Goffman's second book, *Asylums* (1961a), is methodological as well as theoretical. The data were collected during more than four years of observations at mental hospitals, with one of these years representing concentrated observations through fieldwork at St. Elizabeth's Hospital in Washington, D.C. Goff-man wanted to "learn about the social world of the hospital inmate" (1961a:ix) and brilliantly organized his observations and insights into a theoretical perspective.

Goffman's dramaturgy deals with interaction as if it were the product of a closed system. He finds it appropriate, therefore, to study an ideal type of closed system, what he calls a *total institution*. Goffman (1961a:

xiii) defines a *total institution* as "a place of residence and work where a large number of like-situated individuals, cut off from the wider society for an appreciable period of time, together lead an enclosed, formally administered round of life." Mental hospitals clearly fit this definition. Goffman identifies five categories of total institutions:

1. There are institutions established to care for persons felt to be both incapable and harmless; these are the homes for the blind, the aged, the orphaned, and the indigent. (1961a:4)

2. There are places established to care for persons felt to be both incapable of looking after themselves and a threat to the community, albeit an unintended one: TB sanitaria, mental hospitals, and leprosaria. (1961a:4)

3. A third type of a total institution is organized to protect the community against what are felt to be intentional dangers to it, with the welfare of the persons thus sequested not the immediate issue: jails, penitentiaries, P.O.W. camps, and concentration camps. (1961a:4–5)

4. Fourth, there are institutions purportedly established the better to pursue some worklike task and justifying themselves only on these instrumental grounds: army barracks, ships, boarding schools, work camps, colonial compounds, and large mansions from the point of view of those who live in the servants quarters. (1961a:5)

5. Finally, there are those establishments designed as retreats from the world even while often serving as training stations for the religious; examples are abbeys, monasteries, convents and other cloisters. (1961a:5)

Goffman observes that in the larger society, people tend to participate in many groups, eating, working, playing, and praying with different co-participants. In a total institution all things are done together, with the same persons, under a rigid schedule, and under rigid authority. There is a wide gap between the managers or those in authority and the managed or those in subject positions; social mobility between these two groups is greatly restricted. Thus in the mental hospital there are two distinct worlds: the world of the inmate and the world of the staff. Goffman directs most of his attention to analyzing the inmate world and the inmate's behavior within the total institution.

One of the first things that happens to the patient upon entering the hospital is an attempt to strip him/her of the "old" self. Admittance to the hospital represents a shift from a prepatient stage to a patient stage, and the change is a dramatic one. Goffman (1961a:140) states, "I am suggesting that the prepatient starts out with at least a portion of the rights, liberties, and satisfactions of the civilian and ends up on a psychiatric ward stripped of almost everything." Goffman is concerned with how this stripping is made possible. For Goffman (1961a:168) it is a result of the structure of the institution:

> The self, then, can be seen as something that resides in the arrangements prevailing in a social system for its members. The self in this sense is not a property of the person to whom it is attributed, but dwells rather in the pattern of social control that is exerted in connection with the person himself and those around him. This special kind of institutional arrangement does not so much support the self as constitute it.

In discussing the underlife of a mental institution, Goffman makes it clear that he views behavior as being determined by the structure. The patient identifies with the organization and acts partly in accord with the norms of the institution and partly in opposition to them. Goffman asserts that the self represents a balance of cooperation with and opposition to the structure. He views the self as an entity that takes a position somewhere between an identification with the structure and an opposition to it. The self attempts to balance between these two extremes. He suggests that this is true not only of inmates of total institutions but of participants in the larger society as well. People must identify and relate to organizations or social structures in order for self to emerge.

In both mental hospitals and other social situations, actors learn to work the system. The inmate of the mental hospital may present himself/ herself in such a way as to curry favor with the staff in order to secure special privileges. Domination of the weak by the strong also tends to be part of the scene in a mental hospital, just as it is in other institutions. The thrust of Goffman's analysis is to portray the presentation of self. He emphasizes that even in total institutions, individuals are not simply willing products of the system. In any social relationship, "we always find the individual employing methods to keep some distance, some elbow room, between himself and that with which others assume he should be identified" (Goffman, 1961a:319).

Goffman does not limit his sociological analysis to the impact of social structures on a person's behavior as has much of functionalism. For Goffman, passing or transitory situations are a fruitful area of sociological investigation. Behavior in such transitory structures may be analyzed within a dramaturgical framework, just as behavior within institutions may be analyzed through this perspective. Goffman's interest in such temporary structures as gatherings at a bus stop or a cocktail party provide the subject matter for some of his later works.

Further Illustrations of Impression Management

The themes of Goffman's later works are actually extensions of *The Presentation of Self*. In *Encounters: Two Studies of Interaction* (1961b), Goffman continues his interest in describing face-to-face interaction—particularly how people manage the impressions they give off in interacting with others. *Encounters* is a study of impression management in "non-enduring social groups." In it Goffman (p. 4) focuses on face-to-face interaction "when people effectively agree to sustain for a time a single focus of cognitive and visual attention." In analyzing some situations, Goffman still uses his dramaturgical framework, with the individual skillfully playing a role that is partially determined by and partially in reaction to structural constraints. The individual creatively manages the impression of self given off in daily encounters. His discussion of role distance provides one illustration.

Role distance is defined as a "pointed separateness between individual and putative role" (Goffman, 1961b:314). *Role embracement,* or the "admittedly expressed attachment to the role" (Goffman, 1961b:315), varies according to one's social status and the role being enacted. Goffman uses a merry-go-round as one illustration. Until the age of five, Goffman reports, the child wholeheartedly embraces his/her role as a rider of a merry-go-round. By the age of five, an irreverence begins that continues to grow with increasing age. Goffman points out that the role playing of the adult differs from that of the adolescent, and that both adolescent and adult differ from a four-year-old in the degree to which each embraces the role. Role distance and role embracement appear related to the person's status, including age, sex, education, and other related variables. A married female professor may express more distance from her role of "wife" than might a full-time homemaker. A wife and mother of four small children may demonstrate more distance from the role of wife (as a result of a closer attachment to the "mother" role) than she did when she first married or will after her children are grown. A foreman of a factory may find he has less of an attachment to his role as a skilled worker as his supervisory duties increase. Thus there are various degrees of attachment to one's roles, both among persons and within one person's life cycle.

Goffman continued his interest in nonenduring social groups when he studied *Behavior in Public Places: Notes on the Social Organization of Gatherings* (1963a). Here Goffman observed face-to-face contacts in streets, parks, restaurants, theaters, shops, dance halls, meeting halls, and other gathering places, concerning himself with describing the presentation of self in such noninstitutional situations. Although behavior in such public gathering places is not institutionalized in the manner of a church, an office, or a family, people spend much time interacting in such transitory encounters, and they are worthy of sociological concern. Again, persons carefully manage the impressions they give off to others who share these transitory situations.

In *Stigma: Notes on the Management of Spoiled Identity* (1963b), Goffman considers some aspects of a problematic presentation of self. *Stigma* refers to the "persons with handicaps disqualifying them from full social acceptance" (p. 3). The stigmatized include such groups as the blind, minority groups, ex-cons, and even childless married couples. According to Goffman, these people are either *discredited* or *discreditable*. The *discredited* are persons whose stigma is readily visible, such as the physically handicapped person, a member of a minority racial group, a female, a severely obese person, or a dwarf. Once again the structure of the institution and the situation come into play, for stigma is often contingent upon the group into which a person seeks full social acceptance. A female lawyer may be discredited, but a female hairdresser is not. A black businessman may be fully accepted by the black community but may experience stigma when attempting to purchase a home in an elite suburb. Goffman is interested in describing impression management by such stigmatized persons.

In addition to the discredited, there are also those whom Goffman calls the *discreditable*. The *discreditable* are "those whose discrepancy from accepted standards are not immediately apparent" (1963b:5). These individuals present an interesting problem of managing the information that can become known about their respective failings. There may be nothing about the appearance of a well-dressed salesman to reveal that he has spent six months in jail for income tax evasion nor about the young attractive mother to indicate that she is now sterile. The revelation of this type of information must come from other sources than the naked eye.

Much of this book is a collection of anecdotes about the problems of stigma and how stigmatized persons manage their handicap. Stigma, for Goffman, is not an abnormality in the person, as it is caused by varying situations. Anyone can and does encounter stigma, and when he/she does, an attempt will be made to manage the spoiled identity. Goffman (1963b:137–138) emphasizes that stigma is "not so much a set of concrete individuals who can be separated into two piles, the stigmatized and the normal. . . . The normal and the stigmatized are not persons but rather perspectives."

Frame Analysis: An Essay on the Organization of Experience _____

The view that we are all actors on the stage of life is a theme that runs through all of Goffman's works, and he expands on this notion in *Frame Analysis* (1974). He admits (Goffman, 1974:14) that in this work he is dealing with materials that he has dealt with earlier—"another go at analyzing fraud, deceit, con games, shows of various kinds, and the like." Goffman (1974:14) asserts that in this work he is "trying to order my thoughts on these topics, trying to reconstruct a general statement." Although *Frame Analysis* falls short of Goffman's goal of a general theoretical statement, it does represent another illustration of his genius in using dramaturgy.

Frame analysis is basically a study of subjective reality. A *frame* is defined as "definitions of the situation [that] are built up in accordance with the principles of organization which govern events—at least social ones—and our subjective involvement in them" (1974:10–11). In accordance with this definition, his work is subtitled *An Essay on the Organization of Experience*. Goffman (1974:13) emphasizes that his work is not a discussion of the organization of society:

> I make no claim whatsoever to be talking about the core matters of sociology—social organization and social structure. Those matters have been and can continue to be quite nicely studied without reference to frame at all. I am not addressing the structure of social life but the structure of experience individuals have at any moment of their social lives. I personally hold society to be first in every way and any individual's current involvement to be second; this report deals only with matters that are second.

Frames organize the individual's experience of events and contain varying levels of reality. Although they are subjective in terms of emphasis, they are not merely a matter of the mind. Rules and norms govern our activity, and we learn to employ the proper frame for a given situation. In any given activity, we employ a frame defining what is actually going on. Is it a joke, an accident, a mistake, a dream, a deception, a theatrical performance? In other words, we need to read each situation and make sense of it, but we do so employing already existing norms or rules.

Again we can find the theme of impression management that runs through Goffman's works. The self a person presents is in accord with the situation at hand. This self is presented in behavior that is in accord with rules or norms provided by the frame. As Goffman (1974:573–574) observes:

> There is a relation between persons and role. But the relationship answers to the interactive system—to the frame—in which the role is performed and the self of the performers is glimpsed. *Self, then, is not an entity half-concealed behind events, but a changeable formula for managing oneself during them.* Just as the current situation prescribes the official guise behind which we will conceal ourselves, so it provides for where and how we will show through. (Italics added)

In this last work, as in all of his works, Goffman attempts to sensitize sociology to the importance of studying noninstitutional as well as institutional behavior. Goffman has taken it upon himself to analyze events systematically, from pedestrian traffic to cocktail parties, from the position of a seemingly distinterested observer. He attempts an objective description of overt behavior in face-to-face interaction, with particular emphasis on how persons manage the impressions of self that they emit. Without denying the importance of structural analysis in sociology, Goffman chooses to focus on the "individual's current involvements," or actual behavior within situations, which is often neglected in traditional sociological analysis.

A Critical Evaluation of Goffman's Dramaturgy

Goffman's approach to sociology represents a shift toward humanism and away from the scientific model; that is, Goffman is more concerned about studying persons as they appear rather than fitting abstractions of their behavior into preconceived propositions and theories. Both his model of people and his conception of sociological theory represent a departure from the approaches we have considered thus far.[3]

Structural functionalism and its offshoot, exchange theory, view persons as more-or-less determined by social structures. In earlier chapters, we have seen that Merton, Parsons, and Blau, and to some extent Homans, all view persons as products determined by their social structures. Goff-

---

[3] Gamson (1975), in his review essay of *Frame Analysis*, attempts to speculate about its ability to be placed in a naturalistic mode of theory construction. He is particularly interested in methodological questions and the feasibility of training Goffman-like researchers.

man, more than any theorist treated thus far, allows the individual some freedom from his/her role. This may be seen in Goffman's discussion of impression management (which allows for errors or mismanagement), as well as in his concepts of *role distance* and *role embracement,* discussed earlier in this chapter.

Cuzzort and King (1976:254) have astutely observed that Goffman's persons are artists—con artists. Actors in society are constantly at work to maintain impressions of themselves. They don't necessarily act in accord with normative standards; rather they engineer "a convincing impression that these standards are being realized" (Goffman, 1959:251). The assumptions inherent in Goffman's model of people differ from those of other theorists discussed to this point. One basic difference is that Parsons, Merton, Homans, and Blau all view men and women as rationally seeking goals that are useful and valuable to them. Gouldner (1970:383) observes that dramaturgy differs from this view in that it "reaches into and expresses the nature of self as pure commodity utterly devoid of any necessary use-value: it is the sociology of soul selling." Goals are not based upon the usefulness of the item but rather upon whether one makes the desired appearance.

For Goffman, the human being is preoccupied with the kinds of impressions he/she is making on others. Critics have suggested that this is a narrow view of people. As Blumer (1972:52) expressed it:

> Without minimizing the fact that human beings in one another's presence are sensitive to how they are being regarded, it is farfetched to assume that this form of self awareness constitutes the major concern of the human being in handling himself. People in association just do not go around with their attention constantly focused on how they are being regarded and on how they can influence the way in which they are regarded. At various times they do this, and some people do it more than others. But this does not constitute the central content of what the person does in interacting with himself.

The self, as presented by Goffman (1959:253), is not the developing entity that is so important, as we shall see in the following chapter, to symbolic interactionists: "The self, then, as a performed character, is not an organic thing that has a specific location, whose fundamental fate is to be born, to mature, and to die; it is a dramatic effect."

Goffman's treatment of self leaves numerous unanswered questions. Gouldner (1970:380) raises four basic ones that Goffman fails to treat:

1. Why are some selves rather than others selected and presented by the actors?

2. Why do others accept or reject the proffered self?
3. Are some selves more gratifying in their consequences, to self and other?
4. How do power and wealth provide resources that affect the capacity to project self successfully?

Goffman's analysis fails to deal adequately with any of these important questions.

The view of the social world presented by dramaturgy is essentially that of a closed system: "A social establishment is any place surrounded by fixed barriers to perception in which a particular kind of activity regularly takes place" (Goffman, 1959:238). Goffman, as we have seen, is less concerned with the social structure itself than with the subjective manner in which actors organize their experiences. It is the particular situation that provides the data for Goffman's theoretical musings. As Gouldner (1970:379) observes in his evaluation of dramaturgy:

> It is a social theory that dwells upon the episodic and sees life only as it is lived in a narrow interpersonal circumference, a historical and non-institutional, an existence beyond history and society, and one which comes alive only in the fluid, transient "encounter." Unlike Parsons, who sees society as a resilient, solid rubber ball that remains serviceable despite the chunks torn from it, Goffman's image of social life is not of firm, well-hounded social structures, but rather of a loosely stranded, criss-crossing, swaying catwalk along which men dart precariously. In this view, people are acrobatic actors and gamesmen who have, somehow, become disengaged from social structures and are growing detached from even culturally standardized roles. They are seen less as a product *of* the system, than of individuals "working the system" for the enhancement of self.

It is important to remember that Goffman never denies the existence of culture, social structure, or power. In fact he (1959:238) asserts that dramaturgy is but one approach to the study of social facts. An establishment may be viewed structurally, culturally, or politically—but it may also be viewed dramaturgically. In *Frame Analysis* (1974:13), as we have already noted, Goffman sees his concerns as second to the first concern of sociology, which is the study of social structures.

At the same time, Goffman (1971:xv–xvi) is critical of the scientific model as it exists in much of sociology:

> A sort of sympathetic magic seems to be involved, the assumption being that if you go through the motions attributable to science then science will result. But it hasn't. . . . Fields of naturalistic study have not been

uncovered through these methods. Concepts have not emerged that reorder our view of social activity. Frameworks have not been established into which a continuously larger number of facts can be placed. Understanding of ordinary behavior has not been accumulated; distance has.

Goffman himself has used a method of "unsystematic, naturalistic observation" to collect data to support his assertions. In his latest works, he draws heavily from communications media, including newspaper accounts, television programs, and magazines. He artistically takes these observations and creates out of them the sociological approach that he has termed *dramaturgy*. His approach to theory seems to follow more of a humanistic artistic form than scientific propositional theorizing. The result is a creative attempt at theorizing and an insightful account of face-to-face interaction.

Summary

Erving Goffman employs the language and imagery of the theater for his sociological analyses of people presenting themselves to other persons. Their activities and the success of the production are determined by structural props and the fixed structure or transitory situation, as well as the rules or norms governing the performance. Although the structure of the stage and the script is never far removed from Goffman's dramaturgy, the spotlight of analysis rests on the individual actor's performance. His first major work, *The Presentation of Self in Everyday Life,* sets the theme for his subsequent analyses of human behavior. Persons are actors in life's drama according to a script designated by the social milieu. They in part follow the script, and in part they react against it. Persons "work the system" in order to present a favorable image of self.

In his later works, Goffman emphasizes the need for sociologists to study nonenduring social groups. These transitory groups include face-to-face encounters in streets, parks, restaurants, theaters, shops, dance halls, meeting halls, and other gathering places. He also deals with individuals who are stigmatized in some way, focusing on how they manage to present self in spite of some stigma. Again, the emphasis is on impression management, or how men and women attempt to present themselves as they wish others to view them.

Goffman's view of persons as "con artists" in presenting a convincing act for others is a departure from the determinism of structural functionalism. For this reason, Goffman is frequently labeled as a *symbolic interactionist*. As we have seen from Blumer's critique of dramaturgy, this label is possibly a misnomer. Goffman presents *action* but fails to deal adequately with *interaction*. For the symbolic interactionist, *I* plus another in interaction constitutes a *we* that makes self possible. Self is not simply presented in an isolated situation; rather it is in continual process, creatively interpreting and responding to other actors in their social world. This interpreting and creative processual self is the base of Herbert Blumer's symbolic interaction theory, which provides the material for the next chapter.

References

BLUMER, HERBERT
    1972 "Action vs. Interaction." *Society* 9 (April):50–53.
CUZZORT, R. P., and E. W. KING
    1976 *Humanity and Modern Social Thought.* Hinsdale, Ill.: The Dryden Press.
GAMSON, WILLIAM
    1975 "Review Symposium." *Contemporary Sociology* 4 (November):603–607.
GOFFMAN, ERVING
    1959 *The Presentation of Self in Everyday Life.* Garden City, N.Y.: Doubleday Anchor.
    1961a *Asylums: Essays on the Social Situation of Mental Patients and Other Inmates.* Garden City, N.Y.: Doubleday Anchor.
    1961b *Encounters: Two Studies of the Sociology of Interaction.* Indianapolis: The Bobbs-Merrill Co., Inc.
    1963a *Behavior in Public Places: Notes on the Social Organization of Gatherings.* Glencoe, Ill.: The Free Press of Glencoe.
    1963b *Stigma: Notes on the Management of Spoiled Identity.* Englewood Cliffs, N.J.: Prentice-Hall, Inc.
    1971 *Relations in Public.* New York, N.Y.: Harper Colophon Books.
    1974 *Frame Analysis: An Essay on the Organization of Experience.* New York, N.Y.: Harper Colophon Books.
GOULDNER, ALVIN
    1970 *The Coming Crisis of Western Sociology.* New York: Basic Books, Inc.

11

A Symbolic Interactionist Perspective: Man and Meaning

> My purpose is to depicit the nature of human society when seen from the point of view of George Herbert Mead. While Mead gave human society a position of paramount importance in his scheme of thought he did little to outline its character. His central concern was with cardinal problems of philosophy. The development of his ideas of human society was largely limited to handling these problems. His treatment took the form of showing that human group life was the essential condition for the emergence of consciousness, the mind, a world of objects, human beings as organisms possessing selves, and human conduct in the form of constructed acts. . . . In making his brilliant contributions along this line he did not map out a theoretical scheme of human society. However, such a scheme is implicit in his work. It has to be constructed by tracing the implications of the central matters which he analyzed. (Blumer, 1966:535)

Symbolic interaction represents an American school of sociology born of a psychological tradition. The works of American psychologists like William James, James Mark Baldwin, and John Dewey influenced sociologist Charles Horton Cooley, who helped to develop social psychological theory within American sociology. Cooley's (1930) dictum that the imaginations that people have of one another are the solid facts of society served as a reminder of the reality of the subjective world. William Isaac Thomas, a contemporary of Cooley, also stressed the need to study the subjective but not to the neglect of objective facts. This is typified in his assertion that if people define things as real, their subjective definitions have real objective consequences (Thomas, 1923:41–43). What Thomas was reminding sociologists was that the subjective meanings that people attach to the phenomena have objective results or consequences. Social psychology must be aware of both dimensions of reality.

Although sociologists Cooley and Thomas are important figures in symbolic interactionist history, it is their American contemporary of the early twentieth century, philosopher George Herbert Mead, who is often considered the most influential founder of this perspective. Mead accepted and advanced a framework that stressed the importance of *both* overt, or objective, *and* covert, or subjective, behavior for sociological thought. Mead's position is somewhere between Cooley's extreme subjectivism, where only "imaginations" are the subject matter of sociology, and Durkheim's extreme objectivism, where only concrete social phenomena or "social facts" are appropriate for sociological analysis.

In comparing symbolic interaction [1] with the naturalistic perspective, we could say that the latter has stressed the objective aspects of society to the neglect of subjective meaning. The symbolic interactionist tradition offers this neglected dimension to sociological analysis, namely, an analysis of the subjective and interpretative aspects of human behavior. Rather than viewing people as a product determined by the objective structure or situation, symbolic interactionism's person is an at least partially free agent. Instead of treating action as the direct response to a social stimulus, the interactionist approach emphasizes the need for sociology to consider the actor's subjective definition or interpretation of the objective stimulus.

George Herbert Mead accepted the reality of the objective world and its role in the development of human beings, but he also recognized the place of the subjective interpretation of this objective world by the individuals in it. As is apparent from the introductory quotation, Blumer's work is heavily indebted to Mead's. This debt makes it necessary to review briefly Mead's classic formulation of symbolic interaction before we consider his student Herbert Blumer's contribution to this theory.

---

[1] We acknowledge at the outset that this chapter does not deal with the various approaches that are part of symbolic interactionist theory. Kuhn (1964), for example, identifies some major contributions to symbolic interactionist theory that greatly limit Blumer's contributions. As Meltzer and Petras (1972) have observed, Kuhn and Blumer represent two different schools of symbolic interaction: the former is of the more positivistic and naturalistic "Iowa school," whereas Blumer is clearly of the humanistic and interpretative "Chicago school."

Blumer undoubtedly has been the major spokesman for the so-called Chicago school. The dedication of the Stone and Farberman (1970) edited collection on symbolic interactionism speaks to Blumer's importance: "To Herbert Blumer, teacher and scholar, who has kept the perspective of symbolic interaction alive and lively in the continuing dialogue we call social psychology."

Mead's Social Psychology _____

Mead's social psychology was dominated by a processual rather than a static view of social reality. Both people and their social order are in the process of *becoming* rather than being a completed fact. Mead dealt with the intricate matter of how the individual becomes a member of this organization we call society.

Mead's explanation was that the self represents an internalization or subjective interpretation of the objective reality of the larger structure. "Self" is actually a person's internalization of the "generalized other" or the social habits of the larger community. It is a dialectical product of the "I," or the impulsive self, and the "me," or the social side of the person. Thus each person's self is a composite of the biological and psychological "I" and the sociological "me." This self develops as persons learn to "take the role of others" or enter into *games* rather than *play*. In "play" a child is aware of only his/her own behavior. In playing with a doll or a truck, the child need not be aware of the part played by others. When involved in a game, however, the child must consider the role of others who are also involved in the game. This may be illustrated by a baseball game, where each player must be cognizant of the expected and actual behavior of the others who are also players. This same model holds true for life's games, where a person's role is enacted with a recognition of the roles of those around him/her. For example, a husband and father enacts his role with an awareness of the roles being played by his wife and his children. A minister plays his/her role in light of the roles of various members of the congregation. Such role taking enables the actor to share in the perspective of the other actors involved in the game.

Mead points out that people not only are aware of others but also have the capacity to be aware of themselves. Thus persons not only interact with others but interact symbolically with themselves as well. *Symbolic interaction* is accomplished through the use of language, the single most important symbol, and through gesture. Symbols are not accomplished facts; rather they are in the state of continual process. It is this process of conveying *meaning* that is the subject matter of much symbolic interactionist analysis. People in interaction learn to understand conventional symbols, and they earn to employ them to take the roles of the other actors in a game. For example, a performer knows that a standing ovation indicates that the audience has been most pleased with his/her performance. Putting himself/herself into the role of a member of the audience, the performer knows that an encore would be appreciated. It is important to remember, however, that the performer does not have to do an encore; he/she is free to modify interaction by simply taking a curtain call. So it is with all interaction; persons are free to modify the interaction through alternative lines of action. For Mead, the subject matter of sociology is the organized and patterned interaction among diverse actors in social situations. It was Mead's student, Herbert Blumer, who endeavored to keep this Meadean tradition alive during a functionalist era that stressed the social group (rather than the individual) and objective (rather than subjective) reality.

Symbolic Interaction: Perspective and Method

For Blumer (1969:2) symbolic interactionism rests on three premises. These premises are as follows:

1. "That human beings act toward things on the basis of the meanings that things have for them."
2. That these meanings are derived from "the social interaction that one has with one's fellows."
3. That these meanings are modified through an interpretive process.

There is nothing inherent in an object that provides meaning for the person. Take as an example the meaning that may be attached to a snake. For some, a snake is a vile reptile; for naturalists, it is another link in the delicate balance of nature. Whether a person instantly kills a harmless snake in his/her garden or watches it spellbound by nature's beauty depends on the meaning the person ascribes to this object. These meanings are derived from interaction with others. The son whose father was a naturalist and who himself was schooled early in the operation of the animal world may respond quite differently from the lad whose only contact with the snake comes from reading the Genesis account of Adam and Eve's encounter with the serpent. All objects are similarly encountered—not directly, but with meanings attached to them. These meanings are derived from interaction with others, particularly with significant others. As Blumer (1969:4–5) observes, "The meaning of a thing for a person grows out of the ways in which other persons act toward the person with regard to the thing. Their actions operate to define the thing for the person." If a parent responds favorably toward a child who is not afraid of a garden snake, the child will continue such behavior. If, however, parents and playmates both show disapproval of the child, the child may modify not only his/her behavior but the meaning attached to the object.

It is important to remember, however, that our nature lover and snake hater do not automatically internalize two extreme meanings of the object *snake*. Blumer (1969:5) asserts:

> The actor selects, checks, suspends, regroups, and transforms the meanings in light of the situation in which he is placed and the direction of his action. Accordingly, interpretation should not be regarded as a mere automatic application of established meanings but as a formative process in which meanings are used and revised as instruments for the guidance and formation of action.

We might use the illustration of a young female's accepting a ride home every evening from a married male co-worker as an example of this interpretive process. She may accept the ride as simply a gesture of friendliness and neighborliness. On the evening that he asks her if she would like to stop at a local lounge for a drink before going home, another stimulus is introduced that she will have to interpret. Let us suppose that our young woman interprets this action simply as a friendly gesture and stops for a drink. He than proceeds to discuss some of his marital difficulties with her and indicates that he wishes his wife were more like her. The young woman interprets this as an invitation to become romantically involved, at least in a casual way, and begins to decline rides from her co-worker. She begins to question his motivation for being so helpful to her and also his willingness to confide in her. It is possible that she has misinterpreted the married man's message; he may have seen her simply as a good friend. What becomes important is the meaning that she attaches to the question, "Do you need a ride home tonight?" rather than the question itself.

Blumer asserts that persons do not act because of some "forces" out there (as structural functionalists seem to imply) nor because of "inner forces" (as psychological reductionists suggest). Blumer (1969:80) argues:

> Instead of the individual being surrounded by an environment of pre-existing objects which play upon him and call forth his behavior, the proper picture is that he constructs his objects on the basis of his ongoing activity. In any of his countless acts—whether minor, like dressing himself, or major, like organizing himself for a professional career—the individual is designating different objects to himself, giving them meaning, judging their suitability to his action, and making decisions on the basis of the judgment. This is what is meant by interpretation or acting on the basis of symbols.

The human being is thus a conscious and reflective actor who pieces together the objects he or she notes through what Blumer (1969:81) terms the process of *self-indication*. *Self-indication* is a "moving communicative process in which the individual notes things, assesses them, gives them a meaning, and decides to act on the basis of the meaning." This process of self-indication takes place within a social context in which the individual attempts to anticipate the actions of his/her co-actors and to align his/her own actions to their action as he/she interprets it. The young woman in our illustration considers her male co-worker's invitation in light of the context in which it is given and her previous experience, which allows her to assess the question and to give it meaning, and then responds on the basis of this meaning.

The action of human beings is permeated with interpretation and meaning. This action is fitted together and comprises what functionalists have termed *social structure*. Blumer (1969:17) chooses to refer to this social phenomenon as *joint action* or "a social organization of conduct of different acts of diverse participants." Each of these acts flows in processual form, and each interlinks with the processual acts of others. Action for Blumer is far more than the single performance described in Goffman's account of impression management. People engaged in joint action comprise the social structure. An institution such as a church, a business corporation, or a family is simply a "collectivity that engages in joint action." Yet these institutions are not static structures, for the behavior linkages are never identical (although they may be similar) even when patterns are well established. Consider the example of a family comprised of a husband, a wife, and one child. This family is in the continual process of day-to-day living. The marital relationship when the child is two months old may be quite different from when the child is six years old. Similarly the husband's career may assume a greater importance as he climbs the organization ladder, which also affects his family life. There is no simple definition of a husband's role, a wife's role, or parental roles. They develop within the context of the familial structure, which is constantly in a state of flux, responding to the symbolic interactions within the family unit. Blumer (1969:19) asserts the priority of interaction to the structure when he states that it is "the social process in group life that creates and upholds the rules, not the rules that create and uphold group life." In other words, norms, as discussed by structural functionalists, do not determine the behavior of individuals; individuals act in concert to uphold the norms or rules of behavior. A structural functionalist emphasizes that people are products of their respective societies; a symbolic interactionist stresses the other side of the coin, namely, that social structure is the result of persons in interaction.

Society as Symbolic Interaction _____

For Blumer, then, the study of society must be a study of joint action rather than a preoccupation with what he feels to be nebulous systems and elusive functional prerequisites. Society is a result of symbolic interaction among persons, and it is precisely this aspect that should be of concern to sociologists. The peculiarity of the symbolic interactionist approach for Blumer, as we have seen, is that human beings interpret or define each other's actions instead of merely reacting to each other's actions in a stimulus–response fashion. The response of a person is not made directly to the actions of another person but is based instead on the meaning that he/she attaches to such action. Blumer (1969:78–79) asserts, "Thus, human interaction is mediated by the use of symbols, by interpretation, or by ascertaining the meaning of one another's actions. This mediation is equivalent to inserting a process of interpretation between stimulus and response in the case of human behavior." Although all of sociology is concerned with human behavior, frequently it neglects analyzing interpretation or meaning that is attached to such behavior. Interpretation provides a response, but this response is one of "acting on the basis of symbols."

Rather than asserting the priority and dominance of the group or the structure, Blumer (1969:84–85) views group action as a collection of individual actions: "Human society is to be seen as consisting of acting people, and the life of the society is to be seen as consisting of their actions." Blumer extends this idea to point out that such group life is a response to situations in which persons find themselves. These situations may be structured, but Blumer cautions against ignoring the importance of interpretation even in relatively fixed institutions. Blumer (1969:78) observes the following two differences between the structural functionalist and the symbolic interactionist views of society:

> First, from the standpoint of symbolic interaction the organization of human society is the framework inside of which social action takes place and is not the determinant of that action.
> Second, such organization and changes in it are the product of the activity of acting units and not of "forces" which leave such acting units out of account.

Sociology's preoccupation with structure has caused the neglect of interpretative processual action.

Blumer's proposed symbolic interactionism contains a number of "root images" or basic ideas. These root images could be summarized as follows:

1. Society consists of human beings in interaction. These activities are fitted together in complex ways through *joint action,* forming what has come to be known as *organization* or *social structure.*

2. Interaction consists of human activities in response to other human activities. *Nonsymbolic interactions* involve a simple stimulus–response, such as a cough to clear one's throat. *Symbolic interaction* involves "interpretation of the action." If the person in an audience coughs whenever he/she disagrees with a point the speaker is making, coughing becomes a significant symbol used to convey the meaning of disapproval. Language, of course, is the most common significant symbol.

3. Objects have no intrinsic meaning; rather the meaning is a product of symbolic interaction. Objects can be classified into three broad categories: (a) physical objects, such as desks, plants, or cars; (b) social objects, such as mother, teacher, minister, or friend; and (c) abstract objects, such as values, rights, and laws. Blumer (1969:10–11) defines an object as "anything that can be referred to." It is through symbolic interaction that the world of objects is "created, affirmed, transformed, and cast aside." The role of meaning applied to even physical objects may be illustrated by the treatment and use of cattle in the United States as compared with India. The object (cattle) is the same in both societies, but whereas cattle may mean "meat" in America, in India, they are sacred. When viewed in a cross-cultural perspective, even physical objects whose meanings we take for granted may be seen to be socially derived.

4. Human beings not only recognize objects external to themselves, but they are able to view themselves as objects. Thus a young man is able to see himself as a student, a husband, and a new father. This view of self, like all objects, emerges during the process of symbolic interaction.

5. Human action is interpretative action constructed by men and women. As Blumer (1969:15) has noted:

> Fundamentally, action on the part of a human being consists of taking account of various things he notes and forging the line of conduct on the basis of how he interprets them. The things taken into account cover such matters as his wishes and wants, his objectives, the available means for their achievement, the actions and anticipated actions of others, his image of himself, and the likely result of a given line of action.

6. Action is interlinked and fitted together by members of the group; this is known as *joint action. Joint action* may be defined as "a societal organization of conduct of different acts of diverse persons" (Blumer, 1969:17). Most situations of joint action are repetitive and stable, constituting what sociologists have come to call "culture" and "social order." Much of Blumer's theoretical approach to symbolic interactionism has

been developed from his interpretation of Mead. Mead, however, neglected to spell out the appropriate method for symbolic interactionist research. It is to this topic that Blumer has devoted much of his concern.

Methodological Principles of Empirical Science

Blumer is aware of the methodological weaknesses of Mead's philosophical formulation of social psychology. Although philosophy represents an indispensable foundation for this perspective, it is the "empirical world (that) must forever be the central point of concern" (Blumer, 1969:22). Methodology, or the logic of scientific procedure, permits sociologists to embark on their quest for scientific theory. Blumer, however, is critical of the tendency of contemporary sociology to equate methodology with advanced statistical techniques, observing that analysis is but one aspect of methodology. Moreover, he (1969:28) questions the "widespread and deeply entrenched belief in the social and psychological sciences that faithful adherence to what is commonly accepted as the proper protocol of research procedure automatically yields results that are valid for the empirical world." Blumer is also critical of social science's slavish dependence upon preconceived theoretical models and ultrasophisticated research techniques, urging instead a direct return to the empirical world. He (1969:34) emphatically states:

> The road to such empirical validation does not lie in the manipulation of the method of inquiry; it lies in the examination of the empirical social world. It is not to be achieved by formulating and elaborating catchy theories, by devising ingenious models, by seeking to emulate the advanced procedures of the physical sciences, by adopting the newest mathematical and statistical schemes, by coining new concepts, by developing more precise quantitative techniques, or by insisting on adherence to the canons of research design. Such preoccupations, without prejudice to their merit in other respects, are just not headed in the direction that is called for here. What is needed is a return to the empirical social world.

This empirical social world, for Blumer, consists of human beings and their daily activities in the course of living. Knowledge of such intimate behavior can be obtained only through firsthand observation and participation in the group under study; it cannot be obtained by an outsider lacking in familiarity and intimate acquaintance with the group. Thus Blumer (1969:34) proposes that the methodology of symbolic interaction be a direct examination of social phenomena—"a down-to-earth approach to the scientific study of human group life and human conduct."

Blumer proposes two modes of inquiry that would make possible the direct examination of social phenomena: exploration and inspection. *Exploration* is a flexible method allowing the researcher to "move toward a clearer understanding of how one's problem is to be posed, to learn what are the appropriate data, to develop ideas of what are significant lines of relation, and to evolve one's conceptual tools in the light of what one is learning about the area of life" (Blumer, 1969:40). Its main aim is to get a clearer picture of what is going on in the subject area of research by being alert to the need to test and revise observations. Out of such exploration should come what Blumer (1969:147) terms *sensitizing concepts*. Sensitizing concepts put the researcher in touch with what he/she is studying by giving the user "a general sense of reference and guidance in approaching empirical instances" (1969:147). Blumer views numerous concepts, such as culture, institutions, mores, and personality, as sensitizing because although they lack a clear-cut identification, they "rest on a general sense of what is relevant" (1969:147).

Such sensitizing concepts make possible the second mode of inquiry: inspection. Through *inspection* the researcher creatively examines concepts in light of empirical evidence. Blumer (1969:44) compares inspection with the handling of a strange physical object: "we may pick it up, look at it closely, turn it over as we view it, look at it from this or that angle, raise questions as to what it might be, go back and handle it again in light of our questions, try it out, and test it in one way or another." Thus Blumer's approach is definitely empirical, but he tries to avoid what he considers the sterility of the extreme quantitative approach to sociological research—an approach that may be more misleading than helpful in bringing sociology to maturity.

A Critical Evaluation of Blumer's Interactionism

Symbolic interaction has been referred to as "the loyal opposition" in contemporary sociology (Mullins, 1973:75–104). Although acknowledging the existence of patterned behavior, Blumer's symbolic interactionism has continued to question its reification in structural functional concepts, such as *structure, norm,* and *status.* Blumer is also critical of the methodology that has been coupled with the functionalist approach in sociology, a methodology that tends toward quantification rather than understanding. Symbolic interactionism's emphasis has been upon the interpretive *process* of interacting rather than upon a *product* of social groups.

Blumer's symbolic interactionist premises presume a creative and spontaneous rather than a fixed and determined person. As Blumer (1969:14) observes, the view of humanity in symbolic interaction is radically different from other sociological perspectives:

> Instead of being merely an organism that responds to the play of factors on or through it, the human being is seen as an organism that has to deal with what it notes. It meets what it so notes by engaging in a process of self-indication in which it makes an object of what it notes, gives it a meaning, and uses the meaning as the basis for directing its action.

The human being is not merely a *responding organism* but also an *acting organism*, that is, "an organism that has to mold a line of action on the basis of what it takes into account instead of merely releasing a response to the play of some factor on its organization."

By far, Blumer's theory offers the most creative view of people of any theory presented thus far. Blumer denounced sociology's preoccupation with structure long before Homans's call to bring men back into sociological analysis. Although Homans dealt with the individual in his theory, he presented, as we have seen, a very determined portrait of human beings. The deterministic nature of theory led to Dennis Wrong's (1961:183–193) decrying "the oversocialized conception of man in modern sociology." Wrong has criticized this overintegrated view of sociology, which has resulted in an "oversocialized" or deterministic view of people that became rampant as structural functionalism grew in importance.

In short, Blumer kept alive the tradition of G. H. Mead during a period in which the latter's theory was ignored by functionalists. By employing the concept of "role," functionalists had assumed that they brought individuals into their analyses, but this concept was used very differently by them than by interactionists. A brief consideration of the twin concepts of status and role will illustrate the vast difference in usage.

We may recall in our discussion of structural functionalism that status role was seen by Parsons to be the basic unit of the social system. *Status* refers to the position in the system, and *role* is viewed as expected behavior associated with a particular position. A structural functionalist tends to equate status and role in both theory and analysis; a symbolic interactionist sees important differences between the two concepts. Blumer would view a social status (e.g., father, president, student) as a social object to which meaning is attached; this interpretation of the status affects the enactment of the role or behavior. For example, a young girl may learn through interaction with her own mother that motherhood is a status to which she should aspire for fulfillment in life, *or* she may learn that motherhood need not be personally fulfilling in the same manner that career excellence may be. The status of mother would be reacted to and possibly enacted differently based on such early interaction. The role is thus formed and transformed by human interaction rather than being determined by some overpowering structure.

Blumer's conception of society, as we have seen, flows from his model of a voluntary person. Human society is symbolic interaction rather than a reified and autonomous structure. Blumer (1969:84) defies the trend in sociology by refusing to consider society as an entity that exists as an emergent structure.

> Under the perspective of symbolic interaction, social action is lodged in acting individuals who fit their respective lines of action to one another through the process of interpretation; group action is collective action of such individuals. As opposed to this view, sociological conceptions generally lodge social action in the action of society or in some unit of society.

In other words, Blumer emphasizes the need to view society as "acting people" rather than as a source of forces that act upon people. Society is a framework within which humans engage in action.

Blumer's conception of people and society has led him, as we have discussed in this chapter, to consider the methodology appropriate for symbolic interactionist analysis. He insists upon sympathetic introspection, which can best be carried out by the use of life histories, case studies, diaries, letters, nondirective interviews, and participant observation as the best techniques for collecting sociological data. Blumer is clearly toward the humanistic, interpretative end of the naturalistic–humanistic continuum, asserting that human beings must be studied as a distinct subject matter and that this study cannot take its lead from the natural sciences.[2]

---

[2] Of the theorists treated thus far, Blumer's approach to sociology stands closest to that of his former student, Erving Goffman. Blumer (1972:52–53) lauds Goffman's "perceptive analysis" of the everyday and the commonplace that have been neglected in sociology. He also praises his former student's research procedure:

> In the spirit of a scientific pioneer he is ever ready to probe around in fresh directions in place of forcing his investigation into the fixed protocol so frequently demanded in contemporary social science research. Fortunately, his interests are in untangling the empirical world rather than in paying obeisance to some sanctified scheme for doing so. Through the use of choice accounts of human experience he cuts through to important observations that are not yielded by hosts of stylized findings. (Blumer, 1972:53)

Blumer's brand of symbolic interactionism has not been without criticism. The heart of Blumer's theory rests with the concept of *self*, but this concept has not been treated satisfactorily. Stryker (1973:14–15), for example, asserts that sociologists in the tradition of Blumer have been too concerned with the notion of a unitary, undifferentiated self rather than with the self as a complex entity. Perhaps the self may be divided into parts, with these parts being organized hierarchically. This approach, insist critics, would allow for a more empirical approach to the study of self than Blumer's theoretical formulation permits.

Problems with Blumer's conceptualization of self have fed into his view of society. Blumer attempts to avoid reification of concepts—particularly those relating to society. Zeitlin (1973:217) observes that Blumer's approach has resulted in a view of society as "nothing more than a plurality of disembodied selves interacting in structureless situations." Blumer's approach to society makes topics such as stratification, intergroup conflicts, or bureaucracy difficult, if not impossible, to treat.

Blumer's approach to symbolic interactionist theory has also been challenged on methodological grounds by other symbolic interactionists (see, for example, Kuhn, 1964). His humanistic approach to symbolic interaction has come to be termed the *Chicago school*, whereas Manford Kuhn's naturalistic and positivistic approach is referred to as the *Iowa school*. The Iowa school of symbolic interactionism stresses its commonalities with other scientific disciplines and utilizes the more standard techniques of survey research design.

It appears that Mead's and Blumer's symbolic interactionism is incompatible with the natural-science approach to sociology. In fact any movement toward positivism moves the theorist away from what Mead and Blumer consider the heart of symbolic interaction, namely, the dynamic and interpretative nature of social action. Symbolic interactionism, in the tradition of Mead and Blumer, has been seen as the "loyal opposition" to structural functionalism, but it is more than that. It represents a strong humanistic position against the well-rooted scientific or neopositivistic emphasis in contemporary theory.

Summary

Symbolic interactionism represents a break from the view that the individual is a product determined by the society. Rather it conceptualizes the self as being in process and not conforming completely to the idealized, oversocialized man of functionalist theory. Persons apply subjective meaning to their world of objects rather than simply accepting a pre-designated interpretation of the objective reality that they encounter. Moreover the social structure is viewed as a product of the joint actions of its members rather than as a reality *in itself,* as postulated by Émile Durkheim and his present-day functionalist disciples. It is people in inter-action that comprise the group.

Joint actions forming the structure or institution are possible because of symbolic interaction, which uses gestures and language to convey meaning. It is through significant symbols, symbols having shared mean-ings, that objects are interpreted and defined. Meanings are conveyed to others in the interaction process.

The theoretical premises of Blumer's symbolic interactionism lead him to establish methodological guidelines for research. Social action must be studied as a process and in terms of how it is formed. Organization or social structure is thus viewed as an organization of action. Symbolic in-teractionism attempts to explain the way in which participants define, interpret, and meet situations, thus contributing to the structure's forma-tion and/or its change. The processual nature of the formation of both self and social structure cannot be ignored in empirical research.

In spite of his attempts to make methodological statements tied to symbolic interactionist theory, Blumer's concepts are nebulous and diffi-cult to operationalize in empirical research. As members of a discipline that stresses the importance of testing and verifying theory, many soci-ologists (including members of the Iowa school of symbolic interaction-ism) have found Blumer's formulation of symbolic interactionist theory and method impossible to use in *doing* sociology. The future of symbolic interactionism as a sociological perspective remains in doubt. Some of its former theorists have shifted more toward an ethnomethodological per-spective—a theory that shares many of the premises of symbolic inter-actionism but attempts to wed its theory intimately with empirical research. Ethnomethodology is the subject of the following chapter.

References

BLUMER, HERBERT
   1966 "Sociological Implications of the Thought of George Herbert Mead."
        The American Journal of Sociology 71 (March):535–544.
   1969 *Symbolic Interactionism: Perspective and Method.* Englewood Cliffs,
        N.J.: Prentice-Hall, Inc.
   1972 "Action vs. Interaction." *Society* 9 (April):50–53.
COOLEY, CHARLES HORTON
   1930 *Sociological Theory and Social Research.* New York: Holt, Rinehart
        and Winston.

KUHN, MANFORD H.
  1964 "Major Trends in Symbolic Interaction Theory in the Past Twenty-five Years." *Sociological Quarterly* 5 (Winter):61–84.
MELTZER, BERNARD N., and JOHN W. PETRAS
  1972 "The Chicago and Iowa Schools of Symbolic Interactionism." Pp. 43–57 in J. Manis and B. Meltzer (Eds.), *Symbolic Interaction*. Boston: Allyn & Bacon, Inc.
MULLINS, NICHOLAS C.
  1973 *Theories and Theory Groups in Contemporary American Sociology.* New York: Harper & Row, Publishers.
STONE, GREGORY, and HARVEY A. FARBERMAN (Eds.)
  1970 *Social Psychology Through Symbolic Interaction.* Waltham, Mass.: Ginn-Blaisdell.
STRYKER, SHELDON
  1973 "Some Recent Developments in Social Psychology." Prepared as a "refresher lecture" for presentation at the Annual Meeting of the American Sociological Association. Mimeo.
THOMAS, WILLIAM I.
  1923 *The Unadjusted Girl.* Boston: Little, Brown and Company.
WRONG, DENNIS
  1961 "The Oversocialized Conception of Man in Modern Sociology." *American Sociological Review* 26 (April):183–193.
ZEITLIN, IRVING M.
  1973 *Rethinking Sociology: A Critique of Contemporary Theory.* Englewood Cliffs, N.J.: Prentice-Hall, Inc.

12

Ethnomethodology: Studying Taken-for-Granted Aspects of Reality

It has been the purpose of this paper to recommend the hypothesis that scientific rationalities can be employed only as ineffective ideals in the actions governed by the presuppositions of everyday life. The scientific rationalities are neither stable features not sanctionable ideals of daily routines, and any attempt to stabilize these properties or to enforce conformity to them in the conduct of everyday affairs will magnify the senseless character of a person's behavioral environment and multiply the disorganized features of the system of interaction. (Garfinkel, 1967:283)

Garfinkel's ethnomethodology offers a radically different approach to sociological theory. Although he is clearly in the humanistic tradition, insisting that the subject matter of sociology differs greatly from that of the natural sciences, he calls into question the very appearances that sociologists observe as reality. Garfinkel insists that the sociologist, who is called upon to study objectively his/her social world, must doubt the reality of that very world. In neglecting to study people's behavior from a perspective of skepticism and doubt, sociologists, charged Garfinkel, may have created an ordered, scientific reality of human behavior but one that is not real.

Ethnomethodology, as we shall see, is more than an abstract theory of behavior. It is an empirical study of how people make sense of the experiences confronting them daily in their social world. It sets for itself the task of empirically studying a person's construction of reality during the course of his/her daily interaction.

Although this approach developed during the 1950s, with Harold Garfinkel teaching its tenets on the West Coast at UCLA, it was not until the late 1960s and the early 1970s that the larger profession became aware of ethnomethodological developments by Garfinkel, his students, and his students' young protégés. Given the undisputed role of Garfinkel as the founder of this approach, we will center our discussion of ethnomethodology on his formulation of it. Before addressing ourselves to a discussion of Garfinkel's ethnomethodology, however, we will briefly place this school of sociological thought in relation to the other perspectives we have considered.

Although ethnomethodology cannot properly be said to be a direct offshoot of the symbolic interactionist tradition, it does share much with this approach.[1] Commonalities include the focus of analysis on the individual in face-to-face interaction, emphasis on the importance of language, attempts to explain empirical reality from the perspective of the people being studied, awareness of the subjective as well as the objective aspects of society, and criticism of the methodology employed in conventional sociology. With regard to the latter point, ethnomethodology has been especially critical of sociology's failure to depict reality and has launched an even stronger attack on current ways of doing sociology and social psychology than the symbolic interactionists have. The developments in ethnomethodology, as we have noted, are relatively new in contrast to the more established functionalist and symbolic interactionist approaches. Its newness, perhaps, makes ethnomethodology far from a unified body of theoretical knowledge. Stryker (1973:17) has aptly expressed the problem in attempting to discuss ethnomethodology:

> I enter now a territory, where if angels don't fear to tread, they should— and I'm anything but an angel. I'm not at all sure I understand everything that fits the rubric of ethnomethodology, and I'm not helped by the fact that everytime I read someone working in this vein, he/she informs me

---

[1] As symbolic interactionism and ethnomethodology share a subjective view of the social world, Denzin (1969) proposed a synthesis of the two approaches based on their common approach in explaining the social order. Zimmerman and Wieder (1970:289), however, questioned Denzin's understanding of ethnomethodology. "The ethnomethodologist is *not* concerned with providing causal explanations, of observing regular, patterned, repetitive actions by some kind of analysis of the actor's point of view. He is concerned with how members of society go about the task of *seeing, describing,* and *explaining* order in the world in which they live." According to Zimmerman and Wieder, the problem of social order, which has been central in sociological theory, is only peripheral in ethnomethodology. Basically we concur with Zimmerman and Wieder's observations and contend that ethnomethodology is a radically different approach to sociology. We do see, however, that there are points of convergence between symbolic interaction and ethnomethodology.

that the person I've just read is stupid, or vacuous, or misses the point of the whole thing, or whatever.

In spite of the problems of accurately representing ethnomethodology, it has become an important area of discussion in contemporary sociological theory. This is true no less for its critics than for its supporters. In order to avoid the type of problem Stryker describes, of conflicting and contradictory assertions among ethnomethodologists themselves, we will limit our discussion to the founder of ethnomethodology, Harold Garfinkel.[2]

In tracing the origins of ethnomethodology, Mullins (1973:185–186) asserts that it began with Garfinkel, who was a student of functionalist Talcott Parsons. In addition to Garfinkel's exposure to Parsonian theory at Harvard, he also studied with phenomenologist Alfred Schutz at the New School for Social Research. For Schutz, the everyday world is an intersubjective one, shared with the others with whom we interact. To this extent, Schutz's theory shares much with that of symbolic interactionist George Herbert Mead (briefly discussed in the last chapter). Schutz contends, however, that this intersubjective world is made up of multiple realities, with the reality of everyday experience emerging as paramount. It is to this taken-for-granted, common-sense, everyday world that Schutz directs his attention. This reality is one that we accept—bracketing any doubts about it unless the reality is called into question. For example, ordinarily a person wouldn't question whether the electricity failed to operate while he/she was asleep. If the alarm had been set for 6 A.M., however, and a person awoke to the alarm and saw a noonday sun when opening the blinds, a power failure would be a plausible explanation. The same principle of "bracketing doubt" occurs in our everyday interaction with others. We don't wake up daily to question the veracity of our loved ones, the operation of our nation's monetary system, or the reality of our social institutions.[3]

Our common-sense reality and everyday existence may be termed our *practical interest* in the social world. This practical interest may be contrasted to a scientist's *theoretical* or *scientific interest*. Scientific theory at-

[2] Mehan and Wood (1975:vii) observe that ethnomethodology has many quarreling factions but in unison state their attempt: "I neither wish to quarrel nor create another faction. My vision of ethnomethodology sees diversity as a sign of strength." Mehan and Wood's book-length discussion of ethnomethodology offers the interested student a good description of a synthesis of the diversity that is encompassed in the label of *ethnomethodology*.

[3] As we shall see during the course of our discussion of Garfinkel's ethnomethodology, this perspective reverses Schutz's "bracketing of doubt." What the ethnomethodologists attempt to do is to suspend their belief in the reality of a situation, thus "bracketing reality." This process enables them to observe how persons construct their everyday reality.

tempts to observe and understand the world systematically. Here the brackets of doubt may be removed for a close inspection of the phenomenon. People operate, contends Schutz, not according to scientific theory but on a practical level, sharing this intersubjective world with others who also experience it. Schutz's discussion of common-sense reality provided Garfinkel with the perspective for carrying out his studies of ethnomethodology and provides the theoretical base for other ethnomethodological treatises. Ethnomethodology has tried to demonstrate empirically some of the philosophical observations made by Schutz.

What Is Ethnomethodology? _____

Ethnomethodology differs from all of the approaches we have studied thus far in that it criticizes the standard sociological way of tackling the problem of order in society. The reality of social order is seen by sociologists as being something "out there"—a reality that individuals internalize through the social norms reflecting their culture. Ethnomethodologists object to the idea that order has such a reality of its own. They suggest rather that order is attributed to situations by the participants. Thus people try to "make sense" or "make order" out of whatever action or situation they encounter. This principle of ethnomethodology will be further illustrated.

Ethnomethodology is concerned with studying the everyday activities of people—especially the taken-for-granted aspects of social interaction. Garfinkel (1967:11) defines ethnomethodology as "the investigation of indexical expressions and other practical actions as contingent ongoing accomplishments of organized artful practices of everyday life." This approach, which sheds light on the "rational accountability of practical action" includes the following: (1) the distinction between objective and indexical expressions; (2) the reflexivity of practical actions, and (3) the analyzability of actions within their everyday context. This description, given in Garfinkel's inimitable language, requires some explanation.

Put simply, the ethnomethodologist is concerned about how (the method by which) people make sense of their everyday world. The ethnomethodologist is concerned about the way persons ascribe order or patterns to their reality. Language and the meanings attached to such significant symbols are an important source of indexical expressions. *Indexical expressions* are a person's designation of the time and space of an occurrence that may serve as an "index" to locate the happening within the sphere of reality. Usually our everyday indices are less than precise. If someone were to ask a person when she/he last went to a movie, he/

she might respond, "about a month ago." In everyday life we are accustomed to such inexact indexical expressions of time. He/she would not be inclined to respond with a more precise statement, such as, "I last went to a movie on Friday, January 23, of this year. It was the 9:00 showing, which started promptly and let out at 11:12 p.m." Such precise reference of time might be considered an *objective expression* and would be in order on some occasions (for example, on a patient's hospital record sheet to record some physical change). Indexical and objective expressions reflect Schutz's practical and theoretical realities, which indexical expressions being appropriate for everyday, practical activities, and objective expressions being the mode for the scientific realm. Thus it is through language, and particularly the use of indexical expressions, that persons are able to express the order they make of their everyday world.

Garfinkel points out that objective expressions are awkward for most informal discourse, but they are essential to science. The arts are characterized by indexical expressions, but science relies upon objective expressions. Sociology is caught in a dilemma. As a reputed science, it attempts to use objective expressions, but they are superimposed upon the everyday use of indexical expressions by the subjects studied. Garfinkel questions the manner in which scientific reality has been superimposed upon interaction using indexical expressions. For example, standard research instruments in sociology attempt scientific precision, but they are studying people engaged in constructing practical reality. Phenomena such as decision making, social attitudes, sources of influence, and other social processes of concern to sociologists are not enacted in accord with the scientific model but rather with a practical model.

Second, Garfinkel notes that sociologists have not found accounts of "practical action" to be interesting. What he means is that scientific observers take too much for granted in their scientific inquiries of human behavior. In *practical action* Garfinkel (1967:7) includes "many organizationally important and serious matters: . . . resources, aims, excuses, opportunities, tasks, and of course . . . grounds for arguing or foretelling the adequacy of the procedures and the findings they yield." Garfinkel urges the study of such practical action in order to determine what is going on in the first place. An example that we will deal with later in this chapter is a jury. Jurors have been provided with the norms or rules to guide decision making, but men and women of the jury might (and do) set up their own guidelines to determine guilt or innocence. To ignore these taken-for-granted guidelines is to ignore an important aspect of reality.

Third, when sociologists analyze action, they must remember that such action occurs within a larger context. Each action has a history that may be traced to other contexts. This is true for repetitive actions as well as for acts that persons may not have engaged in before. Even though a juror may never have served on a jury previously, he/she uses past experience to guide behavior. Daily living (which does have a continuous history) is not therefore particularly problematic. The repetitiveness of daily events allows any doubts about its reality to be bracketed.

Garfinkel's ethnomethodology challenges the basic sociological concept of order. He appears to assume that there is little that is particularly orderly in social events. The order that is established is established according to norms guiding how people make sense of our their social world. It is only when reality is challenged that the process of making sense or making order out of the world becomes apparent. This process may be illustrated by an analysis of informal conversations, which demonstrate how sense is made out of what is being said.

Illustrating Common Understanding

As we noted earlier in this chapter, informal conversation uses indexical rather than objective expressions. Much is left implicit in everyday conversations, causing the listener to "fill in" additional materials to "make sense" out of conversation. The following is an example of such a common conversation reported by Garfinkel (1967:25–26). The right side of the column gives a possible interpretation to each brief statement actually spoken.

Husband: Dana succeeded in putting a penny in a parking meter today without being picked up.	This afternoon as I was bringing Dana, our four-year-old son, home from nursery school, he succeeded in reaching high enough to put a penny in a parking meter when we parked in a meter zone, whereas before he had always had to be picked up to reach that high.
Wife: Did you take him to the record store?	Since he put a penny in a meter that means that you stopped while he was with you. I know that you stopped at the record store either on the way to get him or on the way back. Was it on the way back, so that he was with you or did you stop there on the way to get him and somewhere else on the way back?
Husband: No, to the shoe repair shop.	No, I stopped at the record store on the way to get him and stopped at the

		shoe repair shop on the way home when he was with me.
Wife:	What for?	I know of one reason why you might have stopped at the shoe repair shop. Why did you stop in fact?
Husband:	I got some new shoe laces for my shoes.	As you will remember I broke a shoe lace on one of my brown oxfords the other day so I stopped to get some new laces.
Wife:	Your loafers need new heels badly.	Something else you could have gotten that I was thinking of. You could have taken in your black loafers which need heels badly. You'd better get them taken care of pretty soon.

Thus there seems to be a difference between what was actually said in the conversation and what was talked about. Put another way, people speak in indexical expressions rather than in objective expressions that might be better illustrated in a comparison of left- and right-hand columns. In conversations there is shared agreement beyond the actual words being spoken. This taken-for-granted, shared communication is what is of interest to the ethnomethodologist.

Studies of the Routine Grounds of Everyday Activities

In an ethnomethodological attempt to challenge taken-for-granted reality and thus to make such taken-for-granted aspects of daily living more apparent, Garfinkel and his students utilized quasi-field experiments. Unlike the conversation quoted, which is a simple report of a conversation and an interpretation of its content, quasi-field experiments involve some manipulation of the subject of study in order to challenge the manner in which he/she constructs a definition of the situation. Take the following case reported by Garfinkel (1967:43) as an illustration:

> On Friday night my husband and I were watching television. My husband remarked that he was tired. I asked, "How are you tired? Physically, mentally, or just bored?"
> (S) I don't know, I guess physically, mainly.
> (E) You mean that your muscles ache or your bones?
> (S) I guess so. Don't be so technical.
> (After more watching)
> (S) All of these old movies have the same kind of old iron bedstead in them.

(E) What do you mean? Do you mean all old movies, or some of them, or just the ones you have seen?
(S) What's the matter with you? You know what I mean.
(E) I wish you would be more specific.
(S) You know what I mean! Drop dead.

In this case, the wife, serving as the experimenter (E), was challenging the manner in which her husband, the subject (S), was constructing his reality. As she deliberately violated the expectation that casual conversation will utilize indexical expressions by demanding objective ones, he became angry, not knowing what to make of her behavior.

To further document some taken-for-granted aspects of society, Garfinkel set up the quasi experiment of having students act as boarders in their own homes. These students were to be extremely polite when dealing with family members, were to speak only when spoken to, and were to avoid getting personal. Garfinkel (1967:47) reports that in the vast majority of the cases, the family members were "stupefied" and "vigorously sought to make the strange actions intelligible and to restore the situation to normal appearances." This and other contrived studies demonstrated how people attempt to make sense out of their everyday affairs— even when little sense can be made of the events themselves. The field experiments were designed to make this reality problematic, causing the subject to try to re-create some kind of organized reality.

Garfinkel performs this same type of analysis on jury decision-making. The process through which jurors reach their decision as to the guilt or innocence of a defendant provides Garfinkel with a noncontrived illustration of this ethnomethodology or "methodology used by the people." A juror is presented with multitudinous bits of information and must decide its "truth" and "reality." The collective knowledge of "facts" of the case yields a jury decision. Garfinkel observes that this decision-making procedure is governed by rules and norms that provide guidelines for a "good juror." Jurors learn the official appropriate behavior for jurors from court instructions, a handbook, and other such places. They also receive unofficial tutoring from TV and movies, from each other, and from high-school-aged children enrolled in civics classes. "Finally, there is the fact that in the course of their ordinary outside affairs, jurors had built up a stock of information about procedures that were in their view merely theoretic, impractical, playful, make-believe, 'high-class,' 'low-class' and so on" (Garfinkel, 1967:110).

The jurors bring with them their rules for constructing reality in daily life. The main difference between this reality and their tasks as jurors is that as jurors, they are called upon to observe events *theoretically*. The uniformities of affairs of everyday, by contrast, are usually problematic. As we have seen in the field experiments, by "playing guest" in their homes, students made the construction of reality problematic for their parents. Similarly, in the quasi-field experimentation where the investigator demanded a full explanation of the obvious in a conversation, the construction of reality was made problematic for the subjects. Usually such everyday realities go by unnoted, primarily because they are nonproblematic. The jurors' realities, however, are only in part nonproblematic; in part they are expected to modify their rules of daily life. The jurors agree to abide by the rules of the court—rules that implicitly require them to restructure some of their everyday conceptions of reality. They are expected to replace their subjective perspectives with objective insights. Garfinkel feels that in practice the jury decision is made only in part according to objective guidelines; another important part is the modified norms of everyday activity. Thus there are aspects of both indexical and objective expressions present in jury decision-making.

Garfinkel makes another ethnomethodological observation on the state of clinic records. Anyone who has tried to use institutional records as a source of data is aware that the information on these records is less than complete. Facts that are supposed to be uniformly recorded on all cases simply are not uniformly recorded. Rather than simply shrugging off the missing data, Garfinkel attempted to develop an explanation of the frequency of such "bad records." Part of the explanation, Garfinkel believes, rests in an economic problem. Agencies operate on fixed budgets. Obvious information, such as age and sex, is invariably noted, but information requiring more detail represents practitioners' time taken from service. The practitioner may neglect to collect the desired information (for example, on occupational history) simply because it takes too long or he/she does not think it represents the best use of the time available. Similarly supervisors may not enforce the collection of this data, reasoning that the time might be spent better in serving the patient's physical needs. Thus there is a rational explanation for the lack of background data on many records. Garfinkel (1967:186–207) discusses it in terms of "good" organizational reasons for "bad" clinic records. The taken-for-granted rule of assessing the utility of the information collected by the staff is one that social science researchers should be aware of.

Rational Properties of Scientific and Common-Sense Activities

These and other observations led Garfinkel to critique the methodology, complete with unrecognized assumptions, of contemporary sociology. Garfinkel asserts that the everyday world operates on a system filled with indexical expressions, whereas sociologists are describing it using objective expressions. By stressing scientific rationality, sociologists are removed from the rationality of daily life. The "definition of the situation" used by persons in their daily lives should not be confused with "scientific knowledge." Both are rational, but each represents a different type or category of rationality. As Garfinkel (1967:270) has stressed:

> the scientific rationalities, in fact, occur as stable properties of actions governed by the attitude of scientific theorizing. By contrast, actions governed by the attitude of daily life are marked by the specific absence of these rationalities either as stable properties or as sanctionable ideals.

The ethnomethodologists have called into question the entire methodology employed by sociology, particularly surveys and interviews. They question whether in the surveys and interviews popularly used by researchers, the subjects are being forced into preconceived molds that belie the reality of everyday life. Two procedures acceptable to ethnomethodologists, but infrequently employed in sociology, are participant observation and quasi-field experiments. Research techniques must guarantee that scientific rationality is not superimposed on the taken-for-granted rationalities of day-to-day life. Garfinkel (1969:283) feels that scientific rationalities can be employed "only as ineffective ideals in the actions governed by the presuppositions of daily life." To attempt to enforce conformity to them in everday conduct will result in a magnification of a "senseless character of a person's behavior" (1969:282), when in fact such behavior when viewed through an ethnomethodologist's eyes is not senseless at all. It is toward this goal of accurately capturing the construction of everyday, common-sense reality that ethnomethodology strives.

Critical Evaluation of Ethnomethodology

In some ways, ethnomethodology resembles Goffman's dramaturgy and Blumer's symbolic interactionism; in other ways, ethnomethodology represents a radical departure from other theoretical orientations. These differences and similarities may be observed in Garfinkel's image of people, his image of society, and his conceptions of sociological theory.

Garfinkel's image of people most closely resembles Goffman's.[4] For

---

[4] In his review of *Frame Analysis,* Davis (1975:601) asserts that Goffman can best be described as a "social constructionist." Goffman

> is always trying to point out the social construction of the seemingly natural— the human fabrication of what most people consider pre-fabricated (the individual, the ritual order, institutions, roles). As a social constructionist, he be-

Goffman, as we have seen, persons are primarily interested in managing the impressions they give off and are guided by tact in so doing. Men and women are analyzed by Goffman as they act in everyday situations and in routine activities. Garfinkel also studies people in daily situations and routines as they maintain reality through tacit understanding. Garfinkel's concern with *tacit understanding* (what men know and know others know) is not unlike Goffman's *tact*. Neither Goffman's nor Garfinkel's person demonstrates the type of rational (goal-oriented) properties found in functionalism and the exchange theories. Although Garfinkel sees a person's behavior as "rational," it is an everyday, practical rationality and *not* scientific or theoretical rationality that is of the greatest importance to sociologists.

Ethnomethodology, which has also been called "sociology of the absurd," [5] skirts the issue of whether persons are determined or whether they are free. As Lyman and Scott (1970:4–5) note:

> The age-old problem of freedom versus determinism is not a problem of objective philosophy but rather of the actor's construction of reality, his image of freedom and constraint. The Sociology of the Absurd views man as being constructed—and of constructing—social reality in every situation.

Thus, according to an ethnomethodological position, "freedom" or "determinism" is not an objective fact, but a subjective disposition of the actor. This emphasis on subjectivism bears a strong resemblance to Blumer's call for the study of meaning or interpretation in sociology.

Ethnomethodology shares with exchange behaviorism, dramaturgy, and symbolic interaction the view that the individual is the principal agent of action. For Homans, Goffman, Blumer, and Garfinkel, it is individuals who serve as the unit of analysis rather than social organizations or social systems. Garfinkel further asserts that individuals are the ones who give the impression of social organization to one another in this

---

gins by separating his subject into its basic elements and then shows how these elements are socially transformed (constructed) into something more elaborate. Particularly in *Frame Analysis* can we see similarities between Goffman's dramaturgy and the ethnomethodological perspective.

[5] Lyman and Scott (1970:1) have developed the theme of ethnomethodology as "the sociology of the absurd." They observe: "*The world is essentially without meaning.* In contrast to that sociology which seeks to discover the *real* meaning of action—a sociological reality, such as the *functional* meaning of social behavior—this new sociology asserts that all systems of belief, including that of conventional sociologists, are arbitrary." This view of the social world is a direct challenge to sociology as we know it and is a radical departure from traditional ways of viewing social order.

process of interaction. He thus calls into question the whole issue of an objective social order or social structure—something that exchange behaviorism and dramaturgy would not do and something that symbolic interactionism skirts.

It is important to emphasize that society, for Garfinkel, has no reality apart from men and women's ability to *convince* others that it is out there. Reality is at best a precarious enterprise that requires a constant process of construction and maintenance. As Turner (1974:330) comments, "The 'sense of order' is not what makes society possible, but the capacity of humans to *actively and continually* create and use rules for persuading each other that there is a real world." Order and organization have no reality apart from our ability to convince each other that it does in fact exist.

As we have seen in this chapter, much ethnomethodology is directed toward criticizing existing sociology. Ethnomethodologists have been critical of the existing methodological techniques employed in sociology and are quick to emphasize their shortcomings. Ironically, however, ethnomethodologists have failed to state their own methodology clearly and precisely (see Coleman, 1968, and Hill and Crittenden, 1968). In a related methodological vein, although professing interest in the operation of taken-for-granted assumptions of everyday life, ethnomethodologists have failed to demonstrate how these assumptions operate (Swanson, 1968) and fail to offer a coherent thesis about the nature of social reality (Coleman, 1968). Thus, as Mullins 1973 points out, as of 1971, ethnomethodology had not produced a positive public contribution to sociology. Its main contribution was a negative one—that of criticizing existing sociological techniques, such as survey and interviews, and of criticizing sociologists' theoretical conception of social order. To date, Mullins's criticism of ethnomethodology's lack of a positive contribution to sociology still stands. Only time will tell whether ethnomethodology will emerge in sociology with a strong substance of use to the discipline or whether it will remain a nebulous perspective.

Summary

The ethnomethodologists are concerned with discovering the essence of experiences in everyday life. They see that everyday reality is primary to knowledge in all sciences as well as to knowledge in sociology. They view social reality as existing and defined by individual actors and not as interpreted by sociologists and other social scientists. Ethnomethodologists emphasize the fact that in interaction people communicate with each other by establishing their interaction setting. In each situation in which individuals are involved, they achieve perceived rules. Because rules vary in every interaction setting, however, one cannot automatically generalize the rules from one setting to another. In each situation, individuals discern the rules of interaction that they assume to exist in that particular situation.

Ethnomethodologists assert that the methods used by individuals in constructing, maintaining, and changing the appearance of social reality can be observed, and that this observation must be the first step in constructing sociological knowledge. The study of the method by which individuals construct daily reality, say ethnomethodologists, will provide the foundations for further sociological knowledge. Thus ethnomethodologists are committed to a study of the methods people use in constructing everyday reality, a subject that they treat as problematic and as suitable material for sociological study.

The ethnomethodologists' works have been the focus of much criticism from both conventional and radical sociologists. Ethnomethodologists, it is asserted, have failed to state their own methodology clearly and precisely, to demonstrate how taken-for-granted assumptions of everyday reality operate, and to offer their own coherent thesis about the nature of social reality. In the face of such criticism, it remains to be seen whether ethnomethodology will remain a viable perspective with the passage of time.

References _____

COLEMAN, JAMES
    1968 "Review Symposium." *American Sociological Review* 33 (February): 126–130.
DAVIS, MURRAY
    1975 "Review Symposium." *Contemporary Sociology* 4 (November):599–602.
DENZIN, NORMAN K.
    1969 "Symbolic Interactionism and Ethnomethodology: A Proposed Synthesis." *American Sociological Review* 34 (December):922–934.
DOUGLAS, JACK D. (Ed.)
    1970 *Understanding Everyday Life*. Chicago: Aldine Publishing Company.
GARFINKEL, HAROLD
    1967 *Studies in Ethnomethodology*. Englewood Cliffs, N.J.: Prentice-Hall, Inc.
HILL, RICHARD J., and KATHLEEN STONE CRITTENDEN (Eds.)
    1968 *Proceedings of the Purdue Symposium on Ethnomethodology*. Lafayette, Ind.: Purdue Research Foundation.

LYMAN, STANFORD M., and MARVIN B. SCOTT
1970 *A Sociology of the Absurd.* New York: Meredith Corporation.

MEHAN, HUGH, and HOUSTON WOOD
1975 *The Reality of Ethnomethodology.* New York: John Wiley & Sons, Inc.

MULLINS, NICHOLAS C.
1973 *Theories and Theory Groups in Contemporary American Sociology.*
New York: Harper & Row, Publishers.

SCHUTZ, ALFRED
1970 *On Phenomenology and Social Relations.* Helmut R. Wagner (Ed.)
Chicago: University of Chicago Press.

STRYKER, SHELDON
1973 "Some Recent Developments in Social Psychology." Prepared as a
refresher lecture for the Annual Meeting of the American Sociological
Association. Mimeo.

TURNER, JOHNATHAN H.
1974 *The Structure of Sociological Theory.* Homewood, Ill.: The Dorsey
Press, Inc.

ZIMMERMAN, DON H., and D. LAWRENCE WIEDER
1970 "Comment on Denzin." Pp. 285–295 in Jack D. Douglas (Ed.), *Understanding Everyday Life.* Chicago: Aldine Publishing Company.

13

The Social Construction of Reality: A Synthesis Between Structuralism and Interactionism

> Sociology is a systematic attempt to see the social world as clearly as possible, to understand it without being swayed by one's own hopes and fears. This ideal of lucidity (one could even call it selfless lucidity) is intended by what Max Weber called the value-freeness of the social sciences. It is often a difficult and painful business. . . . To be a sociologist need not mean that one become either a heartless observer or a propagandist. Rather it should mean that each act of understanding stands in an existential tension with one's own values, even those, indeed especially those, that one holds most passionately. (Berger, 1977:vii)

It might appear that humanistic or interpretative sociology is limited to microsociological concerns rather than macrosociological problems. Naturalistic or positivistic sociology, as we saw in the first section of the text, tends to ignore the individual and focus on the social structure. In contrast, the humanistic theories presented this far tend to emphasize individuals in interaction as the appropriate level of analysis. Yet interpretative sociology need not be limited to social psychological concerns, as demonstrated by the synthesis Peter L. Berger provides between the interactionist and structuralist approaches.

Like Garfinkel, Berger remains indebted to his former professor, Alfred Schutz, and his teachings on the social construction of reality. Whereas Schutz's influence led Garfinkel to ethnomethodological field experiments and attacks on current popular ways of doing sociology, Schutz's work enabled Berger to develop a different theoretical model of how the social world is constructed. Whereas, as we have seen in our discussion of ethnomethodology, Garfinkel's social world exists only as long as actors permit it to exist, Berger's social reality exists of itself and acts back in structuralist fashion upon its human subjects. Unlike Garfinkel, Berger asserts that there is an objective social reality (a concern of Durkheim and later functionalist disciples) but that its meaning is derived from and by the individual's subjective relation to the objective world (a perspective shared by Mead and his symbolic interactionist followers, especially Blumer).

This "painful business" of sociology, alluded to in the opening quotation, not only must walk the tightrope between social psychology and structurally oriented sociology, it must also balance itself between valueless sterility and propaganda. Berger (1977:vii) points to two ways of avoiding the pain and difficulty of doing sociology:

> One way is to segregate the process of sociological understanding from all questions of value to the point where the sociologist tries to fashion himself into an utterly detached observer, or, alternatively, adheres to his own values without any reference to sociological insights. This is either dehumanizing (the individual as such, not just a particular intellectual activity of his, then becomes value-free), or it constitutes a surrender to irrationality (the individual holding on to his values in a realm of the mind that is inaccessible to reasonable argument). The other way, probably the simpler one, is to reject the ideal of value free understanding, to declare it to be impossible, or undesirable, or both. Such rejection then permits the individual to interpret the social world in accordance with his own value preferences—in effect, to see the world as he would like to see it.

Berger is convinced that both positions are wrong: "To be a sociologist need not mean that one becomes either a heartless observer or a propagandist." One's subjective values will be in dialectical tension with one's attempt at objective scholarship.

The attempt to bridge the macro and micro, value-free and value-laden, structuralist and interactionist, as well as theoretical and relevant, sociologies is apparent in Berger's works. He thrusts himself into the middle of the "painful business" of sociology, attempting to analyze the manner in which reality is constructed.

The Social Construction of Reality _____

Berger co-authored his major theoretical treatise *The Social Construction of Reality* (1966) with German sociologist Thomas Luckmann.

Although co-authored, the same theory developed here was presented in Berger's earlier work *Invitation to Sociology* (1963) and is used repeatedly by Berger in his own later analyses. In fact, this work is the cornerstone upon which Berger's writings, both those intended for popular audiences and those intended primarily for social scientists, are grounded.

Berger and Luckmann (1966:1) summarize their theory by stating that "reality is socially constructed" and that the sociology of knowledge must analyze the process by which this occurs. They acknowledge an objective reality by defining *reality* as "a quality appertaining to phenomena that we recognize as having a being independent of our own volition (as we cannot 'wish them away')." Berger and Luckmann observe that we all seek *knowledge* or "the certainty that phenomena are real and that they possess specific characteristics" in our daily lives. Sociology engages in a more particular search for "knowledge" and "reality" that is "somewhere in the middle between the man in the streets and that of the philosopher." The man in the street "knows" his/her reality without taking time to analyze it systematically. The philosopher, on the other hand, is forced to look hard at the validity and the invalidity of knowledge. The sociologist cannot be taken up with the philosophical question of "What is really real?" Rather he/she must focus on how social reality comes about, regardless of its validity. Sociologists do not debate whether or not a chair is really a chair or whether a family is really a family; they take such labels for granted. They accept the apparent realities of society and proceed with analysis from there.

Berger agrees with the phenomenological assertion that there are multiple realities rather than a single reality. (Ethnomethodology, it will be recalled, emphasized the differences between two realities: the daily, taken-for-granted, common-sense reality and the scientific reality.) With Garfinkel, Berger concurs that there is an overriding reality, "the reality of everyday life," which is the more important reality. This reality is perceived as an ordered and patterned reality; it is usually taken for granted and nonproblematic because it is shared with others in *typified* (patterned) interactions. Unlike Garfinkel, however, Berger stresses that this reality of everyday life has both subjective and objective dimensions. The human being is an instrument in creating objective social reality through the *externalization* process, just as he/she is influenced by it through the *internalization* process (reflecting subjective reality). In a dialectical fashion, with thesis and antithesis in operation to produce a synthesis, Berger sees society as a product of people as well as people's being a product of society. We will explore the implications of the subjective and objective dimensions of reality as well as the dialectical process of objectivation, internalization, and externalization in the sections that follow.

SOCIETY AS OBJECTIVE REALITY

Following Durkheim and the structural functional tradition, Berger acknowledges the existence of an objective social reality that can be viewed in terms of societal institutions. This social order, however, is not part of the "nature of things." It does not spring as Minerva did from the head of Zeus; it can be seen only as a "product of human activity" (Berger and Luckmann, 1966:52). Berger agrees with Durkheim that this objective social structure does have a character of its own, but its origins must be seen in terms of human *externalization* or persons interacting in an already existent structure. This externalization further expands the institutionalized social order, making this structure one of continual process rather than of stagnating completion. The objective reality created through externalization, in turn, acts back on persons in society. This dialectical process is ongoing, with externalization and objectivation being but "moments" in history. The third element in the process is *internalization,* or the socialization of the individual into the objective social world (Berger and Luckmann, 1966:61). All three of these elements internalization, externalization, and objectivation—coexist, working on each other in a dialectical manner.

The basic rule governing the objective social world is order. Berger (1977:xv) insists that "sociology leads to the experience that order is *the* primary imperative of social life" and that "society, in its essence, is the imposition of order upon the flux of human experiences." He contends that "social life abhors disorder as nature abhors a vacuum." Berger acknowledges that this social order is precarious, but in functionalist fashion, he views social institutions as tending toward the equilibrium of order.

Berger and Luckmann's (1966:72–79) conceptualization of *role* as the link between the human organism and the social structure also resembles a structural functional formulation. The social structure consists of *typified* or patterned role behaviors—typifications that are reciprocal. Although the individual is not identical with his/her role, he/she does perform the activity within the standards of role performance. These role typologies are "a necessary correlate of the institutionalization of conduct." The roles thus can be said to represent the basic unit of the objective institutional order.

Unlike most functionalist models, however, Berger and Luckmann's emphasizes process along with structure. In a real way, society is never a finished product but remains in the process of becoming. Objectivation thus designates a process through which the social world is becoming a reality with the capacity to constrain and mold its participants. This objective reality of society "protects our sanity by preempting a large number of choices, not only of action but of thought." Yet limited choices do remain, enabling the structure to experience gradual change. Given the fact that for Berger and Luckmann objective reality is but one facet of our complex world, the sociologist must also be attuned to analyzing subjective reality, which may mirror but is not identical to the institutional order.

SOCIETY AS SUBJECTIVE REALITY

If the naturalistic sociologists stress the objective structural order, the interpretative sociologists represent an awareness of the importance of the subjective world of men and women. We have seen how Blumer, Goffman, and Garfinkel each have stressed subjective reality over objective structure. Berger, although devoting much time and theoretical effort to the discussion of structure, places equal emphasis on the subjective world. Objectivation is but one "moment" in the process of constructing reality. The two other "moments" in this dialectical process—internalization, and to a lesser extent, externalization—both represent an attempt to synthesize the two perspectives.

It is through the process of *internalization* or socialization that a person becomes a member of society. In the tradition of social psychology, Berger and Luckmann (1966:130) describe primary socialization as the first socialization that an individual goes through in childhood and the one by which the child is introduced to the objective social world. Individuals encounter the significant others (parents or parent substitutes) who are in charge of a child's socialization. The definitions of reality adhered to by these significant others are posited by the child as objective reality.

Because it is impossible to absorb perfectly any existing reality, the child internalizes his/her interpretation of this reality. Each person has a "version" of reality that he/she accepts as a reflection of the objective world. Berger and Luckmann thus emphasize the existence of multiple realities within our social world. A lower-class child, they note, is not only exposed to a lower-class perspective but "he absorbs it in the idiosyncratic coloration given it by his parents." Class, race, religion, and other such variables may be indicators of an objective reality, but no two individuals of any group are socialized in *exactly* the same manner. There may be great similarities between the lower-class child and his peer living next door, but there are also differences.

Although there is a symmetrical relationship between objective and subjective realities, the two realities are not identical. "What is real 'outside' corresponds to what is real 'within,'" Berger and Luckmann (1966: 133) contend; "Objective reality can readily be 'translated' into subjective reality, and vice versa." They assert that objective and subjective reality do correspond to each other, yet there is always "more" objective reality than can be internalized by any single individual. Socialization is never a perfectly completed process. There are aspects of subjective reality that have not originated in socialization, just as there are aspects of the objective reality that have not been internalized. Berger and Luckmann (1966:147–163) observe further that because socialization is never complete, there is a continual challenge to maintain reality, particularly the need to safeguard the symmetry between the objective and subjective realities.

Externalization is the process by which men and women, all being imperfectly socialized, collectively construct a new reality. Berger insists throughout his works that such change is slow yet persistent. Many of Berger's popular articles appearing in diverse literary journals and magazines deal with what he refers to as a theme of "modernity" (1977), which is central to his sociological thesis and which may be used to demonstrate the externalization process.

Modernity (1977:70) refers to "the transformation of the world brought about by the technological innovations of the last few centuries," with its economic, social, and political dimensions. "It has also brought on a revolution on the level of human consciousness, fundamentally uprooting beliefs, values, and even the emotional texture of life." Internalizing the old social world has become less and less feasible or desirable, with new realities being externalized or constructed that mesh with modern technological changes.

Perhaps a simple illustration will cast light on the highly abstract dialectical process of objectivation, internalization, and externalization. Courtship and marriage patterns are undergoing worldwide changes with the advent of modernity. In industrial societies we see a decrease in family size, the disappearance of arranged marriages, couples selecting a dwelling apart from either set of parents, the emancipation of women, and changes in divorce practices from preindustrial norms. All of these changes in structural norms guiding the institution of marriage have been gradual, with societal members collectively reconstructing new definitions of social reality. In selecting one change in norms governing the family (let us use the decrease in family size made possible by the practice of contraception), we can illustrate the threefold dialectical process of objectivation, internalization, and externalization. Because of urbanization and industrialization, the American birth rate has been on a decline for at least 150 years. For example, birth rates were three and a half times as high in 1800 as in 1930. Yet at the same time, there were strong norms against the dissemination of birth control information in the early twentieth century, as evidenced by the harassment of family-planning promoter Margaret Sanger. The drop in the birth rate even during that time is evidence that contraceptives were being sought and used by Americans despite some legal and church sanctions discouraging such practices. The internalization of objective norms was less than perfect, making possible the reconstruction of a reality that encourages "responsible parenthood," with its decrease in the number of children per family and its increase in the use of effective contraceptive techniques.

THE SOCIAL CONSTRUCTION OF REALITY AND LEGITIMATION

Berger and Luckmann (1966:61) point out in Weberian fashion that this objective institutional world requires *legitimation* or "ways by which it can be explained and justified." The original meanings of a social institution and the process of their construction are either lost or are a part of history. People, however, ascribe meanings to institutions and institutional practices, and this common "hearsay" becomes part of the legitimation process. For example, the exact meaning of American limited institutional democracy created by the founding fathers is known to historians, but little note is taken of it by American citizens, who assume that all persons were intended to have equal representation by and participation in governmental affairs. The Constitution has been legitimized and idealized in the nearly two centuries since it was written. Thus the legitimating factors could be said to arise from interaction among individuals, and the description of this legitimation becomes objectified. Legitimation thus places a "stamp of approval" upon the objective social world.

Berger has been particularly intrigued with the problem of legitimating the modern world. Secularization has been a noteworthy dilemma of modernity because it "has brought with it a massive threat to the plausibility of religious belief and experience" (Berger, 1977:78). Religion, Berger contends, has been the greatest bulwark against a meaningless existence. In other words, religion has been a most effective source of legitimating the social world. Secularization has meant a weakening of the plausibility of the legitimating enterprise. It is in an analysis of the changing religious institutions that Berger applies his theory of the construction of reality through sociohistorical analysis.

The Sacred Canopy: *An Application of Berger's Theoretical Model* _____

In his book *The Sacred Canopy: Elements of a Sociological Theory of Religion* (1967), Berger once again introduces his theoretical dialectical scheme of externalization, objectivation, and internalization. He emphasizes the fact that individuals are both products of and producers of their social institutions. Religion, as a social institution, is subject to the same process that any other institution experiences. In other words, religion has been humanly created, has developed an objective reality, and continues to act upon and to be acted upon by men and women in the modern world.

Berger notes that to discuss society as a world-building enterprise as he has done is to say that it is a *nomizing* activity. *Nomos* is the opposite of *anomie,* or a state of normlessness. If anomie represents a breakdown in the social order, nomos represents order and its normative prescriptions. There is a common nomos or meaning for the larger society in which the individual participates, but as we have already seen, there exist along side it individual or subjective meanings. Berger (1967:20) states, "The social world constitutes a nomos both objectively and subjectively. The objective nomos is given in the process of objectivation as such." Nomos thus becomes the particular state in society to which Berger directs his attention.

In addition to this nomos, there is also what Berger refers to as a *cosmos.* This cosmos transcends everyday reality, going into realms beyond objective verification. It is the cosmos that posits religion, which according to Berger (1967:27) is "a human enterprise by which a sacred cosmos is established." In modern times, we see religious cosmization alongside secular cosmization. Berger observes that science has developed a thoroughly secular attempt at cosmization.

In terms of the social construction of reality, religion has been the most widespread and effective source of legitimation. As Berger (1967: 35) stresses, "the historically crucial part of religion in the process of legitimation is explicable in terms of the unique capacity of religion to 'locate' human phenomena within a cosmic frame of reference." Thus religion can be said to serve two important purposes in man's construction of social reality: (1) it provides nomos, or meaning, to this reality, and (2) it legitimates, or puts a stamp of approval on, this reality.

The crux of Berger's theory of religion is that religion, as we know it, is faltering. Its biggest challenger is the rise of science, which has taken religion's place as a source of explanation. Although science can better explain natural phenomena than can religion, science fails miserably in providing nomos. The autopsy of modern science may be able to determine the medical cause of a child's sudden death, but it is unable to provide the meaning or comfort that traditional religions have provided in time of such tragedy. Belief in an all-good or all-powerful God provides the depth of meaning that science alone is unable to provide.

Using his dialectical theory, Berger traces the rise of secularization historically and notes its effect on religion. Although avoiding a detailed prognosis for the future of religion, Berger does emphasize not only that religion has helped to shape man's everyday reality but that forces (in the form of man's ability to externalize and change reality) are alive that will modify religion in the future. It is history that provides Berger with the data to trace the institutionalization (and thus the objectivation) and possibly the deinstitutionalization of religion in the future. The entire objective world perceived by men and women includes both sacred and secular aspects, with the sacred being represented by religious tenets and the secular by scientific ones. When internalized by modern man, religion does not take the same shape it took when it was internalized by his great-grandparents. With changes in the modern world correlating with changes in the subjective acceptance of a religious reality come changes in the objective institutional church. Men and women are externalizing and are bringing about changes in the objectivation of religious reality through, for example, their rejection of established churches, their less than wholehearted participation even when they are church members, their refusal to accept the tenets of particular churches.

As a theologian as well as a sociologist, Berger reflects his struggle with the "painful business" of doing sociology quoted in opening this chapter. In subsequent works, Berger (1967, 1977) wrestles with his religious perspectives in light of an increasingly secularized world. His own works in the sociology of religion reveal the tension that is an ever-present part of Berger's blend of scientific scholarship and personal values.

An Application of Berger's Theory to Marriage

Berger insists that his theoretical model is useful not only for macro-analyses of society and large institutions but for analyzing even small groups. He and Kellner (1970) attempted to apply the model to the construction of reality in a two-person group, namely, marriage. It is precisely such a small intimate group as the marital dyad that permits individuals "to externalize themselves in reality and to produce for themselves a world in which they can feel at home" (Berger and Kellner, 1970:56).

When two people marry, each must attempt to correlate his/her respective realities with the other's. The marriage partner becomes the most important significant other for the spouse. Thus the objective reality of marriage and the setting up of a new family is a product of the subjective dispositions of the bride and groom; this objective reality also acts back on the couple, affecting their individual subjective realities. For example, marriage may mean the breaking off of old friendships established during singlehood for new friendships that can be jointly shared. Similar changes may take place in eating preferences, recreational activities, decorating choices, and so on. This is a gradual process that goes on throughout marriage.

Conversation or "talking through" issues is a main device through which the new world view is constructed in marriage. Each partner contributes from his or her subjective reality views that are "hashed over" in conversation. These discussions from furniture-style preferences to the number of desired children become part of an objective reality that act back on the married couple. For example, a young woman may have been very uninterested in politics before her marriage. As her husband continues to voice his interest in local political affairs, she may come to identify herself as a political liberal, sharing his views. Similarly she may more clearly define herself as an antique furniture buff who appreciates classical music, also reflecting her husband's tastes. This same process is also occurring with the husband as he develops an interest in ballet and an appreciation of medieval art because of his wife's influence. Two distinct biographies are aired in conversations, and redefinitions occur that will permit the new definitions to be included in the shared reality of marriage.

Berger and Kellner emphasize that the construction of reality in marriage is not a planned occurrence. Rather it is almost automatic as the two marriage partners discover themselves and the world together. Their subjective realities are correlated to produce an objective reality that acts back on its producers. Berger and Kellner (1970:67) observe, "Marriage involves not only stepping into new roles, but, beyond this, stepping into a new world. The *mutuality* of adjustment may again be related to the rise of marital equalitarianism, in which comparable effort is demanded of both partners."

Individuals don't simply step into preexisting marital roles. There are some generally accepted societal norms guiding their respective behaviors (for example, living together, perhaps having children, keeping family contacts, sharing friends), but much of their shared reality is created by themselves. This reality can be said to be objectivated and will act not only upon the couple producing it but upon their friends and their children.

Critique of Berger's Theory

Berger's humanistic theory makes several advances over the ones we have considered thus far. Unlike Goffman, Blumer, and Garfinkel, Berger does not deemphasize or deny the importance of structure to sociological analysis. In utilizing structural theoretical concepts and theoretical insights, Berger is able to move beyond microsociological concerns. History becomes an important data source that helps to describe the development and change of modern social structures. Yet Berger shares with the other mentioned humanistic theorists the importance of treating the subject matter of sociology—namely, the action of men and women in social structures—without losing sight of their flesh and blood makeup. Berger shares other humanist and interpretative sociologies' assumptions about the nature of people and the nature of society.

Berger (1977:xv) defines society as "the imposition of order upon the flux of human experience." This order is a restraining force on men's and women's potential freedom, but this constraint is paradoxically liberating. As Berger (1977:xvi) notes, "Society protects our sanity by preempting a large number of choices, not only of action but of thought." In fact, Berger (1977:xviii) argues in favor of society's constraints:

> The "meaninglessness" of so much social life, which is currently decried as the source of so-called "alienation," is in fact a necessary condition for both individual and collective sanity. The currently fashionable left ideal of "full participation," in the sense that everybody will participate in every decision affecting his life, would, if realized, constitute a nightmare comparable to unending sleeplessness.

Yet although Berger's people are structurally constrained by their objective social reality, they are also potentially free. They can and do help to fashion the social world, but within limits. Berger (1977:xviii) states that sociology "points up the social limits of freedom—the very limits that, in turn, provide the social space for any empirically viable expression of freedom."

Berger describes his theoretical orientation as "conservative humanism." As a conservative he is skeptical of theories that advance notions of rapid social change because he has "profound suspicions about the benefits of whatever is proposed as an alternative to the status quo" (1970:21). As a humanist, he is critical of the shift in the sociological enterprise from theory toward narrowly circumscribed studies (1963:8). In calling for sociology as a humanistic discipline, Berger (1963:168) urges an "openness to the immense richness of human life [which] . . . forces the sociologist to permit 'holes' in the closed walls of his theoretical schemes." Only as a humanistic enterprise that cannot be easily molded into a rigid propositional format for rigid empirical testing can sociology reflect the "richness of human life."

At the same time, as we have already noted, Berger (1977:xviii) is not willing to abandon the model of a value-free discipline:

The *discipline of sociology*, I insist as emphatically as I can, must be value-free, however difficult this might be in some situations. The moment the discipline ceases to be value-free in principle, it ceases to be a science, and becomes nothing but ideology, propaganda, a part of the instrumentarium of political manipulation.

But values continue to be a source of tension and pain for Berger's humanistic sociologist, for "the sociologist who (after all) is also a living human being, must *not* become value free. The moment he does, he betrays his humanity and (in an operation that can simultaneously be called 'false consciousness' and 'bad faith') transforms himself into a ghostly embodiment of abstract science." Berger tackles issues of central significance, including politics and religion, and proceeds with his attempt to engage in this "painful business of sociology." [1] As one reviewer has noted of Berger's latest work: "Berger will doubtless be charged with trying to wear two hats: the mortarboard of 'value-free' sociologist . . . and the biretta of concerned Christian trying to make sense of our bemusing times" (Hassenger, 1978:8). It is precisely in his attempt to develop a humanistic scientific yet relevant theory that Berger's works make an indelible mark on contemporary sociological theoretical perspectives.

Summary

As we have seen, Berger attempts to synthesize the objective social world described by the functionalists with the subjective world emphasized by the social psychologists. He does this within a sociology-of-knowledge framework that analyzes how both objective and subjective reality are constructed by humans.

Objectivation, internalization, and externalization are three processes that go on continuously in history. They represent a gradual dialectical change rather than rapid, revolutionary transitions. There is an objective social world "out there" that shapes individuals; that is, men and women

[1] Berger (1977:viii–ix) himself refers the interested reader to his diverse attempts at wrestling with his values and the issue of modernity:

> I have explicated my understanding of the impact of modernity on human social existence and consciousness in *The Homeless Mind* (New York: Random House, 1973, with Brigitte Berger and Hansfried Kellner). Finally, the reader who wants to know more about my unapologetically *moraliste* approach to politics may turn to *Pyramids of Sacrifice* (New York: Basic Books, 1974), while *A Rumor of Angels* (New York: Doubleday, 1969) is still the longest statement on how I combine being a sociologist with (I'm afraid) a rather heretical Christianity.

are products of their society. Some of this social world exists in the form of laws that reflect our social norms—laws on marriage, protection of property, the making and breaking of contracts, and so on. Other aspects of objective reality are not as readily identifiable but influence everything from our style of dress, manner of speaking, and food preferences to our religious and social values. This objective social reality is mirrored by a child's significant others (although the reality perceived by the child and by his/her significant others is not identical). Children internalize this objective reality through the socialization process, and as adults they continue to internalize the new situations that they encounter in their social world.

Humans, however, are not completely determined by their environment. Put another way, the socialization process is never a complete success. There is room for people to externalize or collectively to shape their social world. Through this externalization, changes occur in the social order—changes that act back on the producers and may act upon subsequent generations. Society is thus a product of men and women, who not only are shaped by society but consciously and unconsciously endeavor to change it.

Berger has applied this theoretical model to both the macrosociological concern with changes in religion as a legitimating institution and the microsociological topic of constructing reality in marriage. It is also a framework that he has endeavored to use in numerous articles on modernity. Throughout both popular and sociological writings, Berger has struggled to develop a sociological model that is humanistic and relevant to the analysis of our real world.

References

BERGER, PETER
  1963 *Invitation to Sociology: A Humanist Perspective.* Garden City, N.Y.: Doubleday and Company, Inc.
  1967 *The Sacred Canopy: Elements of a Sociological Theory of Religion.* Garden City, N.Y.: Doubleday & Company, Inc.
  1970 "Between System and Horde." Pp. 11–82 in Peter L. Berger and Richard Neuhaus (co-authors), *Movement and Revolution.* Garden City, N.Y.: Doubleday & Company, Inc.
  1977 *Facing Up to Modernity: Excursions in Society, Politics and Religion.* New York: Basic Books, Inc.
BERGER, PETER, and HANSFRIED KELLNER
  1970 "Marriage and the Construction of Reality: An Exercise in the Microsociology of Knowledge." Pp. 50–71 in Hans P. Dreitzel (Ed.), *Recent Sociology.* New York: Macmillan Publishing Co., Inc.

BERGER, PETER, and THOMAS LUCKMANN
  1966 *The Social Construction of Reality.* Garden City, N.Y.: Doubleday &
     Company, Inc.
HASSENGER, ROBERT
  1978 "A Sociologist's Faith." *The Chronicle of Higher Education* 15 (January 9):18.

Postscript on Humanistic Sociology

Just as we saw varying degrees of adherence to the tenets of naturalistic sociology, so too we find differing levels of commitment to the ideal type of humanistic sociology. Although the humanists presented are agreed that sociology is different from the natural sciences, their responses to the major differences are not always in harmony. There are points of contrast as well as similarities among the theories presented in this chapter that we will attempt to summarize.

One major point of contrast is the degree to which men and women are free to shape their social world. Of the work of the four theorists presented, Goffman's dramaturgy is decidedly the most deterministic as evidenced by his work on total institutions. Whether within an institution or within a structured situation, Goffman's actors act and react to their surroundings. One gets the impression in reading Goffman's accounts of human behavior that men and women may think they are free—but are not as free as they think they are. They may acquiesce to or they may oppose the script of the drama of life, but whatever they may do, they are reacting to it.

An ingredient that is lacking in Goffman's sociology that is central to Garfinkel's, Blumer's, and Berger's theories is the concept of "meaning." Garfinkel attempts to analyze how "sense" (meaning) is made of an apparently asensical world. Each person, for Garfinkel, struggles to define his/her social experience in such a way that it "makes sense." Whereas Garfinkel works with the issue of common-sense reality on the individual level of analysis, Berger struggles with it on a collective level. A main theoretical issue is how subjective reality (individual-level analysis) stacks up against objective reality (collective-level analysis) and how meaning is derived, particularly in the form of legitimating objective reality. This concept of *meaning*, we have seen, is central to most interpretative sociologies.

Another concept that appears time and again in humanistic sociologies but is usually neglected in naturalistic theory is the concept of *self*. Here again we have witnessed differences as well as similarities. Goffman's self, we would suggest, is multifaceted and much determined by the particular structure or situation the person is in. His person moves from situation to situation with little sense of a personal history that would serve as a base of unity. Blumer's self, if less determined than Goffman's, is also more nebulous. Its strength is that it has far more unity and is capable of more creativity than is Goffman's. Berger's self, it could be argued, represents a synthesis between the creative man of Blumer's theory and the more determined person of Goffman's works.

If the image of humans is not congruent among naturalistic writers, neither is the image of society. Goffman and Berger acknowledge in the structuralist fashion the reality of society. For Goffman even the transitional situation has a reality that affects our performance. Berger, as we have noted, accepts the existence of a social structure—one that may be partially created by its member parts but one that acts back upon its producers. Whereas for both Goffman and Berger, the structure is more than simply the individuals who comprise it, neither Blumer nor Garfinkel would concur with this assumption. Blumer, as we have seen, views institutions as constant processes, simply "joint actions" that are fitted together. Garfinkel seems to go a step beyond in negating the reality of social structures. Any attempt to organize social phenomena, Garfinkel might argue, is not an objective reality but a subjective perception. Organization or structure thus exists in the minds of the multitudinous organizers who daily set about the precarious task of maintaining reality.

Goffman, Blumer, Garfinkel, and Berger share the humanistic belief that the methodology in vogue in sociology due to naturalistic sociology's dominance has failed to depict social reality accurately. In spite of this agreement, their respective methodological solutions differ. Goffman favors "unsystematic, naturalistic observation" as a data base, and Blumer has words of praise for his former student's methodology. Blumer himself has developed some methodological principles in which, like Goffman, he advocates a "down-to-earth approach to the scientific study of human group life and human conduct." Garfinkel, as we have observed, develops quasi-field experiments and participant observations as his source of data for ethnomethodology. Berger alone, undoubtedly because he moves beyond microsociological concerns, adds another dimension to the humanistic data base—that of history. In going beyond a typical humanistic sociological concern for the everyday and commonplace, Berger weds a knowledge of the past with an awareness of the present and makes a limited attempt to develop a prognosis for the future.

Berger may serve as a link between nonevaluative and evaluative theorists. It may well be that his own works are in transition between nonevaluative and evaluative humanism. In earlier works, those interested in applied theoretical concerns seemingly received little support from him. He admitted his skepticism about grand intellectual designs for the improvement of society (1970:20–21). Yet in his latest work, he admits to softening his position toward evaluative sociology (Berger, 1977:xix).

In summary, we may say that humanistic sociology freely relates itself to the humanistic disciplines, including history, philosophy, and the theater. Although insisting that sociology is a science, it also emphasizes that its subject matter differs from that of the natural sciences. Its assumptions about the relative freedom of people take a different emphasis from naturalistic sociology's more deterministic model. There is less emphasis on elements or parts that comprise the structural whole, and there is more stress on the activity of men and women in relation to what sociologists term the *social structure*. Most important is the study of the meaning or interpretation of human action, which is central to interpretative sociology. It is precisely the ability of men and women to interpret their social world that makes them different from the rest of nature. The differences between the naturalistic and the humanistic sociological assumptions often lead the two groups down different methodological paths. The naturalists are concerned with the development of so-called quantitative techniques than can more precisely measure social phenomena. The humanists, as we have seen, are frequent critics of this approach, advocating the use of more qualitative research procedures.

References

BERGER, PETER L.
     1970 "Between System and Horde." Pp. 11–82 in Peter L. Berger and
          Richard Neuhaus (co-authors), *Movement and Revolution*. Garden
          City, N.Y.: Doubleday & Company, Inc.
     1977 *Facing Up to Modernity: Excursions in Society, Politics, and Religion*.
          New York: Basic Books, Inc.

CONTRIBUTORS TO
EVALUATIVE
SOCIOLOGY

part III

14

A Call for Sociological Imagination: A Blend of Social Psychology and Conflict Structuralism

> The sociological imagination enables its possessor to understand the larger historical scene in terms of its meaning for the inner life and the external career of a variety of individuals. It enables him to take into account how individuals, in the welter of their daily experience, often become falsely conscious of their social positions. Within that welter, the framework of modern society is sought and within that framework the psychologies of a variety of men and women are formulated. By such means the personal uneasiness of individuals is focused upon explicit troubles and the indifference of publics is transformed into involvement with public issues. (Mills: 1959b:5)

A frequent criticism leveled against both naturalistic functional analysis and humanistic social psychological theories has been their neglect of the topic of conflict. Whereas the functionalist emphasis on integration has often downplayed social conflict, the interactionist emphasis on the individual as the unit of sociological analysis has been unable to develop theories dealing adequately with the macrosociological phenomenon of coercion and conflict. Structurally oriented theorists, including Lewis Coser (Chapter 5), Ralf Dahrendorf (Chapter 6), and Peter Blau (Chapter 4), have rendered some of the functionalist-directed criticism regarding conflict obsolete, demonstrating that the issue of social conflict can be dealt with from a structurally based position. Similarly there is no reason that social psychological theories cannot treat of conflict, particularly when such theories attempt to move beyond the analysis of small-group behavior.

C. Wright Mills represents a theorist who never lost sight of social psychological principles yet endeavored to link them to the sociological concern with structure. Structural concerns also moved him to an analysis of social issues and applied or evaluative sociological theory. Mills's works as a reform-oriented sociologist demonstrate that the conflict of interests is one of the social facts of life. In his concern for larger issues (a neglect of many social psychologists), however, he did not lose sight of the individual (a problem of much structural functionalist theory). Throughout his major works, we see Mills's awareness of the relationship of individuals to the structures in which they live.

As exemplified by the introductory quotation, it was the late C. Wright Mills who heralded an early call in the 1950s for "sociological imagination." It was to be a blend of two "research ways," identified by Mills as the macroscopic and the molecular. The *macroscopic* deals with "total social structures in a comparative way; their scope that of the world historian; they attempt to generate types of historical phenomena, and in a systematic way, to connect the various institutional spheres of society, and then relate them to prevailing types of men and women" (1953:267). The works of Weber, Marx, Simmel, and Mannheim are all examples of macroscopic research ways. The *molecular* is characterized by "small-scale problems and by its generally statistical models of verification" (1953:267). According to Mills (1953:267), "Shying away from social philosophy, it often appears as technique and little else." With regard to the "macroscopic" versus the "molecular" research way, Mills (1953:268) commented: "The more socially or politically significant our problems and work (the more macroscopic), the less rigorous is our solution and the less certain our knowledge (the less molecular)." Mills's solution to this dilemma is to shuttle back and forth between the two levels, allowing us to work grandly on the macroscopic levels while moving minutely on the molecular level for adequate illustrative data.

Mills's call for "sociological imagination" was critical of much that has gone on under the guise of science. He (1954:22) has few kind words for the extreme naturalistic sociologists, whom he terms "The Scientists," and who he feels would "love to wear white coats with an I.B.M. symbol of some sort on the breast pocket. They are out to do with society and history what they believe physicists have done with nature." Mills feels that this perspective is wanting because of ignorance of three things: (1) the important place of ideas in human history; (2) the nature of power and its relation to knowledge; and (3) the meaning of moral action and the place of knowledge within it. Mills's own sociological theory attempts to keep these three elements central in his analysis.

Mills is also quite critical of another group of sociologists, whom he terms "The Grand Theorists." Talcott Parsons (whom we discussed in Chapter 8) serves as the example par excellence of grand theory. "The Grand Theorists" represent a partially organized attempt to withdraw from the effort to describe plainly, explain, and understand human conduct and society, says Mills (1954:23): "in turgid prose they set forth the disordered contents of their reading of eminent nineteenth-century sociologists, and in the process mistake their own beginnings for a finished result." Although Mills died prior to some of Parsons major theoretical revisions, it is highly doubtful that Mills would have been any more impressed with Parsons's later works.

Mills does express his admiration for a third group of sociologists, who are interested in the meaning of phenomena to the society and who try to place it in historical context. These sociologists tend to be well versed in the works of the classics, showing similar concerns to those of classical sociologists Max Weber, Georg Simmel, Gaetano Mosca, and Karl Mannheim. Such sociologists blend their concern for a relevant sociological theory with a knowledge and use of history and biography. Mills credits those sociologists, who are interested in a relevant sociological theory and who use history and biography as sources of data, with having "sociological imagination."

Mills then is often seen as the father of the rebirth of reform-oriented sociology. He worked feverishly to return sociology to the public—to rescue it from what he feared were the clutches of a bankrupt nonevaluative position. He tried to restore in sociology's leaders a concern for the issues of the day. Although C. Wright Mills died in the early 1960s, many of his works seem to have more relevance today than when he first wrote them.

Mills's Social Psychological Base

Mills took his Ph.D. at the University of Wisconsin in 1941 under two masters of classical theory, Hans Gerth and Howard Becker. Especially under the mentorship of Gerth, with whom Mills edited and translated essays of Max Weber, Mills became immersed in the German sociological tradition. This interest in and knowledge of classical theory that Mills shared with Gerth led to their collaboration on a social psychological discussion of social institutions titled *Character and Social Struc-ture* (1953).[1] This work is divided into four parts, each of which works toward the goal of better understanding how men and women are shaped by their sociocultural milieu. In Part I of the volume, Gerth and Mills (1953:4) introduce the social psychological perspective:

> The social psychologist attempts to describe and explain the conduct and the motivations of men and women in various types of societies. He asks how the external conduct and inner life of one individual interplay with those of others. He seeks to describe the types of persons usually found in different types of societies, and then to explain them by tracing their interrelations with their societies.

Character structure is linked to social structure—including kinship, re-ligion, economics, the military, and politics—through the persons' social role.

Part II of the book focuses on the relation between character and social structure and upon the components of each. Gerth and Mills assert that men and women are unique creatures because of the particular con-stellation of biological organism, psychic structure, and role-playing per-son within each character structure. The human being is a biological entity complete with psychic makeup of feelings, sensations, and impulses anchored in this organism. Using their biological and psychic equipment, men and women act out roles in society. The social role that Gerth and Mills use to analytically fashion their concept of social structure becomes the major link between the character and social structure or institutions. Thus the political order consists of those institutions "within which men acquire, wield or influence the distribution of power and authority within social structures" (Gerth and Mills, 1953:26). The economic order is made up of those institutions "by which men organize labor, resources, and technical implements in order to produce and distribute goods and services" (Gerth and Mills, 1953:26). The military order "is composed of institutions in which men organize legitimate violence and supervise its use" (Gerth and Mills, 1953:26). What is important to remember from

---

[1] Scimecca (1977:37) emphasizes the seminal nature of *Character and Social Structure* in understanding all of Mills's subsequent works. He describes it as synthe-sizing "the social behaviorism or personality formation of the pragmatists with the emphasis upon social structure of Max Weber and the German sociologists." We con-cur with Scimecca's observation that many sociologists have failed to see the theo-retical model in Mills's works because they have not paid close enough attention to *Character and Social Structure,* which could be seen as a theoretical framework for Mills's later works.

Gerth and Mills's discussion of the interrelationship of character and social structure is that neither persons nor institutions have an independent existence. Persons and institutions are both interdependent, having reciprocal effects through the linkage of both by social roles. A person exists as a mother-wife and is tied to the kinship order; she is Protestant, Catholic, Jewish, or "other" and linked to the religious order; she is a business executive or a factory worker and related to the economic institution. It is only through interaction with others in more-or-less structured settings that a person fully emerges, and it is only through persons' acting out social roles that institutions exist.

In Part III of *Character and Social Structure*, Gerth and Mills (1953: 165) examine "the general mechanisms by which persons and institutions are related." They discuss the importance of the social controls provided through institutions. In a manner true to their social psychological orientation, the importance of language and other "symbol spheres" that define situations is emphasized. Part III, like Parts I and II, contains discussions that would be similar to points made by the social psychologists we have treated earlier in this text.

In Part IV of the Gerth and Mills volume, however, the concern shifts to dynamics and the importance of history to a full appreciation of social psychology. Blumer, Goffman, Homans, and Garfinkel, although sharing a common concern for making individual behavior the unit of analysis, could be said to be ahistorical, leaving history out of their analyses. Gerth and Mills (1953:480) emphasize the limits that history may place on men and women:

> Man is a unique animal species in that he is also an historical development. It is in terms of this development that he must be defined, and in terms of it no single formula will fit him. Neither his anatomy nor his psyche fix (*sic*) his destiny. He creates his own destiny as he responds to his experienced situation, and both his situation and his experiences of it are the complicated products of the historical epoch which he enacts. That is why he does not create his destiny as an individual but as a member of a society. Only within the limits of his place in an historical epoch can man as an individual shape himself, but we do not yet know, we can never know, the limits to which men collectively might remake themselves.

This interweaving of social psychology with social history is an approach that remained with Mills throughout his sociological career. His awareness of history kept him mindful of the fact of social conflict and the need for sociology to analyze it. It helps to explain the emphasis Mills placed on biography and history as sources of sociological data.

C. Wright Mills and the
Study of Power _____

During the 1950s, Mills addressed what he considered to be the great agonies and issues of the age—from Castro's Cuba to the possible causes of a third world war. One of Mills's overriding concerns in analyzing these "agonies," and one that appears to have great relevance for today, was his concern with the study of power. He saw social life as consisting of a continual struggle for power—sometimes physical confrontation in war but more frequently a symbolic and political struggle. Mills was perhaps more interested in decision making and the power structure than he was in coercive power, which is the "final form of power." Rooting his study firmly in a historical perspective, Mills (1963:25) observed, "I should contend that 'men are free to make history,' but that some men are indeed much freer than others. For such freedom requires access to the means of decision and of power by which history can be made."

It is important to keep in mind that Mills (who died in 1963) was writing at the height of the structural functionalist era. At this time, the conflict perspective, even conflict structuralism, was far from being in vogue. The emphasis, moreover, was on a nonevaluative, value-free sociology that remained aloof from the problems of the day. Although Mills was interested in studying society scientifically, he emphasized that social scientists should be concerned with sociology's direct relevance to urgent public issues. He believed that as a social scientist, the sociologist should be concerned with making a difference in the quality of human life in our time. Horowitz (1965:17) summarizes Mills's sociological concern as follows:

> The impulse to return sociology to the public from whence it emanated, to deprofessionalize it in fact, had as its basis Mills' recognition that in his natural state, man is essentially irrational, a creature who responds to impulses, political slogans, status symbols, etc. and sociology could provide that means by which man casts off an egoistic, sectarian and mythic pride and grows to maturity. Sociology helps men "know where they stand, where they may be going, and what—if anything—they can do about the present as history and the future as responsibility."

Mills's writings were intended to be applied and to bring about change. Human behavior is frequently irrational, according to Mills, and it remains sociology's task to expose its irrationality. Through such exposition, perhaps men and women would be less likely to respond irrationally to impulses, political slogans, and status symbols. It is within this context that Mills wrote numerous essays on power and politics, did his study on white-collar workers, and wrote a treatise on power holders in the United States.

White Collar: The American Middle Classes

Mills acknowledges that the middle classes developed as an unexpected buffer between entrepreneurs and wage workers. Karl Marx, the classical theorist who wrote about the plight of the workers in the nineteenth century, failed to see the development of a broadly based middle class in industrial society. This "new cast of actors, performing the major routine of twentieth-century society" (Mills, 1951:4) are not, however, independent like the entrepreneurs of an earlier age. The new middle class has grown as a percentage of the American population. It is made up of managers, salaried workers, professionals, salespeople, and office workers. Many of these white-collar workers, as Mills describes them, are pitiful figures who are increasingly losing personal power. Their plight is characterized by an estrangement or alienation from work as well as from themselves.

Mills builds on Marx's theory of alienation in developing his thesis on white-collar workers. Marx asserted that it was work that separated men from the animal world. Human beings expressed their humanity through their labor, be it the work of a farmer, a blacksmith, a physician, or a shopowner. Modern industry, spurred by the capitalist system, made it increasingly difficult to express humanity through labor. A farmer could toil and see the fruits of his harvest; a shopowner could work and be rewarded by the success of his own business enterprise; a physician could heal and experience the satisfaction of making his fellowman whole. Industrialization under capitalism, Marx asserted, was succeeding in creating more and more personally meaningless jobs. Because the persons employed in these jobs were denied the basic form of human expression through their work, they became estranged from themselves, from each other, and from nature.

It was the Marxian issue of alienation that served as a basis for Mills's discussion of the American middle class. Mills (1951:xvi–xvii) expressed it in the following manner:

> In the case of the white-collar man, the alienation of the wage-worker from the products of his work is carried one step nearer to its Kafka-like completion. The salaried employee does not make anything, although

he may handle much that he greatly desires but cannot have. No product of craftsmanship can be his to contemplate with pleasure as it is being created or after it is made. Being alienated from any product of his labor, and going year after year through the same paper routine, he turns his leisure all the more frenziedly to the *ersatz* diversion that is sold him, and partakes of the synthetic excitement that neither eases nor releases. He is bored at work and restless at play, and this terrible alternation wears him out.

To develop this thesis, Mills used the theoretical framework that he and Gerth had developed in *Character and Social Structure*. The white-collar worker must be placed in his/her historical epoch with an understanding of his/her social structure. Then some attempt must be made to combine a psychological analysis with this sociological framework of social structure.

Mills (1951:3–12) uses history to recount the world of the small entrepreneur of an era gone by. Mills describes him as "a free man, not a man exploited, an independent man, not a man bound by tradition" in a structure where "individual freedom seemed the principle of social order." The lack of security faced by the small entrepreneur in a modern changing society has led him/her to sacrifice his/her independence for a "somewhat indignant search for some political means of security." The changes in the white-collar class since 1900 have represented, in general, a decline in its position. These trends include (1) a loss of prestige when compared with the old-type entrepreneur; (2) a drop in real income "until it is only slightly above, and in several important cases lower than, the average income of various wage-working groups"; (3) the mechanization of office work, which threatens the very existence of many white-collar jobs; and (4) a limiting of the autonomy of the office worker (Mills, 1952:32–33). Moreover much of the work done by white-collar workers is routinized and boring, with little reason given to hope for more intriguing office work in the future.

Mills's treatise on the white-collar worker has been criticized for "damning without mercy or possibility of redemption the ways of the existing middle class" (Riesman, 1951:513). Perhaps Mills does overstate his case on the problems of lower-rung office workers who have exchanged blue collars for white collars; moving from foundry to office, they have made only illusory gains. Perhaps too Mills romanticizes the era gone by, selecting and focusing on the most positive aspects of being an entrepreneur. Yet Mills does focus attention on an important element of middle-class life, namely, the absence of any significant power. Mills emphasizes that middle-class workers, even professionals, are generally devoid of both the personal power to control their own lives and the political power to shape the nation.

The Power Elite _____

The question of power—power on a higher level than that generally discussed in *White Collar*—is the topic of another Mills classic, *The Power Elite*. For Mills, there was a decisive split between those who share in the highest levels of the power structure and those who do not. In Weberian fashion, Mills views power as the ability to have one's own will prevail, even in the face of opposition. The *power elite* are those men and women who, in stark contrast to the middle class, are in pivotal positions to make decisions having major consequences.

As Mills analyzes the American social structure, major national power to make crucial decisions rests with the leaders of big business, the political leaders, and the military leaders. Within the economic, political, and military domains are the important forces of history. All other institutions, including the family, the church, the university, and labor are off to the side, possibly reacting to national policy decisions but unable to influence them. The big three—business, government, and the military—have each been growing in size and domain during the twentieth century. Moreover this triumverate forms a type of interlocking directorate of great historical consequence.

Thus, had Mills lived to see them, he would not have been surprised by the scandals uncovered during the Watergate investigations. The alleged payoff of the dairymen to the Nixon campaign in exchange for higher milk prices, the ITT scandal, and the multimillionnaire Howard Hughes's financial involvement in Republican politics all point to the interconnection of big business and the highest levels of government. Mills asserts that this interconnection can be observed further in the facile movement of top-echelon leaders from one branch of the triumverate to another. The movement of a Robert McNamara from the presidency of an automobile-manufacturing firm to the cabinet of President Johnson and appointment of a General Alexander Haig as chief-of-staff in the Nixon administration provide more recent examples of what Mills was describing.

Mills (1959a:19) treats the power elite as a social class of men of similar origin and education, who have "psychological and social bases for their unity resting upon the fact that they are of similar social type and leading to the fact of their easy intermingling." Mills admits that his thesis does not apply to all epochs of history. He believes, however, that it holds true in the twentieth century, which is witnessing the development of a centralized power elite that was not possible in an earlier era. Mills (1959a:27–28) observes that it is fashionable but fallacious "to suppose that there is no power elite," and he tries to dispel the mythic "image of a society in which voluntary associations and classic publics hold the keys to power." This pluralistic view of power does not take into account that there are different levels of power within the country. Mills (1959a:30–31) would acknowledge that although a middle-level power may operate according to balance and compromise theories, the top level that deals with national and international issues does not. When discussing decisions of "war and peace" or "slump and poverty," Mills asserts that these decisions are made by a power elite composed of the big three.

One of the biggest myths exposed by Mills (1959a:242) is "the theory of balance," where "Americans cling to the idea that the government is a sort of automatic machine, regulated by the balancing of competing interests." Americans frequently assume that Congress acts as a check on the president, while the Supreme Court serves to rule on the maintenance of a balance of power. Even if there were a balance in the three branches of government (a situation that Mills believes is highly doubtful), Mills asks us to consider who it is that represents American citizens in Congress. He asserts (1959a:248) that they are not "rank and file citizens":

> They represent those who have been successful in entrepreneurial and professional endeavors. Older men, they are of the privileged white, native-born of native parents, Protestant Americans. They are college graduates and they are at least solid upper-middle class in income and status. On the average, they have had no experience of wage or lower salaried work. They are, in short, in and of the new and old upper classes of local society.

In reality, however, the power of Congress has been greatly curtailed while the power of the president has become enlarged. At the time of this writing it appears that the Watergate scandal and its aftermath have halted, or at least reduced, the growth of presidential powers, but it does not appear that Congress as a body has been able to fill the leadership void. At best, our theory of checks and balances, Mills (1959a:266) asserts, held only during specific historical epochs:

> Those who still hold that the power system reflects the balancing society often confuse the present era with earlier times of American history, and confuse the top and bottom levels of the present system with its middle levels. When it is generalized into a master model of the power system, the theory of balance becomes historically unspecific; whereas in fact, as a model, it should be specified as applicable only to certain phases of United States development—notably the Jacksonian period and, under quite differing circumstances, the early and middle New Deal.

The concentration of political power at top levels of government is but one dimension of the power elite. Early in American history, from the time of the Revolution through the first quarter of the nineteenth century, the political institutions were central to top-level national decisions. After the Supreme Court decision of 1886 that protected corporations, power shifted from the government toward economic institutions. The New Deal under Franklin D. Roosevelt was a response to economic failure, leading to a coalition of a governmental and an economic power elite. Mills asserts that in the present epoch, it is nearly impossible to separate big business from big government, with military power being on the ascent since World War II. Mills (1959a:275) feels that "the military structure of America is now in considerable part a political structure." This is so, according to Mills, because of a shift in focus of the power elite from national problems to international issues, giving greater voice to big military leaders in the process of decision making. Mills (1959a: 275–276) describes the economic situation in America as "military capitalism," where "the economy is at once a permanent-war economy and a private-corporation economy."

Mills's discussion of the power elite is almost prophetic when viewed in light of the turmoil of more recent historical events on the American scene. When both a president and his vice-president are forced to resign over separate issues and when other nationally known politicians are indicted, the morality of government leaders has been seriously questioned. In 1959 Mills offered the following sociological explanation for this type of corruption in government:

> From this point of view, the most important question, for instance, about the campaign funds of ambitious young politicans is not whether the politicians are morally insensitive, but whether or not any young man in American politics, who has come so far and so fast, could well have done so today without possessing or acquiring a somewhat blunted moral sensibility. Many of the problems of "white-collar crime" and of relaxed public morality, of high-priced vice and of fading personal integrity, are problems of *structural* immorality. (1959a:243)

A Critical Evaluation of Mills's Theory

Mills's image of people, society, and sociology partially runs counter to the structural-functionalist theoretical trends of his own time. Whereas much sociology asserted that people are socially determined yet rational, Mills presented a possible freedom and irrationality. Functionalists, for example, were prone to view individuals as being more-or-less determined by their social structure, whereas interactionists would have been more in agreement with Mills's allowing social actors some freedom. At the same time, most sociological theorists have posited a rational, goal-oriented person as the actor in society. Mills, as we shall see, depicts the irrational side of men's and women's behavior. In exposing this irrationality, Mills hoped that some people would be disposed to attempt to alter the social structure. Mills also modified the dominant approach to the nature of society. Whereas society was reportedly ordered and patterned for both functionalists and interactionists, Mills emphasized society as a battleground for competing interest. In an era when scientific, positivistic, value-free sociology was presented as an ideal, Mills questioned the sterility of academic sociology.

Mills's view of people reflects a strain between the person as a social product and the person as a creator of the social structure. Much like Karl Marx, who wrote to raise the consciousness of the working class, Mills hoped to expose the irrational behavior of men and women. In recognizing their irrational response to status symbols and political slogans, perhaps they could alter their social history. Thus, for Mills, if people became aware of their basically irrational nature, they might revise their view of themselves and ultimately change their society. In recognizing, for example, that the social structure is such that honesty in politics is difficult, if not impossible, to maintain, voters might be less responsive to political slogans. Or in demonstrating that the democratic ideals hold less actuality than they may have in the past, people might conflict with the interests that have led to a power elite.

Yet at the same time, Mills recognized that historical institutions do shape individuals. The political office holder might not be as free as he or she might like to be from controlling and monied interests. Much white-collar crime, observes Mills (1959a:243) is a result of "structural immorality." Cuzzort and King (1976:144) made the following observation of Mills's view of people as interrelated with the social structure:

> Although Mills claimed that power has its locus within supporting institutions, he still was concerned with the fact that it is individuals who make decisions and are responsible for the consequences. Mills was torn on the one hand by an analytic perspective that properly locates the individual within the broader system and on the other by a humanistic sensitivity that made him critical of an apparent inability of powerful individuals to assert their autonomy.

This tension between individual freedom and structural determinism is apparent within Mills's work on power. Mills asserted that while *all* men and women are free to make history, *some* do indeed have much greater freedom than others. Thus the person Mills depicts is partially free and partially determined, depending upon his or her position among the power elite. At the same time, Mills allows for collective action among socially aware citizens to block the power moves of the elite and to be creators of their own destiny.

Social structure, particularly the social power structure, has a reality for Mills—a reality that has determined the fate and destiny of those who live within it. In fact, Mills has been criticized both for overestimating the power of some social institutions (particularly the military) and for underestimating the actual power of the masses.[2] It appears that Mills's analysis of the power structure treats men and women as pawns of the elite whose fate is determined by the social actions of the elite. At the same time, Mills expresses the hope that political confrontation with the wielders of power could correct the situation. Thus the socio-historical situation is an objective one, capable of determining the lives of people; yet it is one that could be changed and guided by rational action.

Mills's vision of sociology is consistent with his image of people and society. Sociology, if it is to achieve its potential, must be more than a fact-finding exercise and more than grand, abstract thinking. As we have discussed earlier in this chapter, Mills advocated the use of "sociological imagination," which studies significant issues and is willing to examine social problems. Mills urged sociologists toward humanistic, evaluative theory, designed to improve the social world in which we live. In a sense, sociological knowledge was, in some degree, to become part of everyone's knowledge so that it could be implemented with social action.

In warning sociologists against the dangers of scientism,[3] Mills sug-

---

[2] For examples of such criticism see Aptheker (1968), Bell (1958), Dahl (1958), and Parsons (1960). Scimecca (1977:92) observes that such pluralistic criticisms often concentrate on local affairs rather than on the national scene, thereby not really addressing Mills's theory.

[3] There is a twofold criticism of sociology as scientism (Douglas, 1970:3–27): (1) scientism uses the rhetoric of science rather than scientific results to convince audiences and (2) scientism tends to concern itself only with areas where reward (in terms of research grants, status awarded by colleagues, and so on) is great. Because of scientism, critics contend, sociology has witnessed a proliferation of technical terms, quantitative methods and formalized theory that has not yielded a better understanding of the social world. Moreover important topics of potential sociological concern have been neglected in areas that have not been of particular concern to government or private interests. It was of scientism, rather than of sociology as a user of scientific method, that Mills was critical. Such scientism stands in the way of the pursuit of relevant knowledge.

gested appropriate data sources for supporting theory. As is characteristic of many theorists with a conflict orientation, Mills emphasized the importance of a historical perspective. In line with a social psychological approach to sociology, Mills supplemented this historical data with biography. Mills (1959b:143) insisted:

> Social science deals with problems of biography, of history, and of their intersections within social structures. That these three—biography, history, society—are co-ordinate points of the proper study of man has been a major platform on which I have stood when criticizing several current schools of sociology whose practitioners have abandoned this classic tradition. The problems of our time—which now include the problem of man's very nature—cannot be stated adequately without consistent practice of the view that history is the shank of social study, and recognition of the need to develop further a psychology of man that is sociologically grounded and historically relevant.

Mills's own work shows his commitment to dealing with relevant social issues. He followed his own rule of "intellectual craftsmanship" in integrating his life with his scholarship and in taking a personal stand in dealing with social issues—particularly the issue of power in contemporary society.

Summary

Mills's call for "sociological imagination" was critical of the naturalistic model that was dominant in contemporary sociology. He indicted American sociology for its abstract empiricism, which was more preoccupied with the methods it used than with relevant questions. For Mills (1959b:5), "the sociological imagination is the ability to grasp history and biography and the relations between the two within society." It was this sociological imagination that Mills tried to exercise in his own work. Theory could not be abstract, grand theory with few or no data to support it (as Mills contended Parsons's work was), nor could it be abstract empiricism with data but little or no relevant theory. Mills merged his interest in classical theory with his burning concern for social issues in both *The Power Elite* and *White Collar*. Data for both theses were collected from historical accounts and biographical sources, including newspaper accounts, biographies, and journal reports. Thus Mills's works not only are relevant but attempt to merge data and theory for the study of social issues.

One of the best known of Mills's many works is *The Power Elite*, which advances the thesis of an interlocking power triumverate of big business, big government, and big military. Mills believed it within the ability of only a relatively few men and women in American society to make decisions of national and international consequences. It was only through a growing public consciousness of the power situation in the United States, furthered by sociological interest in relevant issues, that any hope for a truly responsive government could be realized.

Mills's works represent evaluative, humanistic sociological theory. His model of people is clearly humanistic, building on the work of the father of interactionist theory, George Herbert Mead. Yet he adds to this social psychological emphasis the dimension of history and an awareness of the influencing power of social structures. His belief in the freedom of men and women to alter history made him demand a restoration of sociology to the public. Sociology, for Mills, must not become impotent in its ability to influence social change because of its fascination with a natural-science model. The call for "sociological imagination" is a call for a relevant sociology central to concerns of our age.

References _____

APTHEKER, H.
   1968 "Power in America." Pp. 133–164 in W. Domhoff and H. B. Ballard (Eds.), *C. Wright Mills and the Power Elite*. Boston: Beacon Press.
BELL, DANIEL
   1958 "The Power Elite Reconsidered." *American Journal of Sociology* 64 (November):238–250.
CUZZORT, R. P., and E. W. KING
   1976 *Humanity and Modern Social Thought*. Hinsdale, Ill.: The Dryden Press.
DAHL, R.
   1958 "A Critique of the Ruling Elite Model." *The American Political Science Review* 52 (June):463–469.
DOUGLAS, JACK D.
   1970 *Freedom and Tyranny: Social Problems in a Technological Society*. New York: Alfred A. Knopf, Inc.
GERTH, HANS, and C. WRIGHT MILLS
   1946 *From Max Weber: Essays in Sociology*. New York: Oxford University Press.
   1953 *Character and Social Structure: The Psychology of Social Institutions*. New York: Harcourt, Brace and World, Inc.

HOROWITZ, IRVING L.
  1965 "An Introduction to C. Wright Mills." Pp. 1–20 in I. L. Horowitz
       (Ed.), *Power, Politics and People: The Collected Essays of C. Wright
       Mills,* New York: Ballantine Books.
MILLS, C. WRIGHT
  1951 *White Collar: The American Middle Classes.* New York: Oxford Uni-
       versity Press, Inc.
  1952 "A Look at the White Collar." Office Management Series; No. 131.
       New York: American Management Association. Reprinted pp. 140–149
       in I. L. Horowitz (Ed.), *Power, Politics and People: The Collected
       Essays of C. Wright Mills.* New York: Ballantine Books.
  1953 "Two Styles of Research in Current Social Studies." *Philosophy of
       Science* 20 (October):226–275.
  1954 "IBM Plus Reality Plus Humanism = Sociology." *Saturday Review
       of Literature* (May 1):22–23, 54.
  1959a *The Power Elite.* New York: Oxford University Press.
  1959b *The Sociological Imagination.* New York: Oxford University Press.
PARSONS, TALCOTT
  1960 "The Distribution of Power in American Society." *World Politics* 13
       (October):112–128.
RIESMAN, DAVID
  1951 "White Collar: The American Middle Classes." *American Journal of
       Sociology* 57 (April):513.
SCIMECCA, JOSEPH A.
  1977 *The Sociological Theory of C. Wright Mills.* Port Washington, N.Y.:
       Kennikat Press.

15

The Active Society: An Evaluative Synthesis of Naturalism and Humanism

> Most sociologists, the author included, feel that such combination of theory and methods is the very foundation on which sociology as a science ought to be built and is in fact being constructed. But many of us feel that something is lacking.
>
> What is lacking most is *social analysis,* the systematic exploration of social issues; that is, concern with the methodological questions of sociological analysis of the great issues of our age, which tend to involve the study of macroscopic units. The subject of social analysis, though, is the issues, not the sociological building stones; the focus is on the instruments to be utilized to elevate the analysis of societal issues, to improve on our amateur, intuitive, or journalistic sociology. (Etzioni, 1969:133–134)

Well-known theories in contemporary sociology have been, as we have seen in this text, primarily limited to nonevaluative concerns. Writers tended to suspend their personal judgments, biases, and dreams in an attempt to create value-free schemes. The dictates of theory construction limited theory to discussions of society *as it exists* rather than the drawing up of blueprints of social change. Social problems, although admittedly part of the structure, were often viewed as pathologies that were not to be dwelt on excessively. Thus most of the perspectives we have considered are analytical theories that aimed at describing society rather than working to harness sociological knowledge to improve the social order. The analogy frequently presented to a beginning student was that of sociology's being akin to physics rather than engineering. Sociology had to endeavor to discover the laws of social behavior, just as physics seeks the laws of physical matter. Other applied fields might utilize sociology's knowledge, just as engineering relies on the laws discovered by physics. Sociology's theories, however, were to be untainted by hints of application, including proposals for the improvement of the social order.

With the advent of the social turmoil of the 1960s came an increasing awareness of the artificiality of the dichotomy between nonevaluative and applied or evaluative sociology. Attempts were made to develop programs and courses in sociology that would train students for planned social intervention.[1] Some humanistic sociologists, such as C. Wright Mills (see Chapter 14), had long been concerned with the applicability of sociological knowledge to the betterment of society. By the late 1960s, a number of well-trained naturalistic sociologists were joining the ranks of humanistic sociologists in their concern for creating a better society. Members of the latter group, including distinguished scholars and researchers like Paul Lazarsfeld, Philip M. Hauser, and Peter Rossi, did not abandon their more naturalistic orientation in their quest for sociological relevance. In view of the resurgence of interest in applied sociology, it was not surprising to see the development of evaluative theorizing. One such attempt to synthesize a basically natural-science model of sociology with that of an evaluative approach to theory is to be found in the works of Amitai Etzioni.

Etzioni—particularly in what he considers his "life's work," *The Active Society* (1968)—has sought to reconcile social science theory with an active participation in social change. Etzioni (1968:viii–ix) states:

> We wish to illustrate that social science theory can be scientifically valid, can be intellectually relevant, and can serve as a springboard for active participation. Factual statements and value judgments can be systematically articulated without being fused or confused. Sociological imagination can enrich rather than replace social science. We reject the idea that there is no more to social analysis than neutral research, just as we reject the notion that the truth value of a statement is measured by the service it renders to the advancement of a cause.

The theoretical model employed is a cybernetic one, basic to general or modern systems theory (see Chapter 8). Etzioni (1968:x) attempts to answer four basic questions through his model:

[1] For examples of books dealing with the concerns of applied sociology, see Louis A. Zurcher, Jr., and Charles M. Bonjean's (Eds.), *Planned Social Intervention* (Chandler Publishing Co.: 1970); Paul F. Lazarsfeld, William H. Sewell, and Harold L. Wilenski (Eds.), *The Uses of Sociology* (Basic Books: 1967); and Carol H. Weiss (Ed.), *Evaluating Action Programs* (Allyn & Bacon, Inc.: 1972).

1. How is a person's future controlled?
2. How can his or her history be made less by fate and more by rational, yet spontaneous action?
3. How is the individual actor guided?
4. How authentic are the forces of his or her self-control?

Etzioni's answers to these questions are derived through a synthesis of existing perspectives into a cybernetic model. He works to provide a theoretical framework from which propositions may be derived and tested and within which data may be codified.

The Active Society: *A Theory of Societal and Political Processes*

An *active* society is one in which people are in charge of the social world in which they live. This stands in contrast to a *passive* society, in which people are controlled by outside forces or by active others. Social laws, says Etzioni, can be altered by people in an active society. In such a world, men and women are creators, shaping their society to meet their needs. The active orientation has three major components: self-conscious and knowing actors, one or more goals the actors are committed to realize, and access to the power to change the social order (Etzioni, 1968:4). Such activity, however, is not without constraints, for every action brings about counteraction. The active person is one, therefore, who does not simply do anything he or she wishes. Such a person must seek knowledge or information to act intelligently. He or she must be committed to defer personal rewards in favor of a higher realization of societal goals.

What Etzioni is proposing is a "theory of societal self-control." Just as physicists have harnessed nuclear energy, so must sociologists learn to harness societal energy. Etzioni (1968:7) observes that in the realm of machines, there are two revolutions: the mechanization of work and the mechanization of the control of the machines that do the work. In the social order, there is a similar two-step revolution. The development of modern organization is analagous to the "mechanization of work" and represents the sociological machine as being an efficient way of getting things done. Now we must witness the development of *control* over these sociological machines of organization through societal guidance.

Etzioni believes that knowledge is a key to understanding and realizing such a self-guiding society. Scientific knowledge, including the knowledge of social science, will be used in societal transformation. Etzioni

(1968:16) describes his attempted study of this transformation of society in the following manner:

> It is the exploration of a society that knows itself, is committed to moving toward a fuller realization of its values, that commands the levers such transformation requires, and is able to set limits on its capacity for self-alteration—lest it become self-mutilation. This would be an active society.

Foundations for a Theory of Macroscopic Action

Etzioni's theory represents a synthesis between the partial approaches that we have labeled *naturalistic* and *humanistic*. He is opposed to the view that human relations are purely mechanistic and can be studied in an identical manner to chemical or physical relations. Similarly he is in disagreement with the segmented position at the opposite extreme, which sees "little importance in the mechanical aspects of action" and views interpretative explanations provided through the study of significant symbols as *the* key variables. Etzioni (1968:26–29) assumes that both theoretical perspectives must be taken into any account of an active society. He emphasizes, "Control is possible in principle because, on the one hand, the units of action, while they exist in the mechanical world, also respond to symbols." Such control is dependent upon three basic elements: (1) a group of actors possessing knowledge; (2) one or more goals that the group or actor is committed to realize; and (3) access to power, which includes the manipulation of symbols allowing the resetting of the social code. Thus to be "active" is to have knowledge, to be committed, and to have power.

Etzioni acknowledges that although men and women have the capacity to act, there are constraints imposed on this action. Once again he finds fault with existing theoretical perspectives. The collectivistic approach favored by the functionalists assumes that men and women are simply products of their social systems. The social order is seen as unfolding without any human control. At the other extreme is the astructural theory of someone like C. Wright Mills. Etzioni feels that Mills's power elite represents a voluntaristic approach that describes a group of persons who can pretty much run the social order as they will. Etzioni's theory of societal guidance attempts a convergence of "collectivism" and "voluntarism." It views men and women as capable of societal action, but it also identifies constraints or limits upon this action. These constraints are not viewed as "givens" (as they are in a structural functionalist perspective) but they are a result, at least in part, of past actions or past choices. Thus even the constraints of the present are to some extent the result of past voluntaristic actions.

After presenting these assumptions or postulates about the nature of the person as actor and society as both a product of past actions and responsive to present activity, Etzioni identifies some of the basic elements of his theory of societal guidance. Etzioni classifies social relations into three types: normative, utilitarian, and coercive. A *normative relation*, emphasized in functionalist analysis, entails shared norms and values. Primitive communities and *Gemeinschaft*-like organizations (such as the family) are examples of such relationships, where persons treat each other as goals and mutual commitments that are nonrational. *Utilitarian relations* are the rational relations of social exchange, where there is a payoff for each party. (See Chapters 3 and 4 for discussions of exchange theory.) In *coercive relationships*, persons treat each other as objects, and commitments may be either rational or nonrational. Coercion, asserts Etzioni, entails the use, or the threatened use, of force by one actor against another actor. These three bases of the social order are *ideal types*, which usually do not appear in their pure forms. Social relations in reality are a mixture of these three forms.

Two important independent variables in a theory of societal guidance are collectivities and the state. *Collectivities* are groups based upon a set of normative interests and/or values that are shared by their members. The concept of collectivities is similar to the Marxist concept of *class*, in which the members of a class may become aware of similar interests and unite to form a base of action. In addition to the cohesive relations provided through collectivities, there is a need for *control networks*. According to Etzioni's theory, control networks, as represented by the state, must exist before a society can be an active one. Both integration, or cohesiveness, and control may be normative, utilitarian, or coercive relationships.

The control center, represented by the state, is comprised of two kinds of subunits—elites and implementation mechanisms—which link the control center with the member units who are under control. Elites, in Etzioni's theory, are not equated with a "ruling class." An *elite* is a "control unit that specializes in the cybernetic functions of knowledge-processing and decision-making and in the application of power" (Etzioni, 1968:113). These elites do not form a superior class, nor need they have leadership qualities. The term *elite* refers to a role (rather than a class), whose task it is to process knowledge, make decisions, and give commands.

Cybernetic Factor I: Knowledge _____

When the cybernetic model has been applied in social science, knowledge or information is viewed as the form of energy being transformed in the system. As we have seen in a previous section of this chapter, control in an active society is contingent upon a group of actors possessing knowledge. Etzioni asserts that knowledge is an essential ingredient in the ability of a society to guide itself. In his rewriting of Etzioni's theory for a wider audience, Warren Breed (1971:36–41) provides some illustrations of past knowledge failure. One such example comes from the poor information possessed on Vietnam and the commitments made despite ignorance and misinformation. Another illustration may be seen in the unsuccessful 1960s "war on poverty." The possession and use of social knowledge should help to alleviate such failures in the future.

Knowledge, although an essential ingredient in this cybernetic model, does not operate alone. Decision making and power are two other cybernetic elements that must be considered in the model. Given the increase in available knowledge, education becomes increasingly important in industrialized societies. Knowledge makes societal consciousness and social action possible in an active society. Etzioni (1968:223) hypothesizes that "an actor who is conscious of his societal environment and of himself and his internal controls will be more active than an actor with otherwise similar characteristics who is not conscious." Such consciousness entails seeing a phenomenon in context, "being aware of its place in a larger frame of reference" (Etzioni, 1968:226). Awareness that the easy availability of firearms supports a high homicide rate may influence public opinion toward the support of gun-control legislation. Knowledge of the political favoritism spawned by the high cost of campaigning may lend public support to both ceilings on large political contributions and ceilings on the amount spent in any campaign. Consciousness is linked, however, with the other elements (knowledge, decision making, and power) of the cybernetic model of an active society. Etzioni (1968:238–239) advances the following propositions relating consciousness and activity:

1. An increase in consciousness is expected to generate activation only when either the other elements of the active orientation are also increasing or the other elements are more advanced than societal consciousness.
2. When consciousness is at a high level but commitment is low, we expect a societal equivalent of "I don't give a damn" (e.g., a "decadent society").

3. When consciousness is at a high level but knowledge is low, the main effect of consciousness may be to heighten the actor's sense of being unable to cope with his problems (e.g., the economic crisis facing the nation in the 1970s, where recession and inflation have become bedfellows).

Cybernetic Factor II: Decision Making

Knowledge, as we have seen, is a key cybernetic control element. In an active society, however, such knowledge must be put into practice. This is accomplished by decision making, which is the link in the cybernetic model between knowledge (consciousness and commitment) and power. Etzioni (1968:249–250) emphasizes, "It is, thus, mainly through the decision-making processes that vague and abstract societal commitments, whose directions are indicated by the values and goals to which the actor subscribes, are translated into specific commitments to one or more specific courses of action."

The theory of societal guidance assumes that decision makers have options within the broader limiting factors of a society. *Decision* implies a conscious choice between two or more alternatives. Etzioni identifies two methods of decision making: the rational model and incrementalism.

The *rational model* of decision making presupposes four main requirements (Etzioni, 1968:264): (1) information about alternative courses of action and the consequences of each; (2) calculation of the alternative outcomes in terms of their meaning for the various values; (3) a set of agreed-upon values on the basis of which to select goals and to judge the consequences of alternative courses of action; and (4) an exhaustive survey of all relevant alternatives. The fourth requirement—having *all* necessary information—is an impossible one to meet. Information, despite improvements in communication, will always be imperfect, making the rational model utopian as far as practice is concerned.

The alternative model of *incrementalism,* or "muddling through," is less demanding than the rationalistic model. This model settles for relatively satisfactory decisions rather than the best possible one, advocating the use of a piecemeal strategy. Etzioni (1968:270) describes it as follows:

Using this strategy, decision-makers do not attempt a comprehensive survey and evaluation. They do not investigate all alternative policies but only those which differ incrementally (i.e., to a limited degree) from existing policies. In addition, only a relatively small number of means is considered. This greatly reduces the scope and, therefore, the cost of the necessary information and computations.

Decisions are more frequently based on this model than on the rational one. Etzioni argues, however, that this model reflects the values and ends of the most powerful groups rather than those that might be best for the larger society. Moreover it is a perspective that tends to be tolerant of slow, drifting changes. Incrementalism has been described as staggering through history like a drunk, pulling one disjointed incremented foot after another!

Etzioni advances a third approach to decision making, which he terms *mixed scanning*. Mixed scanning represents an active approach to the decision-making process that combines rational decision-making and incrementalism. Mixed scanning involves exploring rationally the possible actions, omitting details and specifications, coupled with incrementalism. Etzioni (1968:284) provides the illustration of a weather satellite and its two cameras as an example of mixed scanning. One camera takes broad-angle pictures covering large segments of the sky at one time, while the other camera takes bit-by-bit detailed information of a much smaller segment of the sky. The broad-angle camera scans the sky for problems that the other camera may zero in on for details.

Etzioni asserts that mixed scanning is already being employed by scientists as well as executives and that this decision-making process is an effective one. It combines the collection, processing, and evaluation of information with the process of making choices. This decision-making model overcomes the problems of a rationalistic and incrementalist model to ensure an active society.

There remains an additional component in the cybernetic model discussed by Etzioni: the phenomenon of power. Power cannot be ignored in decision making. Although Etzioni recognizes power as a component in decision making, he regards it as a key *implementing* factor, rather than as one of the cybernetic factors, in an active society.

Implementing Factor I: Power _____

Power is defined by Etzioni in the Weberian fashion as "a capacity to overcome part or all of the resistance, to introduce changes in the face of opposition" (Etzioni, 1968:314). Etzioni finds it useful to distinguish between *power* and *assets* in his discussion of power. *Assets* represent a power base or a power potential. The advantage of such a distinction is that it enables the sociologist to explain submission even where there is no actual use of power. Power represents actualized power, and *assets* refers to potential power.

Actualized power presents a dilemma: to use power means to generate resistance against it. Although society needs control (and power ensures the meeting of this need), societal members may desire freedom. Etzioni attempts to explore the question of the kind of power that will best meet both needs.

In discussing assets and power, Etzioni identifies three types: utilitarian, persuasive, and coercive. *Utilitarian assets* include economic possessions, technical and administrative capabilities, labor, and the like. *Utilitarian power* is applied when those who possess these assets use them to bring others into line. *Coercive assets* are weapons, installations, and labor that are used by the military, the police, and so on. *Coercive power* is force and results when one unit uses coercive assets to impose a preferred line of conduct on others. *Persuasive power* is exercised through the manipulation of symbols in order to mobilize support. Etzioni suggests that persuasive power is the least alienating or estranging (leading to resistance) and that the application of force is the most alienating. He further proposes that within postmodern societies, the trend is away from coercive power toward utilitarian power. This ensures a lower level of alienation, making the society more responsive to its members.

The type of power employed varies with the goals to be achieved. Etzioni (1968:370–373) asserts that cultural goals (such as education, socialization, entertainment) are usually realized through normative control. Other power is often not required and alienation is low. Production goals (manufacture of goods and distribution of services) are served more effectively by utilitarian power. Etzioni (1968:371) observes how nursing shifted from normative to utilitarian behavior as it left its Florence Nightingale days and became a bureaucratically organized profession. Order goals (such as the control of crime) involve the use of coercive power or force. Such power, as we have noted, is highly alienating, contributing, at least in part, to the failure of prisons to resocialize criminals.

In general, the movement is away from coercive control toward normative control. In a postmodern society, emphasis shifts away from both coercive and utilitarian forms of control toward the normative. This may be evidenced in trends in the labor force that could lead to less bureaucratic work and more self-guiding, nonalienating types of positions. Etzioni (1968:380) summarizes as follows:

> The historical, "secular" trends seem to be toward less coercion and toward more utilitarian and especially more normative compliance, with an increase in the utilitarian controls of "have-not" countries to the degree

that they develop economically and a relative increase in the options for normative guidance in developed societies as they enter the postmodern period. The more active a society—the greater the number of citizens whom it involves and is responsive to—the more it is expected to rely on normative guidance, for the lower level of resulting alienation makes it more effective, and normative guidance, in turn, further reduces the level of alienation.

Societal Consensus and Responsiveness

Etzioni views society as a loose mosaic of subcollectivities or subgroups. Examples of these groups include the family, religious and ethnic groups, racial collectivities, classes, and voluntary associations. These subcollectivities feed the politically active larger collectivities, such as the state. Etzioni (1968:441) suggests that "the state and, more generally, the society-wide political processes deal much more with organizations that represent sub-collectivities and their combinations than with organizations that have no collective base." Thus, in the postmodern society, it is not the individual to whom society is responsible, but rather it is responsible to the collectivity or group acting in unison.

The state, however, does not simply execute the wishes of the collectivity; it does have power of its own. The self-guiding society should have a blend of two basic components: control (as found in totalitarian countries) and consensus building (as emphasized in democratic societies). Etzioni believes that the means of accomplishing this task would be to use less coercion and persuasion and more education in democratic societies. There should be a "planned freedom" or guidance that allows members of the society to be free. Etzioni asserts that this has been the trend occurring in postmodern democratic societies, where control has been increasing but it is a control that allows for greater freedom. One example might be the social security system. Most workers are required by law to pay a certain percentage of their earnings into social security or some other retirement fund. Although this is a form of control, it also provides the "freedom" of knowing that one will be receiving some income after retirement from the labor force.

A truly responsive society is aware of the needs of all of its members, not simply the most powerful collectivities. The ideal of the active society is one of near equality. Groups must be permitted to mobilize and must be granted access to power positions.

From Alienating to Active Society _____

Although the United States may be said to be moving toward an active society, it would be a mistake to think that the active society has in fact arrived. It is something that must be planned or worked toward. Alienation or unresponsiveness of the world to the person is still very much a part of the American way. What we have, basically, is an *inauthentic society*, or one that gives the appearance of responsiveness while underneath it is in fact alienating. The roots of this alienation, says Etzioni (1968:618), lie not in the individual psyche but in the societal and political structure. It is the structure that must be changed if alienation is to be reduced.

Etzioni (1968:622–626) observes that the concepts of alienation and inauthenticity assume the existence of basic human needs that the active society must allow to be met. He attempts to provide an incomplete list of such needs. They include the following:

1. The need for affection, also referred to as the need for solidarity, cohesion, or love.
2. The need for recognition, also referred to as the need for self-esteem, achievement, or approval.
3. The need for context or the need for orientation, consistency, synthesis, meaning, or "wholeness."
4. The need for repeated gratification allowing frequent and predictable rewards.

In addition to the needs for affection, recognition, "context," and repeated gratification, men and women need variance. By *variance* Etzioni means that a society must allow for a variety of social roles and norms. This would allow an outlet for the diversity among people due to personality and/or socialization differences.

These "needs" are not intended to be an exhaustive list of all basic human needs. Nor are they to be accepted as givens. Etzioni emphasizes the role of empirical research in providing knowledge of the desired goals for members of a society. Achieving an active society is possible only when adequate knowledge achieved through scientific research illuminates the way for society's actors.

Critique of The Active Society _____

Etzioni has described *The Active Society* as his "life's work," and he tries to "summarize its main points in every public presentation" he has given (Etzioni, 1973:31). Within this magnum opus, Etzioni clearly provides his model of people, society, and sociological theory.

Etzioni's image of people resembles that of naturalistic theory in general and Parsonian theory in specific. Like Parsons, Etzioni views human behavior as voluntaristic and goal-oriented but still contingent upon the particular social structure in which persons live. We see this clearly in Etzioni's discussion of alienating versus active societies. Although men and women have basic human needs (such as variance, affection, recognition, context, and gratification), these needs may be thwarted by the structure. The result of thwarting these needs is an alienated person. Yet actors may—if they have access to knowledge, decision making, and power—alter their society. Etzioni recognizes the importance of being aware of the individual, but he steers clear of social psychologism. As Friedrichs (1970:39) observes, he "would veer from any reification of the 'individual' and move instead toward such terms as 'role' and 'social unit.' "

The individual, for Etzioni as for Parsons, is not the main unit of sociological analysis. Although his theory is based upon assumptions about the "determined" yet "free" essence of human behavior, it is society or the social group that is of theoretical importance. Friedrichs (1970:39) compares Etzioni with Parsons on this issue: "Both Parsons and Etzioni link respect for functional analysis with a benevolent image of society and emphasize the significance of consensus, Etzioni going so far as to endow collectivities with 'selves' and to speak of the 'general' or 'shared will.' " Society, there can be no doubt, forms the units of analysis for Etzioni and is the subject matter of his sociology.

Etzioni, like Parsons in his general systems theory, assumes a cybernetic model of society. In this model it is knowledge that is the form of energy being transformed in society. This element, along with decision making and power, are the three prime components in the social system. Etzioni's society clearly is not a static model but rather is malleable and capable of being transformed. Etzioni is not fascinated with social order but assumes social entropy and the inevitability of conflict.

Etzioni's model is not unlike other macrotheoretical models, bearing a resemblance to Parsonian theory and to a more general modern systems approach. Where Etzioni moves away from Parsons is in his insistence that sociological theory deal with relevant issues. Although not as critical of naturalistic, nonevaluative sociology as C. Wright Mills, Etzioni (1966: 317; 1968:133) does reflect Mills's concern about sociology's need to deal with social issues:

> What is lacking in American sociology is *social analysis,* the *systematic* exploration of societal issues, that is, concern with the methodological

questions of sociological analysis of the great issues of our age, which invariably involves the study of macroscopic units.

Etzioni (1969:134) does not favor the abolishment of academic sociology. Rather he asserts there is a "need to add to 'sociology as a science' (as the institutionalized desire to know) the systematic concern with the application of knowledge (the institutionalized desire to help)." For Etzioni, sociology remains a science much like the natural sciences, but there is a critical need to supplement this scientific knowledge with training in the application of such knowledge.[2]

Summary

The Active Society is an attempt to synthesize various perspectives in sociological theory into a single political and economic analysis of society. In it can be found the functionalist concern with social structure as well as the Marxian belief in the need to transform the structure into a responsive society. It attempts to combine scientific theorizing with evaluative social planning. Although macroscopic in orientation, it recognizes the reality of social psychological needs that are either thwarted or met through the social structure. Using a cybernetic model, *The Active Society* represents a theory of both structure and change.

What is needed for an active society are (1) a group of actors possessing knowledge; (2) one or more goals that the actor is committed to realize; and (3) access to the power to execute the decisions based on societal knowledge. To be "active" requires knowledge, a decision-making process, and access to power. Etzioni discusses the expansion and state of knowledge in the twentieth century. He then considers this knowledge in relation to the decision-making process, identifying both the strengths and the weaknesses of the rational model versus the more commonly used alternative model of incrementalism. Etzioni then advances a third model for decision making, a combination of the rationalist and the incrementalist models, which he terms *mixed scanning*. This decision-making process is implemented through use of utilitarian, coercive, or persuasive power.

---

[2] For a more concrete illustration of Etzioni's concerns with the need for evaluative work in sociology, see *Genetic Fix: The Next Technological Revolution* (1973). In a personal account of his participation in a conference with both natural and social scientists on the implications of work in genetics, Etzioni "attempts to focus attention on the profound implications of genetic engineering."

The phenomenon of power distinguishes the active society from both the passive and the inauthentic one. A passive society is unresponsive to the needs of its members and subjects them to forces they neither comprehend nor desire. Highly alienating structures rely heavily on coercion and manipulation; these brutalize and dehumanize the rulers as well as the ruled. An inauthentic society provides the appearance of responsiveness while the underlying conditions are alienating. Active societies strive for authenticity. They allow transformation of the structure to meet the basic needs of the societal actors.

Etzioni's work may be used to demonstrate the model of a scientifically oriented yet evaluative sociological theory. His theoretical constructions include a nonevaluative general systems base combined with evaluative social analysis. He attempts to break down the dichotomy between pure and applied theory, demonstrating that social analysis and its concern for the issues of our age will enhance our theoretical products.

References

BREED, WARREN
  1971 *The Self-Guiding Society.* New York: The Free Press.
ETZIONI, AMITAI
  1966 "Social Analysis as Sociological Vocation." Pp. 317–323 in Arthur B. Shostak (Ed.), *Sociology in Action.* Homewood, Ill.: The Dorsey Press, Inc.
  1968 *The Active Society.* New York: The Free Press.
  1973 *Genetic Fix: The Next Technological Revolution.* New York: Harper & Row, Publishers.
FRIEDRICHS, ROBERT
  1970 *A Sociology of Sociology.* New York: The Free Press.

16

The Coming of Post-Industrial Society: A Venture into Social Forecasting

> It is almost old-fashioned today to admit to an interest in ideas. The language of the social sciences is one of *hypotheses, parameters, variables,* and *paradigms.*
>
> . . .
>
> My concerns are different. I am interested in social description and in explanation, in sketching a broad reality rather than the controlled, but abstracted, testing of hypotheses. It is not necessarily less "scientific" than academic sociology. Nor is it really "literary." It is sociology as a "perspective," as a way of becoming sophisticated about the world. It is at one with academic sociology in using similar concepts (group, status, social mobility), and with literary analysis in the interest in the moral component of social action. (Bell, 1960:15)

The theoretical endeavors of Daniel Bell represent an attempt to deal with sociological problems from a critical standpoint in hopes of bridging the gap between academic sociology and the humanistic disciplines. Topics that he has dealt with include an analysis of "the exhaustion of the political ideas of the fifties" (Bell, 1960); looking at "future consequences of public policy decisions, to anticipate future problems, and to begin the design of alternative solutions so that our society has more options and can make a moral choice" (Bell, 1968); and "the cultural contradictions of capitalism" (Bell, 1976). Although each of these works employs Bell's sociological framework, the major aim is directed toward social analysis rather than abstract social theory. Like Mills and Etzioni, Bell is committed to a relevant sociology that is willing to tackle large-scale societal problems.

Bell's particular approach to sociology has been termed *social forecasting*. Social forecasting blends the macrotheoretical perspective that has been part of the classical sociological perspective with a renewed interest in a "relevant" and "useful" sociology that speaks to the conditions of our times. Bell (1973) distinguishes "social forecasting" from earlier sociological attempts at prediction. *Prediction* deals with the outcome of events (such as who will win an election or who will lose a war), but such prediction cannot be formalized—that is, prediction cannot be made subject to rules (Bell, 1973:3–4). *Social forecasting*, on the other hand, attempts to outline the probabilities of an array of historical tendencies. It is possible only where "there are regularities and recurrences of phenomena" or where there are persisting trends whose direction "can be plotted within statistical time series or be formulated as historical tendencies." Bell emphasizes that "forecasting is possible only where one can assume a high degree of rationality on the part of the men who influence events" (Bell, 1973:4).

Such rationality, however, is frequently absent in many human situations. This is particularly true in politics, where many privileges and prejudices, rather than consistent rational behavior, characterize human events. If this is the case, of what use are social forecasters? Bell observes, "Though they cannot predict results, they can specify the *constraints* or limits within which policy decisions can be made effective" (1973:4). Thus the specification of such constraints is the task of social forecasting.

There are other modes of forecasting besides the sociological one. These include technological forecasting, which identifies the constraints in technological developments; demographic forecasting, which provides projected population statistics; economic forecasting, including simple market surveys, the construction of consumer price indexes, rate of employment, and so on, which serve as indicators of business activity; and political forecasting, dealing with trends in the political sphere. The most important difference between these types and social forecasting is that social forecasting utilizes sociological variables (rather than technological, demographic, economic, or political variables) as the independent variables that affect the behavior of other variables. Examples may be found in the attempts to link social indicators (such as crime rates and educational figures) in a sociological model, as may be illustrated by the sociohistorical analysis of Tocqueville's *Democracy in America* or Max Weber's socioeconomic theory of bureaucratization and the pervasive process of rationalization.

Bell's two recent treatises *The Coming of Post-Industrial Society* (1973) and *The Cultural Contradictions of Capitalism* (1976) may be considered in tandem as examples of his social forecasting. In the preface to *The Cultural Contradictions of Capitalism,* Bell (1976:xi) succinctly spells out the interrelationship between the two works:

> This book stands in a dialectical relation to my previous book, *The Coming of Post-Industrial Society.* In that volume, I sought to show how technology (including intellectual technology) and the codification of theoretical knowledge as a new principle for innovation and policy were reshaping the techno-economic order, and with it, the stratification system of the society as well. In these essays, I deal with culture, especially the ideal of modernity, and with the problems of managing a complex polity when the values of the society stress unrestrained appetite. The contradictions I see in contemporary capitalism derive from the unraveling of the threads which had once held the culture and the economy together, and from the influence of the hedonism which has become the prevailing value in our society.

In *Post-Industrial Society,* Bell (1973:13) is "concerned chiefly with the social structural and political consequences of the post-industrial society." In *Cultural Contradictions* (1976:10), Bell treats the third analytical division of society, namely, the culture. Together these two books provide Bell's model of society and his sociological theory.

The Coming of Post-Industrial Society

Bell's major hypothesis is that the Western world is in transition from an industrial to a postindustrial society. This concept of a postindustrial society can be better understood through an analysis of the five dimensions or components of the term (Bell, 1973:14–33).

The first dimension concerns the economic sector, where there has been a change from goods producing to services. As a nation becomes more industrialized, a greater percentage of the labor force moves from farming or agriculture into the manufacturing sector of the economy. As national incomes rise, in part a consequence of the transition, there is a greater demand for services. Bell (1973:15) observes that, "The United States today is the only nation in the world in which the service sector accounts for more than half of the total employment and more than half of the Gross National Product."

The second dimension occurs in the realm of the occupational sphere. Here there is a change in the kind of work done, with the preeminence of the professional and technical class: "In the United States, by 1956, the number of white-collar workers, for the first time in the history of industrial civilization, outnumbered the blue-collar workers in the occupational structure" (Bell, 1973:17). By the 1970s, the white-collar workers outnumbered the blue-collar workers by more than five to four (Bell, 1973:17). Even more startling has been the growth of professional and technical employment. This group, made up of scientists, engineers, technicians, medical and health personnel, teachers, and other such occupations, is the heart of the postindustrial society.

A third dimension of the postindustrial society is the "centrality of theoretical knowledge as the source of innovation and of policy formation for the society" (Bell, 1973:14). Changes in the knowledge dimension may be seen in major difference between industrial and postindustrial society. Industrial society is mainly concerned with the coordination of machines and men in the production of goods. Bell (1973:20) observes, "Post-industrial society is organized around knowledge, for the purpose of social control and the directing of innovation and change; and this in turn gives rise to new social relationships and new structures that have to be managed politically." In postindustrial societies, there is a primacy of abstract theoretical knowledge over concrete empirical knowledge (e.g., inventions). This theoretical knowledge is central as a source of policy decisions.

The fourth dimension is a future orientation, which controls technology and technological assessment. In other words, the postindustrial society may be able to plan and control technological growth rather than simply "letting it happen."

The fifth dimension involves decision making and the creation of a new "intellectual technology." This dimension is concerned with the method or manner of gaining knowledge. *Intellectual technology* includes the use of scientific knowledge to specify ways of doing things in a *reproducible* manner through the substitution of problem-solving rules for intuitive judgments.

What Bell analyzes in his first major theoretical statement is the change in the character of knowledge and the structure of the postindustrial society. This includes the vast growth and branching of science, the rise of a new intellectual technology, and the codification of theoretical knowledge. This shift in the type of knowledge has had its effect on the economy of our society. It is toward the changing shape of the economy that Bell directs his attention.

FROM GOODS TO SERVICES: THE CHANGING
SHAPE OF THE ECONOMY

The concept of a postindustrial society gains in meaning as we compare it with the attributes of a preindustrial and an industrial society. Most of the world, including the vast continents of Asia, Africa, and Latin America, still exist in the preindustrial state. The economic sector consists primarily of extraction through agriculture, mining, fishing, and timber. Life, then, is still primarily a game against nature, dependent upon the seasons of the year, the nature of the soil, and the availability of water. Industrial societies, including Western Europe, the Soviet Union, and Japan, are goods producing. Bell (1973:126) describes them in the following manner:

> Life is a game against fabricated nature. The world has become technical and rationalized. The machine predominates, and the rhythms of life are mechanically paced: time is chronological, methodical, evenly spaced. Energy has replaced raw muscle and provides the power that is the basis of productivity—the art of making more with less—and is respon sible for the mass output of goods which characterizes industrial society. Energy and machines transform the nature of work.

The postindustrial society, of which the United States is an example, is based on services. Rather than being a "game against nature" or a "game against fabricated nature," it is essentially a game between persons. Rather than depending on "raw muscle power" (as do preindustrial societies) or "energy" (as do industrial societies), postindustrial societies rely on information. The professional, being in possession of the desired information, is increasingly in demand in the postindustrial society.

The concern of social forecasting, however, is more than a simple description of the materialization of a postindustrial society. The task of social forecasting is to identify some of the constraints on change toward such a service-oriented society. One such constraint on change is the "constraint of productivity" (Bell, 1973:155). Bell observes that productivity and output grow much faster in goods than in services. In services there is a relation between persons rather than between person and machine. Because the dependence is upon persons who continually must be paid for services, costs are continually rising. This is true for education, a live concert, or a physician's services. The output of services is difficult to increase because of relations that are fixed by time components.

Related to this constraint on the increase of service productivity is the "constraint of inflation." The cost of services is rising at a much more rapid rate than is the cost of goods. Bell (1973:156–157) observes that from 1965 to 1970, the price of an automobile rose 15 per cent, durable goods (televisions, appliances, furniture) rose 18 per cent, and the price of services (medical care, schooling, recreation, insurance) had gone up 42.5 per cent. Problems with inflation have continued to mount during the years since 1970, with little hope being offered for any immediate solution.

A third constraint, one that is related to inflation, is that American manufactured goods are pricing themselves out of the world market. This has led American labor, which has been traditionally committed to free trade, to become heavily protectionist. Because of the increase in costs and the limitations of protectionism, there may be less room for experimentation in the labor force to change working conditions. The cost may be too great in terms of dollars and cents.

Bell asserts that the largest constraint is "the very multiplicity of competing demands in the polity itself" (1973:159). A postindustrial society is increasingly a communal society where the public cries for a better quality of life in such arenas as environment, recreation, and culture. Bell (1973:159) comments, "But all this involves two problems: we don't really know, given our lack of social-science knowledge, how to do many of these things effectively; equally important, since there may not be enough money to satisfy all or even most of the claims, how do we decide what to do first?"

THE DIMENSIONS OF KNOWLEDGE AND TECHNOLOGY: THE NEW CLASS STRUCTURE OF POSTINDUSTRIAL SOCIETY

Bell asserts that there have been major structural changes in society affecting knowledge and technology. Not only has there been an exponential growth in the rate of discoveries, but the scale of life has increased from even the industrial period. Bell (1973:172) observes:

> An individual today, on the job, in school, in the neighborhood, in a professional or social milieu, knows immediately hundreds of persons and, if one considers the extraordinary mobility of our lives—geographical, occupational, and social—during a lifetime one comes to know, as acquaintances or friends, several thousand. And through the windows of the mass media, and because of the enlargement of the political world and the multiplication of the dimensions of culture—the number of persons (and places) that one *knows of* accelerates at a steeply exponential rate.

Not only has there been a growth of knowledge, with sources of innovation being increasingly within the realm of *theoretical* knowledge, an analysis of the gross national product reflects that a larger share of the employment of a postindustrial society is within the knowledge sphere. Bell estimated that by 1975, approximately 25 per cent of the labor force in the United States would have at least two years of college education, with a total of 15 per cent of the labor force being employed in the professional and technical labor force. Postindustrial society becomes increasingly dependent upon the educated class of the country. In order to plan for the future, it is important to analyze the knowledge class and its distribution in the occupational world.

Bell (1973:262) theorizes that politics will play a bigger role in the postindustrial society than it has ever played before. Rather than the market's determining decision making, the decision to allocate resources will be made more and more by the political center or government. Because interests and values are diverse, conflict and tension over scarce monetary resources are probably unavoidable.

Bell (1973:263–264) outlines some of the crucial decisions that will have to be faced about the future of a postindustrial society. These include (1) the method of financing higher education, which characterizes the postindustrial society; (2) the evaluation of research, the results of which can be used for future allocation of scarce research resources; (3) the determination of the conditions and settings for creativity and productivity; (4) the process by which technological discoveries made in a laboratory may be transferred more readily into production; (5) analysis of the pace at which knowledge develops and the manner in which teachers can keep up with the latest developments; and (6) the problems of monitoring social change.

TENSION BETWEEN ECONOMIZING AND SOCIOLOGIZING MODES

In a postindustrial society, there will be an enormous growth in nonprofit areas outside business and government. These include schools, hospitals, research institutes, and voluntary and civic associations. At the same time, the business corporation remains (at least for a while) the heart of the society. The corporation, therefore, cannot be ignored in a study of the post industrial society. The economizing mode that characterizes the corporation will exist in tension alongside the sociologizing mode characterized by the nonprofit, service sector of the society. Bell analyzes the characteristics of both modes and their future in the postindustrial society.

The Economizing Mode. Until the rise of industrialization, it was nearly impossible for a society to achieve a steady increase in wealth and a rising standard of living through the use of peaceful means. Economic life had been very much of a zero-sum game, with one nation of winners achieving its wealth by war, plunder, expropriations, and so on at the expense of another group. The increased productivity resulted from the combined efforts of the engineers who designed the machines and the economists, who were able to assist in the increased efficiency of production. This resulted in a new mode of life, which Bell (1973:275) terms *economizing:*

> Economizing is the science of the best allocation of scarce resources among competing ends; it is the essential technique for the reduction of "waste"—as this is measured by the calculus stipulated by the regnant accounting technique. The conditions of economizing are a market mechanism as the arbiter of allocation, and a fluid price system which is responsive to the shifting patterns of supply and demand.

In other words, the *economizing mode* represents the best allocation of scarce resources among competing ends. With it comes a rational division of labor, the programming of production, and an attempt to locate the best mix of capital and labor at relative prices. We associate economizing with "maximization," "optimization," and "least cost." As is becoming more and more apparent in an age of shortages and pollution, this economizing mode has serious limitations. First, it measures only economic goods, neglecting such items as beautiful scenery, pure water, sunshine, working satisfaction, and the like. Second, it takes no account of externalities (or "external costs"), which may be shifted to other private parties or to society as a whole. One example of such a social cost is air and water pollution. A third problem with the economizing mode is that "the value system of the American society emphasizes, as the primary consideration, the satisfaction of individual private consumption; the result is an imbalance between public goods and private goods" (Bell, 1973:280). Taxes, for example, are frequently viewed as something "taken away" rather than money collectively spent for the public good. Thus the economizing mode is based on the proposition that *individual* satisfaction is the unit in which costs and benefits are to be calculated. Bell suggests another mode, the sociologizing mode, which might serve as a better account system in the postindustrial society.

The Sociologizing Mode. Bell (1973:283) defines the sociologizing mode as "the effort to judge a society's needs in a more conscious fashion and . . . to do so on the basis of some explicit conception of the 'public interest.'" This mode involves two fundamental questions: (1) the conscious establishment of social justice by the inclusion of all persons in the society, and (2) the realization that social goods are subject to communal or political, rather than individual, demand. The sociologizing mode must attempt a rational course of public planning. Bell (1973:284) observes, "The major sociological problem ahead will be the test of our ability to *foresee* the effects of social and technological change and to *construct alternative courses* in accordance with different valuations of ends, at different costs."

Bell emphasizes that corporations cannot simply be subject to the economizing mode as they have in the past; they must also obligate themselves to the sociologizing mode. Social responsibility will become an even more critical issue in the years to come than it is today. Some of the issues on which the corporation must become subordinated to public interests include workers' job satisfaction, employment of minority groups, responsibilities to the community, and responsibility for the environment. In the long run, the corporation will lose some of its overwhelming power as the trend continues toward a noncapitalistic society.

The Power Structure of the Postindustrial Society

Bell (1973:43) observes that the emergence of a new kind of society brings into question the distributions of wealth, power, and status. With regard to the stratification and power system, the postindustrial society may be compared with the earlier preindustrial and industrial types. Stratification and power systems are based on the allocation of scarce resources. The major resource of preindustrial societies is land; in industrial societies, machines; and in postindustrial societies, knowledge. The dominant figures of each system are those who possess the desired resource. In preindustrial societies, the landowner and the military (who protected the land) were in control, their power based on force. Businessmen are in key power positions in industrial societies, their power based on indirect influence in politics. In the postindustrial society, the university and research institutes are places of power, with scientists and research men and women being the dominant figures. The means of power will be a balance of rational technical forces (provided by the scientists) and the calculating political forces (exerted by the power elite). Politics will thus play an ever-increasing role in postindustrial society—and politics is not primarily a rational system in the same sense as are technology and science.

What Bell (1973:375) attempts to do is to outline a scheme for the social structure of a postindustrial society. The stratification system is based on knowledge, with the professional class being the highest ranking. This class includes scientists, technologists, administrators, and those working toward the development of artistic or religious cultural knowledge. This class is followed by technicians and semiprofessionals, clerical workers and salespersons, and finally, blue-collar workers. This class system based on knowledge is one in which achievement and personal ability (rather than ascription or inheritance) become increasingly important.

The postindustrial society does not represent a radical restructuring of society. Rather it is a change in the character of the structure. As Bell (1973:487) expresses it:

> In descriptive terms, there are three components: in the economic sector, there is a shift from manufacturing to services; in technology, it is the centrality of new science-based industries; in sociological terms, it is the rise of new technical elites and the advent of a new principle of stratification.

One of the biggest changes in this society is the shift from the emphasis on a *reality of nature* (as in preindustrial society) to the *reality of technics* (as in the industrial order) to the *reality of the social world* (as in postindustrial society). It is the task of men and women—experiencing recipirical consciousness of self and other—to construct an improved social world.

The Cultural Contradictions of Capitalism _____

Bell (1976:10) has analytically divided society into the technoeconomic structure, the polity, and the culture. The *technoeconomic structure,* with its concern about the organization of production and the allocation of goods and services, and the *polity,* with its concern about the legitimate use of force and the regulation of conflict in the arena of social justice and power, are the topics of Bell's first theoretical treatise just described. *Culture,* the concern of his companion theoretical work, is defined more narrowly than culture anthropologically understood as "the arena of *expressive symbolism:* those efforts, in painting, poetry, and fiction, or within the religious forms of litany, liturgy, and ritual, which seek to explore and express the meanings of human existence in some imaginative form" (Bell, 1976:12).

Bell's thesis, as indicated by the title of the 1976 work, is that there is a cultural contradiction of capitalism. Specifically there is a "disjunction between the kind of organization and the norms demanded in the economic realm, and the norms of self-realization that are now central in the culture" (Bell, 1976:15). In the past, our Western culture, which historically had been fused with religion, had norms guided by the Protestant ethic that were joined to capitalism. These cultural norms and the capitalistic economic system have not only become "unjoined" but also contradictory. Capitalism goes on as our economic system, but our modern cultural system faces a "spiritual crisis" (Bell, 1976:28).

Bell (1976:37) succinctly summarizes his argument as follows:

> what I find striking today is the radical disjunction between the social structure (the techno-economic order) and the culture. The former is ruled by an economic principle defined in terms of efficiency and functional rationality, the organization of production through the ordering of things, including men as things. The latter is prodigal, promiscuous, dominated by an anti-rational, anti-intellectual temper in which the self is taken as the touchstone of cultural judgments, and the effect on the self is the measure of the aesthetic worth of experience. The character structure inherited from the nineteenth century, with its emphasis on self-discipline, delayed gratification, and restraint, is still relevant to the demands of the techno-economic structure; but it clashes sharply with the culture, where such bourgeois values have been completely rejected.

Bell credits the breakdown of religious belief in God and the immortal soul with creating this crisis in self-consciousness that has led to the extreme individualism characterizing modern culture. Bell (1976:71) traces the erosion of Puritanism and the Protestant ethic, which not only left "capitalism with no moral or transcendental ethic" but also left room for the development of a "new liberation" of self-centered, hedonistic cultural norms that exist in "extraordinary contradiction within the social structure itself."

Bell, although squarely facing the problems he feels are confronting modernity, is not a reactionary. He is not calling for a return to the "good old days" but rather reaffirms his faith in the liberal tradition. What he calls for (1976:281–282) is a powerful ideology that can serve as a cultural base for our social structure:

> This basis must be created by conjoining three actions: the reaffirmation of our past, for only if we know the inheritance from the past can we become aware of the obligation to our posterity; recognition of the limits of resources and the priority of needs, individual and social, over unlimited appetite and wants; and agreement upon a conception of equity which gives all persons a sense of fairness and inclusion in the society and which promotes a situation where, within the relevant spheres, people *become* more equal so that they can be *treated* equally.

Critique of Social Forecasting _____

Bell's social forecasting represents a blend of structural functionalism and conflict structuralism in an attempt to identify some of the constraints facing society. Therefore the assumptions upon which it is based are part of the sociological tradition. In Bell's discussion of modernity are found the basic assumptions that society exists, that sociological theory describes the structure and changes of structure within society, and that men and women are products of their social worlds. These basic structuralist assumptions, as we have seen in detail in previous chapters, are contained in much naturalistic sociological theory. Bell's social forecasting, however, makes additional assumptions that may be viewed as corollaries of these three basic assumptions.

Society, for Bell, is a structure in which power relations are important for analysis. In this sense, Bell accepts a Marxian view of the social structure. Where Marx saw property as the basis for social class, however, Bell contends that knowledge has replaced property as the main source of power. This assumption has been questioned by Coser (1975:218), who observes that Bell demonstrates that modern society increasingly depends on the activities of men and women of knowledge *but* that Bell fails to demonstrate their relation to power: "He [Bell] does not seem seriously to entertain the notion that the employers and funding agencies, both public and private, who employ them or contract for their work, may in fact direct their activities much more than they themselves direct them." The degree to which knowledge holds the key to the power positions in the social structure may be seriously questioned.

Bell's theory of social structure has also been criticized for its economic determinism. Floud (1971), for example, notes that Bell has accepted Marx's view of the relationship of the economic order to the social structure. In so doing, Bell classifies societies according to their economic structures without sufficient regard for other social institutions. This same criticism of economic determinism has been level against Bell's theory by Janowitz (1974). Janowitz is particularly concerned about Bell's failure to recognize the importance of the political structure as an independent variable and about his failure to acknowledge the prior and continuing impact of the political process on the occupational and social structure. Scientists may indeed have knowledge, but when they wield power, perhaps it is more because of their astuteness in the area of politics than their specialty knowledge. In lobbying and through the formation of pressure groups—and not from the ivory university towers—knowledge holders have made their presence felt.

Theorists who have no quarrel with the approach that views the social structure as the appropriate subject matter of sociology have questioned Bell's description of this structure and the functioning of his postindustrial society. Others have questioned indeed whether there is any postindustrial society or whether society is not still in the industrial stage. Stearns (1974), for example, observes that simply reporting a speedup of change within a society, as Bell has done, does not warrant the assertion that our society has moved into a new age.

Sociological theory, for Bell, is responsible for describing the patterns within the social structure and the changes to which such a structure is subject. This theory should be capable of being utilized to forecast social trends. Although this aim is laudable, forecasting is impossible if the current situation is not adequately analyzed. We have seen that critics have not fully accepted Bell's analysis of the postindustrial society. Some have questioned the degree to which any systematic theory is present in Bell's work. Olsen (1974:236), for example, charges that *The Coming of Post-Industrial Society* fails to present an integrated thesis, consisting instead "of a maze of insightful and intriguing but poorly organized ideas." Olsen further asserts that although attempting to describe American society, Bell's work does not constitute any explanatory theory, which should be the goal of theory construction. Based on these criticisms, it is apparent that Bell's conception of the goal of his sociological endeavors (which is expressed in the lead quotation for this chapter) is at odds with others' conception of theory.

Being primarily interested in macrosociological analysis, Bell does not deal with the social psychological issue of the relationship between the individual and his/her social structure. He does, however, address some comments to the nature of people. In the earliest epochs of human history, the individual was shaped by the collective struggle against nature. In the industrial era, men and women became less dependent on nature and more involved in a "game against fabricated nature," where the technical order was substituted for the natural one. Bell (1973:487–489) suggests that in the postindustrial society, human relations become more important, but he does not analyze the essence of these interpersonal relationships. Inherent in his thesis, however, is the basic need of persons to be controlled by their social structure, although, as we have seen, the constraints have moved from nature, to technology, and finally toward a "game between persons." Bell (1973:488) asserts, "Society itself becomes a web of consciousness, a form of imagination to be realized as a social construction." In the postindustrial society, the constraints of the past eras vanish, and new ones remain to be developed.

The basic nature of man, however, remains. As Bell (1973:488–489) states:

But what does not vanish is the duplex nature of man himself—the murderous aggression, from primal impulse, to tear apart and destroy; and the search for order, in art and life, as the bending of will to harmonious shape. It is this ineradicable tension which defines the social world and which permits the view of Utopia that is perhaps more realistic than the here-and-now millennium on earth that modern man has sought. Utopia has always been conceived as a design of harmony and perfection in the relations between men. In the wisdom of the ancients, Utopia was a fruitful impossibility, a conception of the desirable which men should always strive to attain but which the very nature of things, could not be achieved. And yet, by its very idea, Utopia would serve as a standard of judgment on men, an ideal by which to measure the real.

Bell's analysis of the social structure does not claim to be Utopian. In his discussion of social reality as he views it, we are able to identify some of the forces at work that are shaping men and women and their society. This type of theoretical approach, perhaps, better prepares us to shape the social world in which we live.

Summary

Social forecasting represents an attempt to use theory to specify the sociological constraints on the development of future society. Bell's attempt at social forecasting is specifically concerned with the social structural and political consequences of the postindustrial society.

Bell hypothesizes that the Western world is in a transition from an industrial to a postindustrial society. This has been represented by a change from goods producing to the production of services, by a change from blue-collar work to a preeminence of professionals and technicians, by a centralizing of technical knowledge, by a future orientation, and by a concern for guiding decision making. In discussing these changes, Bell outlines some of the crucial decisions that will have to be faced in a postindustrial society. These include the financing of higher education, the evaluation of research, and the analysis of the pace at which knowledge develops. He further observes that the profit corporation will become subordinate to nonprofit areas, including government, schools, hospitals, and research institutes. The economizing mode, with its competitive laws, will be replaced with a conscious, decision-making, sociological mode. Social responsibility, predicts Bell, will become an even more critical issue than it is today.

Bell's attempt at social forecasting relies on a use of history as well as on current empirical data, particularly large-scale census data, to cast light on the future. Not only are research data central to supporting Bell's thesis, but research itself is a central ingredient in a postindustrial society. Scientific sociological research and evaluation comes closer to being merged with humanistic concerns for improving society.

References

BELL, DANIEL
  1960 *The End of Ideology.* Glencoe, Ill.: The Free Press of Glencoe.
  1968 *Toward the Year 2000.* Boston: Houghton Mifflin Company.
  1973 *The Coming of Post-Industrial Society: A Venture in Social Forecasting.* New York: Basic Books.
  1976 *The Cultural Contradiction of Capitalism.* New York: Basic Books, Inc.
COSER, LEWIS
  1975 "Structure and Conflict." Pp. 210–219 in Peter M. Blau (Ed.), *Approaches to the Study of Social Structure.* New York: The Free Press.
FLOUD, JEAN
  1971 "A Critique of Bell." *Survey* 17 (Winter):25–37.
JANOWITZ, MORRIS
  1974 "Review Symposium." *American Journal of Sociology* 80 (July): 230–236.
OLSEN, MARVIN E.
  1974 "Review Symposium." *American Journal of Sociology* 80 (July): 236–241.
STEARNS, PETER M.
  1974 "Is There a Post-industrial Society?" *Society* 11:10–22.

17

Reflexive Sociology: A Critical Study of Society

> The renewal of sociology is of course one aspect of the reconstruction of society. Clearly, we cannot have a reconstructed society without a critical revamping of our established ways of thinking about society. . . . The new society we want is, among other things, a society that will enable men better to see *what is* and say *what is* about themselves and their social world. In other words, the very purpose of a new society is, in *some* part, to create a new sociology." (Gouldner, 1973:82)

As the citation suggests, Alvin W. Gouldner is committed to the intimate relationship of theory and society. He describes one of his major works, *The Coming Crisis of Western Sociology* (1970), as being "meant primarily to begin a discussion concerning the proper relation of sociology to society, and therefore of theory to practice" (p. 82). Gouldner's continued commitment to a responsible criticism of both society and sociology and his own attempt to develop relevant theory makes him a leading spokesperson for humanistic evaluative theory. As he himself acknowledges (1973:89), "theorists must make a *personal commitment* to the theory and to the goals on behalf of which they enact it.

Gouldner's theory is *not*, according to his self-admission, a holistic work that analyzes and remedies problems of the modern world. It represents instead a critical questioning stance on both society and sociology. Gouldner (1976:xvi) describes himself as an "outlaw" and as a "Socratic," for whom nothing is too sacred for the probe of critical, scholarly analysis. At the same time, he does not pretend to have advanced a theory to replace what he criticizes:

> The Socratic does not believe he must pay a ransom—by offering a positive doctrine—for his right to criticize. Not preaching any positive

doctrine, the Socratic will not exchange one unexamined life for another, and he therefore subverts both the present and the antipresent. Being the critic of all positive doctrines, searching out their limits, the Socratic is necessarily suspect in the eyes of all who offer (and all who *ache* for) a positive doctrine. In the end, then the establishment *and* those who aspire to succeed it—in other words, both the old and the young—will accuse him of "poisoning the mind of the youth." Thus Socratics are, and are made outlaws. (1976:xvi)

Gouldner plays well his self-reputed role as "outlaw" and "Socratic." He has attacked the old theories, particularly the functionalism or "academic sociology" that has constituted American theory. At the same time he is critical of Marxism, although his leanings are more Marxist than functionalist. Thus both the "old" academic sociologists and the more youthful Marxists are disconcerted by the criticisms proffered by this "outlaw."

Gouldner's major works plus two as yet projected volumes constitute an attempt to trace the development and crises of Western political culture and sociology. He contends that any viable history of social theory written today must be "one part history, one part sociology, and one part criticism" (1966:5). Beginning with his discussion of the relation between social theory and classical Greek writings in *Enter Plato* (1966), continuing with his much-discussed *The Coming Crisis of Western Sociology* (1970), and further developed in *The Dialectic of Ideology and Technology* (1976), Gouldner employs different measures of history, sociology, and criticism as the basic ingredients of his theoretical efforts. *The Coming Crisis* represented an attack on orthodox American sociology, and *The Dialectic of Ideology* continues to critically analyze dominant problems of ideology. *Enter Plato* represents Gouldner's earliest efforts to trace the social bases of social theory. *The Coming Crisis* continues this same task but shifts attention from the past to the present state of theory. Through *The Coming Crisis,* Gouldner sought to demystify academic sociology. Through his more recent *The Dialectic of Ideology* (plus two projected works still to be written), Gouldner seeks to demystify Marxism.

Gouldner's works over the past decade represent a systematic attempt to analyze sociology critically in order to understand society better. Sociology and society are interdependent, with the former reflecting the value assumptions of the latter. This critical sociology must be directed toward proposing humanistic solutions as remedies for the ills it uncovers. Gouldner (1966:130) notes that modern sociologists "have been trained to analyze, study, and understand modern social problems," but they have not "been well trained or encouraged to try their hands at 'solving' social tensions." Gouldner (1966:131) emphasizes, "The social scientist has no right . . . to tell others what they should or must do. But it would seem that they do have a right, if not a responsibility, to inform men about what they *might* do to relieve human suffering and to discover alternative social arrangements. This is the task that Gouldner has set for himself and one with which he continues to struggle as he pursues the task of doing sociology.

The Coming Crisis of Western Sociology

The Coming Crisis was one of several books appearing this decade that critically evaluated the feasibility of a value-free sociology. It took its place among other works in the *sociology of sociology*, doing a critical sociological analysis of the state of the discipline.[1] Proponents of the sociology of sociology argue that the discipline has not been the product of value-free and detached persons in search of some kind of elusive "sociological truth." Rather, sociology is a product of men and women living at a particular time and in a particular milieu. It is within this socio-cultural framework that contemporary sociological theory must be analyzed.

Gouldner (1970:26) calls for a sociology of sociology that recognizes that sociologists are members of the "one race of men" with the same foibles, biases, and distortions. The sociologists of sociology should attempt to delineate some of the assumptions, both the explicitly formulated and the unlabeled or background assumptions, in order to make themselves more aware of the biases present in the field. Gouldner (1970: 34) notes, "To understand the impending crisis in sociology, therefore, it is necessary to understand the dominant intellectual schemes and theories; it is necessary to see the ways in which their background assumptions, by no means new, are being brought to a painful dissonance by new developments in the larger society."

In *The Coming Crisis* Gouldner traces the development of functionalism in American sociology—an approach that he contends has dominated sociology for several decades but that is now under strong attack.

[1] Sociology of sociology is a subdivision of the larger perspective of the sociology of knowledge that attempts to study, using the sociological method of research and analysis, the development of sociology itself. The sociology of knowledge relates the development of knowledge—whether it be scientific, religious, artistic, or philosophical—to the historico-socio-cultural milieu in which this knowledge arises. The sociology of sociology looks at the relationship of a particular area of knowledge—sociology—in relation to its social context. Theories are then presented to describe, and partially explain, the development of sociology as a field of knowledge.

This approach represents a kind of "goodness of fit" between our society and sociological theory. American functionalism, with its roots in positivism and its faith in ultimate progress, fitted well with an American society emerging as a world power. The United States survived a depression, was victorious in a world war, and consolidated its gains as a world power in the 1950s. Clouds of conflict overcast the brilliance of the progress of the first half of the twentieth century during the 1960s, pointing to a crisis not only in society but also within sociology. Parsonian functionalism, with its emphasis on order, was being challenged by alienated young scholars who sought new sociological theories. (Many of the theories discussed by Gouldner, including the works of C. Wright Mills, Erving Goffman, Harold Garfinkel, and George Homans, have been treated in this text.) In brief, functionalism as a theory was much rooted in the history of American social structure. The crisis it now faces as the once-dominant approach to sociology is also very much based in historical and cultural changes within the society itself.

What is the "solution" to the crisis of Western sociology and Western society? For Gouldner, the solution is already under way in the form of a narrowing chasm between Marxist and capitalist countries, which is also reflected in a convergence between Marxism and functionalism in sociology. Gouldner (1970:449) observes:

> If I have not misread the signs, there is a basic shift impending on both sides of this great historical division. As I have said, some Functionalists have in recent times manifested a clear and open drift toward Marxism. Correspondingly, many Marxists in the Soviet Bloc as elsewhere, manifest a growing attraction to Academic Sociology, including Functionalism and even Parsons himself. The Functionalist heirs of the Positivist tradition and the adherents of Marxism are moving now, each toward the other, cautiously and tentatively, to be sure, but moving, nonetheless.

Gouldner calls for the development of what he terms *reflexive sociology* to better understand where sociology is going and where it has been. A reflexive sociology is true to the scholastic goals of the sociology of knowledge, which attempts to analyze the development of knowledge within its sociocultural milieu. Reflexive sociology would attempt to probe the sociocultural roots of sociology, just as sociology scrutinizes and probes the development of other areas of knowledge. Gouldner beckons the reflexive sociologist to be aware of his/her personal and cultural biases —as best he/she can—in order to better realize the goal of an independent sociology characterized by scholarship and relevance.

In attempting to move toward a reflexive sociology, Gouldner "confesses" his own assumptions underlying his conception of sociology. He acknowledges that "no man can be his own critic," yet he asserts that it is important for him to attempt to lay bare his own assumptions (Gould-ner, 1970:481). Consistent with his criticism of Western sociology, he proposes that a self-selecting bias occurs in theorizing. Theorists fre-quently take certain "facets" as "givens" while rejecting those that are discomforting. As Gouldner (1970:484) comments:

> Commonly, the social theorist in trying to reduce a tension between a social event or process that he takes to be real and some value which this has violated. Much of theory-work is initiated by a dissonance between an imputed reality and certain values, or by the indeterminate value of an imputed reality. Theory-making, then, is often an effort to cope with threat; it is an effort to cope with a threat to something in which the theorist himself is deeply and personally implicated and which he holds dear.

Gouldner, like all other theorists, then, is deeply involved personally in his sociology. He must admit that his own knowledge of the social world is very much a part of his self-knowledge, his own position in the social world, and his efforts to change the world.

In his discussion of the development of American sociological theory, Gouldner is assuming an elite that not only supports sociology but that desires a return on its investment. Gouldner (1970:408) contends, "It [reflexive sociology] recognizes that the development of sociology de-pends on a societal support that permits growth in certain directions but simultaneously limits it in other ways and thus warps its character." In other words, vested interests can and do destroy the value neutrality of sociology. The reflexive sociologist must therefore be involved in soul-searching lest he/she sell his/her soul.

Gouldner in fact assumes that a good deal of soul selling has oc-curred and continues to occur within sociology. He asserts that the liberal ideologies of many pre-World War II sociologists have been coopted to serve a welfare state. Gouldner (1970:500) asserts, "Liberal sociologists have thus become the technical cadres of national governance. Here, in the post-World War II period, there has been a marriage of the sociolo-gist's liberalism and his career interests." Sociologists, according to Gould-ner, are a part of the welfare state, supporting and benefiting from the system and making it difficult, if not impossible, to critique it. In this ca-pacity as a beneficiary of the welfare state, the sociologist is expected to present an optimistic image of American society. Such sociologists are not free agents but must act in the interests of the liberal establishment and sell their training and expertise in this marketplace. Gouldner (1970:501) contends, "It has, in other words, become a function of the 'sunshine so-ciologist' to assure American society that the cloudy glass of water is really safe rather than dangerous to drink." Sociology thus fails to be in a position to objectively critique and study many aspects of American society.

Gouldner is convinced that a liberal ideology underlies both sociology and our contemporary welfare state. The reflexive sociologist must be willing to dissect and analyze liberal as well as conservative ideologies. Gouldner continues to analyze the role of ideology in contemporary society in his latest work, *The Dialectic of Ideology and Technology* (1976).

The Dialectic of Ideology and Technology

The inseparable connection between society and sociology, with their common underlying assumptions, is further developed in Gouldner's latest work. Whereas *The Coming Crisis* focused on sociology and its demystification, *The Dialectic* attempts to expose the problems with ideology facing modern people. Just as Gouldner had to discuss the social structure in order to demystify academic American sociology, he makes frequent allusions to problems in sociology as he attempts to demystify the ideology of both capitalism and socialism.

Gouldner contends that ideology has been duly noted and criticized in sociology but is infrequently the subject of systematic study and analysis. The conventional social science view of ideology fails on three counts: its one-sidedness, its ahistoricity, and its nonreflexivity. It is one-sided in its failure to look carefully at both sides of the ideological coin, noting its ideal claims as well as its surrounding reality. The social science view is ahistorical, not paying adequate attention to the complexities of the historical origins of ideologies. It is nonreflexive in that "it glimpses, but never really grasps, the way it *itself* is ideologized because of its own structural situation" (Gouldner, 1976:4).

Goldner repeats important assertions made in his earlier writings regarding the relationship between ideology and social science. From its earliest conceptions, sociology was not far removed from ideology. Although it has usually sought to study ideology as something "out there," sociology must be reflexive, recognizing that ideology is also "in here"— within the discipline. As Gouldner (1976:10) notes,

> The boundary between ideology and sociology, then, is not some long-forgotten outpost that the march of intellectual empire has left behind unwatched. Ideology is not some acne condition that sociology outgrows in its maturity. It remains, rather, a boundary wall that is manned, watched, and recurrently repaired.

For Gouldner, therefore, it is essential to understand and study ideology in order to understand sociology better and move it closer to its own rationality. His own work is an attempt to transcend both ideology and social science as commonly understood, representing "part of an effort to lay a basis for developing a third form of discourse that eludes the pretentiousness, false consciousness, and limits of both social science and ideology" (Gouldner, 1976:19).

Gouldner contends that modern ideology is based on and rooted in Protestantism's conception of the rights and powers of individuals. Although religion continues to lose ground, this conception of rights and powers has been enshrined in secular thought. In its rhetoric of rationality, "it justified the course of action it proposed, by the logic and evidence it summoned on behalf of its views of the social world, rather than by invoking faith, tradition, revelation or the authority of the speaker (Gouldner, 1976:30). Secularized modern ideology has in fact enhanced the Calvinist conception of individual rights and powers. It has further promoted the conception "that life here on earth is capable of being perfected by human knowledge and effort" (Gouldner, 1976:30). In a secularized world there is no Supreme Being who puts limits on human powers. People become all-powerful, knowing no limits to their potency. These powers are ideologically accorded not simply to a few great leaders or rulers but reputedly to the people at large. Yet at the same time, modern ideology is not utopian—it does not assume the perfectability of society. Although it expands the potency of the masses, Gouldner contends, "Ideology is countertragic because it seeks to better, not to perfect the world, offering what is 'only' a substantial improvement" (Gouldner, 1976:75).

Thus ideology, according to Gouldner, is a secularized idea-system that is defined as rational. In an age of reason, ideologies gain ascendance with a lessening of religious influence. Ideology is not only a belief system that purports to be rationally defensible, it is also wed to practice. Its development has been made possible through mass literacy and the mass media. Using the symbols and the communication technology of the modern world, ideology can be packaged and distributed to the public.

Yet modern ideology has failed. Although its faith in man's potential progress may be romantically pleasing, it faces difficult times in an age of crises and shortages. Gouldner recognizes that our modern ideology has failed to actualize its promise. Gouldner calls for reflexive consideration, going beyond the typically one-sided approach to ideology—an approach with proponents being silent on its weaknesses and critics being blind to possible virtues. Self-reflexivity would bring us closer to critical self-examination so that the ideology's ideal values and real enacting of them would be brought into closer harmony. As it now stands, ideological ideals are far from the real culture in which they are embodied.

Changes appear to be under way in capitalistic countries where technocratic consciousness has failed as an ideology. Gouldner (1976:248) contends that in a society "with an expanding GNP, the executive political class, at the societal level and in charge of various scientized bureaucracies, is habituated to expect obedience without ideological convictions." Those in charge within the society are likely to assume the self-evidence of a need for obedience to the system without making necessary ideological appeals to the masses. Gouldner (1976:249) observes possible ideological developments as being made possible by a "fundamental contradiction of capitalist political economy" that

> is based on a system of "indirect rule" that requires operating mechanisms of ideological integration, yet at the same time, its own leading elites and classes inhibit the effective maintenance of the very ideological mechanisms required for their own social reproduction. The hegemonic and dominant classes suspect and oppose those pursuing an ideological politics, seeing it as the politics of unsocialized outsiders who do not play according to "the rules of the game."

Gouldner asserts that ideology is an important component of modern society. Although modern ideology has failed, it attempted to serve as a contemporary replacement for religion that provided transcendence and legitimation in a technological world. It appears, however, that the ideology emphasizing man's potential for progress has lost some of its force and that new ideologies are still in the process of being born. Gouldner (1976:245–246) contends that technology (including consumerism, productivity, and science), with its emphasis on enjoyment of life, is not an ideology. Rather it "*represses* the ideological problem and inhibits ideological creativity and adaptation." Gouldner (1976:246) notes:

> What then governs mass conduct is not a new *belief* in the moral rightness of technology but, rather, *the sheer experience of gratification* with it. Let the technology remain unchanged, but let the gratification level decline, and the matter is put to the test. This is exactly the test inadvertently provided when wars and depressions occur. We then see that it is not science and technology, nor even their continued development, that suffices to maintain the morale and loyalty of modern citizens. There remains an abiding need for a justificatory ideology. Growing rationalization, technological hardware, the scientization of bureaucracy, do not circumvent this need. They never did.

The question of needed legitimation for modern society can be found in classical sociological writings, particularly in those of Durkheim and Weber, who recognized the decreased potency of religion as a legitimating force. Gouldner's search for a new legitimating ideology reechoes classical writings. His own response (1976:245) is that the ecology movement may function "as the ideology appropriate for a time of austerity, of material shortages, of declining or static standards of living, of the conservation of energy supplies and raw materials." In addition to ecology, other ideologies, including new religions, quasi religions, and occultist movements are also developing, emphasizing the "dematerialization" of daily life.

Not only has ideology failed in Western capitalist societies, but it is also experiencing failure in socialist countries. Just as technology has served limited groups rather than being a moral force binding society together, socialist ideology has served smaller interest groups at the expense of the whole. There is a tension in both socialist and capitalist societies between ideological discourse that denies the legitimacy of partisan interests and the reality of partisanship. Recognition of the inherent contradiction between the part and the whole, the individual and society, private and public interests is necessary for a more rational and plausible ideology.

The task of sociology and social theory is to be critical of itself and of existing ideologies. It must be grounded in "justifiable interests and values" and "willing to take responsibility for these, making continuous effort to deepen its reflexive understanding of its own commitments" (Gouldner, 1976:293). Gouldner (1976:293–294) summarizes the best of critical or reflexive theory as follows:

> This means that, when it is at its best, critical theory eschews all temptations to claims of moral elitism and superiority, as well as all posturings of innocence. It never imagines—when it is at its best—that its own self-understanding can be taken at face value, or that its commitments are lacking in ambiguities or even contradictions. Critical theory makes a distinction between what it is and what it hopes to be. Affirming human emancipation as a goal, it never allows itself to intimate—when it is at its best—that it itself has already achieved that emancipation and never allows itself to forget that it, too, possesses a repressive potential. It knows that its own rationality, too, is limited by the world in which it exists and by the social positioning of those speaking for it.

Gouldner is aware that reflexive sociology will be a constant struggle, yet he calls on it to struggle to be aware of its place in the world so as to better understand the society whose task it is to study.

Critique of Reflexive Sociology _____

It is appropriate for the last theorist to be discussed in this text to be committed to the need for a sociology of sociology. Reflexive sociology, as advanced by Gouldner, emphasizes the importance of being aware of the assumptions underlying sociological theory. In the final section of each chapter, we have attempted to alert the reader to some of the expressed and unexpressed assumptions of each theory. Given Gouldner's call for reflexive sociology, it is not surprising that he has frequently noted various underlying assumptions in his work regarding the nature of people, the nature of society, and the appropriate model for sociological theory.

Gouldner's reflexive ideology and reflexive sociology assumes that men and women are partially free agents and partially determined creatures. As he notes:

> I assume that all men are capable of reason, and that through this they are capable of understanding themselves and other men. At the same time, however, men also participate in a variety of other conditions, they are moved by a variety of forces—biological, ecological, psychological and historical—which invisibly control their behavior in the form of irrational, compulsive, or purely "natural" forces or laws. (1973:101)

Thus the image of humans is partially that of persons capable of a "full humanity" and partially that of dependent objects, "not essentially different from lesser animals or even inanimate objects which cannot be moved by an appeal to reason or by self-examination" (1973:101). Gouldner (1973:101–102) emphasizes this paradoxical situation as follows:

> Men thus simultaneously dwell in two worlds, they exist as both subject and object, as creatures of triumphant reason and of reason baffled; as linguistical creatures capable of a unique responsiveness to symbols of their own emission and as dumb creatures moved by pre-symbolic forces; whose behavior is often patterned by invisible ecological scarcities, by bone structure, by hormones, by brawn and brain, and evolutionarily implanted imperatives.

Gouldner assumes, however, that men and women can achieve a greater degree of rationality than currently is demonstrated. It is the task of social science to bring mankind into a greater rationality: "It is the special function of these social sciences continuously to dissolve man's opaqueness to himself; to help him understand those forces that act upon him that he ordinarily finds unintelligible; and to help him transform these natural forces that use him as an object into humanly controllable forces under his control" (1973:102). Social science, according to Gouldner, should help to liberate people from being objects into persons capable of more voluntary action.[2]

Gouldner's assumption of man's rationality and potential for voluntary action reveals in part an interactionist's concern with meaning, language, and symbols. Sociology must develop a tradition "whose function it is to engage men's understanding, to ask for and interpret the *meaning* of events, and to mediate between the world and man in his quest for meaning" (1973:103). At the same time, however, Gouldner remains cognizant of the deterministic side of man and his kinship with other "dumb objects." Sociology can facilitate a union between "dumb energies and rationality" (1973:104).

Gouldner appears to accept without question the reality of society. It is through and within social structures that social action takes place. Gouldner's acceptance of society's existence is congruent with most sociological views of social structure.[3] Where Gouldner parts company with other sociological structuralists is in his insistence that the study of society and the study of sociology itself are intimately intertwined. Sociology not only studies the social structure, it also helps to create and to order it.

---

[2] Gouldner's increasing awareness of man's ability to transcend a deterministic, objectlike nature may be evidenced in his revision of his stance on the universal norm of reciprocity. Gouldner recognized the heuristic value of the concept of reciprocity, which underlies much functionalist thought (see Chapter 2 of this text). He also noted the weakness of the concept and promised to develop it further. In a subsequent paper discussing "The Importance of Something for Nothing," Gouldner notes:

> If men were guided solely by the norm of reciprocity many who needed help might never receive it and would be destroyed or deeply discontent. At any given time there are some persons who cannot reciprocate benefits they once received. . . . Moreover, to the extent that men can empathize with the weak and poor, or to the degree that they can imagine themselves as some day weak and in need of air, their exclusive operation in terms of a norm of reciprocity may create a foreboding awareness of the precariousness of their own future position. . . . (Gouldner, 1973:260–261)

[3] It is not without significance that in the discussion of the rise of sociology in the United States in *The Coming Crisis of Western Sociology*, the absence of any reference to the Chicago school of sociology and to the social psychological tradition developed there is conspicuous. George Herbert Mead, Charles Horton Cooley, W. I. Thomas, and other figures in the symbolic interactionist tradition are not even mentioned. For Gouldner, the contest is not between symbolic interactionism and functionalism, two important schools of American social thought, but between functionalism and Marxism, two structurally oriented theories.

Sociologists are not "out there" studying something they have somehow escaped; rather they are very much involved personally in what they study. Hence Gouldner's call is for both reflexive sociology and a reflexive society, including its legitimating ideology.

As we have seen throughout this chapter, Gouldner advocates a reflexive theory. Questioning the feasibility of a completely value-neutral [4] sociology, Gouldner admonishes sociologists to be aware of the assumptions and interests underlying their work. He notes (1973:100–101):

> In short, what is sought is truth as *practical* reason, practical because relevant to the understanding and transformation of our daily lives and the historically shaped society in which we live. We want to understand our social world and ourselves and others in it, so that we may change it in ways that enable us to understand it still better, to have fuller rational discourse in it, so that we may better be able to change it, and so on.

Gouldner (1973:25) is critical of sociology's blindly patterning itself after what it considers to be the ideal physical science. Sociology must deal with more than technical proficiency. It must be willing to take stands and be committed to a moral sense. Gouldner (1973:25) observes that science, including sociology, has both constructive and destructive potentialities. Sociologists should be aware of both: "Nor does this in any degree detract from the indispensable norms of scientific objectivity; it merely insists that these differ radically from moral indifference" (1973:25).

Gouldner is thus critical of the use of a natural-science model for sociology. The application of this model to the study of humans "think-afied" people, making them objects of control just as things are. It was expected that social science could be used to control people just as physical science is used to control nature (Gouldner, 1970:492). In this sense, the scientific model dehumanizes men and women.

Gouldner calls for a renewal of thought within sociology. A reflexive sociology must be aware of the relation between sociology and society as well as between theory and practice. Gouldner is confident that through the critical analysis of current theory, an emancipatory and liberating sociology may be developed.

---

[4] Gouldner (1961) was one of the first contemporary theorists to challenge the prevalent image of sociology as a value-free science. Its widespread acceptance and distortion in some sociological circles led Gouldner (1973:27) to "fear that the myth of a value-free, social science is about to be supplanted by still another myth and that the once glib acceptance of the value-free doctrine is about to be superceded by a new but no less glib rejection of it."

Summary

The works of Alvin W. Gouldner represent more of a metatheory (a theory about theory) than a new theory to explain the development of society. While critiquing existing theory, Gouldner calls for a renewal in sociological theory to bridge the gap between science and humanism as well as between theory and practice.

Gouldner's call is for reflexive sociology, a sociology that is not afraid to analyze itself with the same probing methods used to study other topics. Such an approach must be willing to lay bare its assumptions and to seek actively to uncover its biases and distortions. At the risk of being criticized for "navel gazing" rather than engaging in the practical business of doing sociology, Gouldner emphasizes the need for self-knowledge. Men and women are more than puppets on a string; they have an ability to reflect on who they are in society and where they are in relation to its tradition.

Gouldner attempts to expose the biases and assumptions underlying contemporary American sociology. He analyzes the crises facing modern sociology with the lessening of functionalism's dominance of the field, yet the lack of an adequate strong alternative model. He attempts to demonstrate how in American functionalism may be found an ideal of value-free sociology along with the reality that the sociological enterprise is heavily funded by the welfare state. He is concerned by the pretentiousness and false consciousness that he feels permeates academic sociology.

The same society that spawned American sociology and its current crisis is facing a crisis in the failure of ideology. The old ideology of individual rights and powers is faltering, and a new ideology seeks to be born. Just as sociology must be reflexive, so must society be reflexive in analyzing its own ideology. False consciousness is prevalent within the modern capitalistic world.

The call is for reflexivity—self-awareness—in the analysis of both sociology and society. It is a call for the increased rationality that such self-knowledge makes possible. It is a call for theory, but a relevant theory wed to practice.

References

GOULDNER, ALVIN W.
    1961 "Anti-Minotaur: The Myth of a Value-free Sociology." Presidential
        Address given at the annual meeting of the Society for the Study of

Social Problems. Published in *Social Problems* 9 (Winter, 1962):199–212.
1966 *Enter Plato.* New York: Harper Torchbooks.
1970 *The Coming Crisis of Western Sociology.* New York: Basic Books, Inc.
1973 *For Sociology.* New York: Basic Books, Inc.
1976 *The Dialetic of Ideology and Technology.* New York: Seabury.

Glossary

Action (rational action)

The process of seeking an end or goal (e.g., organization, leadership) with the most appropriate means (e.g., impersonal organization, qualified leadership).

Active society—Amitai Etzioni

A society in which people are in charge of and in control of the society in which they live; assumes knowledge upon which decision making is based and the power to implement the decisions.

Adaptation—Talcott Parsons

The functional imperative that refers to the ability of the system to secure what it needs from the environment and to distribute these resources through the entire system; for society this function is met through the economy.

Adaptive upgrading—Talcott Parsons

The evolutionary process by which a wider range of resources is made available to social units so that their functioning is freed from some of the ascriptive restrictions imposed on less evolved units; for example, educational function's being met by newly emergent institutions (schools, vocational colleges, universities) instead of the family.

Anomie—Robert Merton

A state of nonconformity that results from a disjuncture between cultural goals and institutionalized means available to obtain these goals; for example, a high rate of unemployment (means) is a disjuncture for many in living a middle-class way of life (end).

Appearances—Erving Goffman

The stimuli of the personal front that function at the time to tell us of the performer's social status; for example, a white coat and a stethoscope for a physician.

Assets—Amitai Etzioni

A power base or power potential; may be utilitarian (based on exchange), coercive (based on force), or persuasive (based on a manipulation of symbols).

Authority

Legitimate power; power residing with the position in society rather than with the person exercising the power.

Class

An aggregation of persons in a society who stand in a similar position with respect to force or some specific form of institutionalized power, privilege, or prestige; persons who stand in relation to each other by virtue of common interests (e.g., holding property, money).

Class system—Gerhard Lenski

A hierarchy of classes ranked in terms of some single criterion; for example, political class, property class, occupational class.

Coercive relations—Amitai Etzioni

An ideal type of social relations that entails the use of force or the threatened use of force by one actor against another.

Collectivities—Amitai Etzioni
Groups based upon a set of normative interests and/or values that are shared by their members; similar to the Marxist concept of *class.*

Constraints—Daniel Bell
Limits of the social structure within which effective policy decisions may be made; for example, limits to available natural resources, problems of inflation, limits of available educational and training facilities.

Control networks—Amitai Etzioni
Supplements the cohesive relations of the collectivities that helps to guide a society; for example, the state.

Core value—Lewis Coser
A central component of a relationship (in contrast to a peripheral issue), an attack upon which threatens the social group upon which it is based.

Cosmos—Peter Berger
That which transcends everyday reality, going into realms beyond objective verification; the concern of religion rather than sociology.

Cybernetics
The study of communication among men, animals, and machines, with particular emphasis on the feedback of information and the function of feedback in the process of control (see also *feedback*).

Decomposition of capital—Ralf Dahrendorf
The dispersion of the ownership of the means of production in a capitalistic economic system.

Decomposition of labor—Ralf Dahrendorf
The increasing stratification of the working class in modern industrial society.

Deductive theory
The method of theory construction that moves from general, abstract, logical statements toward specific propositions that may be empirically tested (see also *inductive theory*).

Differentiation—Talcott Parsons
The evolutionary process by which a unit or a subsystem having a well-defined place in the society divides into units that differ in both structure and functional significance for the wider system.

Dilemma—Peter Blau
One of the dialectical forces of social change that requires a choice between equally desirable alternatives: a "mixed game" where partners have both competing and conflicting interests; threat to the devaluation of a reward because of too frequent giving of it; multiple causations of an act, yielding both desirable and undesirable consequences; and the "dilemma of leadership."

Dilemma of leadership—Peter Blau
Conflict between the gaining of power and the process of winning approval.

Distributive justice—George Homans
The expectation that rewards will be proportional to costs in exchange situations.

Dramaturgy—Erving Goffman
An approach that uses the language and imagery of the theater to describe the subjective as well as the objective fact of social interaction.

Dysfunction—Robert Merton
Any item or social usage that contributes to the breakdown of a social system.

Economizing mode—Daniel Bell
The mode of life that emphasizes the best allocation of social resources among competing ends; emphasizes maximization-of-production and least-cost principles (see also *sociologizing mode*).

Elite—Amitai Etzioni
A role or control unit that specializes in the cybernetic functions of knowledge processing and decision making in the application of power.

Emergence—Peter Blau
The process by which a social structure develops an existence; the attribution of independent properties to social groups, asserting that a social group is more than the simple sum of its individual parts.

Equilibrium
A state of balance or normalcy within a social system.

Ethnomethodology—Harold Garfinkel
The investigation of indexical expressions and other practical actions as contingent ongoing accomplishments of organized artful practices of everyday life; the process by which individuals construct their social reality.

Exogenous variables
Variables that remain outside the new causal theoretical model and that are an unidentified and/or unexplained source of change.

Externalization—Peter Berger
The "moment" in the dialectical process in which individuals collectively and gradually change the patterned objective social world; the process by which imperfectly socialized men and women collectively construct a new reality.

External system—George Homans
The larger environment, which includes an internal system that is being studied; for example, a friendship group within a large factory.

Face-to-face interaction—Erving Goffman
The reciprocal influence of individuals upon one another's actions when in one another's immediate presence.

Feedback
A process in which knowledge of the results of past performance (by an individual, a group, or a machine) leads to modification of future performance, thereby keeping performance effectively directed toward the attainment of a goal.

Fiduciary system—Talcott Parsons
The trusteeship roles that bearers and transmitters of the cultural tradition play with regard to the rest of society; a subsystem that acts as a trustee of some interest of the society.

Frame—Erving Goffman
Definitions of the situation that are built up in accordance with the principles of organization that govern events and our subjective involvement with them.

Front region—Erving Goffman
That part of the individual's performance that regularly functions in a gen-

eral and fixed fashion to define the situation for those who observe the performance, including both a setting and a "personal front" of appearance and manner.

Function

The part that any recurrent social activity, such as a funeral ceremony or the punishment of a crime plays in the social life as a whole. A positive function contributes to the maintenance of the structure; a negative function or "dysfunction" breaks down the structure.

Functional alternatives—Robert Merton

The functionalist concept that asserts that a cultural item or practice may be replaced with another in meeting any functional prerequisite.

Functional imperatives—Talcott Parsons

Those needs that must be met for any living system—including the action system and its subsystem of the social system—to survive—(see also *latent pattern maintenance, integration, goal attainment,* and *adaptation*).

Functional prerequisites (or imperatives)

A concept in traditional functionalism (and central to Parsonian theory) that asserts that certain needs must be met in order for a social system to survive.

Functional unity of society

A pre-Mertonian functionalist assumption that asserted that all parts of the social system work together without producing persistent conflicts that can neither be resolved nor regulated.

Game against fabricated nature—Daniel Bell

Economy of industrial societies, where mechanical energy provides the power that is the basis of productivity.

Game against nature—Daniel Bell

An economy based on extraction through agriculture, mining, fishing, and timber, which is dependent upon the seasons of the year, the nature of the soil, the availability of water, and so on.

Game between persons—Daniel Bell

An economy based primarily on the exchange of services, as characterized by the United States.

Game theory

A mathematical approach to theory construction, which emphasizes how people should behave if they were acting rationally and in accord with the principle of game strategy (see also *zero-sum* and *non-zero-sum games*).

Goal attainment—Talcott Parsons

The functional imperative dealing with the question of meeting the ends or purposes of the system and of establishing priorities among these goals. This imperative is met in society through the polity.

Group—George Homans

A number of persons who communicate with one another often over a span of time, and who are few enough so that each person is able to communicate with the others face-to-face.

Humanism

An approach to the study of sociology that asserts the uniqueness of human nature, making sociology's subject matter intrinsically different from the subject matter of the natural sciences asserts sociology's kinship with the humanistic disciplines, including history, drama, and philosophy (see also *interpretative sociology*).

Humanistic theory

The approach to sociology that aims not so much for precise theory construction as for understanding human behavior. Human behavior is not viewed as being analagous to the study of the natural sciences. (See also *naturalistic sociology*.)

Impression management—Erving Goffman

The artful practice of interaction in which the person attempts to select the correct frame and to minimize any stigma in presenting himself to others (see also *frame analysis* and *stigma*).

Inauthentic society—Amitai Etzioni

A society that gives the appearance of being active and responsive while underneath it is passive and alienating.

Inclusion—Talcott Parsons

The evolutionary process through which newly emergent resources are integrated into the larger structure.

Incrementalism—Amitai Etzioni

The decision-making model that "muddles through" or settles for relatively satisfactory decisions rather than the best possible one; piecemeal, bit-by-bit decision-making. (See also *rational model of decision making* and *mixed scanning*.)

Indexical expression—Harold Garfinkel

A person's designation of time and space of an occurrence that may serve as an "index" to locate the happening within the sphere of reality.

Indispensability

The prevailing postulate in pre-Mertonian functionalism that asserts that every cultural item fulfills some vital task in the working of a system.

Inductive theory

The method of theory construction that moves from specific findings toward more general and abstract principles (see also *deductive theory*).

Inspection—Herbert Blumer

The mode of inquiry that allows the researcher to examine concepts creatively in light of impersonal evidence (rather than preconceived biases or frameworks).

Instrumental–consummatory axis—Talcott Parsons

Functional imperatives that deal with the means (instrumental) necessary to attain an end or goal (consummatory).

Integration—Talcott Parsons

The functional imperative dealing with the problem of coordinating and fitting together the parts of the system into a functioning whole. This imperative is met in society through the societal community.

Interaction—George Homans

Some unit of activity that is stimulated by the activity of another.

Internal–external axis—Talcott Parsons

Functional imperatives that deal with the needs of the internal system or the needs of the system in dealing with the environment (external).

Internalization—Peter Berger

The "moment" in the dialectical process of reality construction through which socialization occurs.

Internal system—George Homans

The group under analysis comprised of interdependent parts (see also *external system*).

Interpretative sociology

An approach to sociology that emphasizes the importance of subjective interpretation or meaning attached to social phenomena (see also *humanistic sociology*).

Joint action—Herbert Blumer

A social organization of conduct of different acts of diverse participants; the process of institutionalization.

Latent function—Robert Merton

Those unintended and unrecognized consequences of a cultural practice that contribute to the adjustment or adaptation of the system.

Legitimation—Peter Berger

Ways of explaining and justifying the social world. Religion was the primary legitimating force in premodern societies.

Macroscopic research—C. Wright Mills

Research dealing with total social structures in a comparative way; for example, works of Weber, Marx, and Manneheim. (See also *molecular research*.)

Manifest function—Robert Merton

Those objective and intended consequences of a cultural practice that contribute to the adjustment or adaptation of the system.

Manifest group—Ralf Dahrendorf

A group that develops around a recognized common interest, seeking a role in the authority structure (see *quasi group*).

Manner—Erving Goffman

Those stimuli of the personal front that function at the time to warn us of the interaction role that the performer will expect us to play in the oncoming situation.

Middle-range theory—Robert Merton

Those theories that lie between the minor but necessary working hypotheses that evolve in abundance during day-to-day research and the all-inclusive systematic efforts to develop a unified theory that will explain all the observed uniformities of social behavior, social organization, and societal changes.

Mixed-scanning decision-making—Amitai Etzioni

Represents an active approach to the decision-making process, involving rational exploration of possible actions, omitting details and specifications, for example the operation of a weather satellite; an intermediate position between rational decision-making, which requires attention to all possible alternatives, and the incrementalist process of "muddling through" without sufficient information.

Molecular research methods—C. Wright Mills

Research dealing with small-scale problems and its generally statistical models of verification (see also *macroscopic research*).

Multiple roles—Robert Merton

A plurality of interlocking positions and expected behaviors, each involving a role set; for example, a woman's simultaneous positions of wife, mother, college president, church board member, and head of the annual charity drive.

Naturalistic sociology

An approach to the study of sociology that likens the social sciences to the natural sciences (see also *humanism*).

Naturalistic theory

A perspective in sociology that would view sociological theory as necessarily using the model of physics, chemistry, or some other natural science as the appropriate model for theory construction (see also *humanistic theory*).

Net balance of consequences—Robert Merton

The analytical practice in functionalism that weighs both positive and negative functions of a cultural practice to determine its total impact on the system.

New causal theory

The approach to mathematical sociology that applies statistical analysis to patterns in empirical observations and that attempts to use such patterned data to construct theory.

Nomos—Peter Berger

The world-building enterprise through which the social world is ordered; opposite of anomie or state of normlessness.

Nonrealistic conflict—Lewis Coser

Conflict that is not occasioned by the rival ends of the antagonists but by the need for tension release of at least one of them; for example, "scapegoating" in racial discrimination.

Non-zero-sum game

A model of games based on principles of both cooperation and conflict that does not assume a "winner-take-all" outcome; for example, prisoner's dilemma or battle of the sexes (see also *game theory*).

Normative relations—Amitai Etzioni

An ideal type of social relations emphasizing shared norms and values, where the goal of the relationship is tradition-based and often nonrational (see also *utilitarian* and *coercive relations*).

Object—Herbert Blumer

Anything that may be referred to: *physical* objects, such as desks, cars, and dress; *social* objects, including social roles; *abstract* objects, such as values, rights, and laws.

Objectivation—Peter Berger

The "moment" in the dialectical process of reality construction that defines objective social reality.

Objective expressions—Harold Garfinkel

Precise references of time and space that locate the happening within a theoretical or scientific context; for example, the importance of noting the precise time of events in a hospital or in a scientific experiment in contrast to the more "indexical" designation of time in daily conversation (see also *indexical expressions*).

Opposition ideals—Peter Blau

Media of reorganization and change, such as establishing a third party in a two-party system.

Particularistic standards—Peter Blau

Status attributes that are valued only by the in-group, such as religious or political beliefs (see also *universalistic standards*).

Passive society—Amitai Etzioni

A society in which people are controlled by outside forces or by active others.

Pattern maintenance—Talcott Parsons

Functional imperative or prerequisite that deals with the problem of how to ensure continuity of action in a system according to some order or norm. This function is met by the *fiduciary system* in society.

Pattern variables—Talcott Parsons

A means of categorizing action or of classifying types of roles in social systems. This fivefold scheme is based on Toennies's typology of *Gemeinschaft* and *Gesellschaft*.

Performance—Erving Goffman

The total activity of a given participant in a social situation.

Power

The ability of persons or groups to impose their will on others even in the face of opposition or resistance.

Power elite—C. Wright Mills

Those men and women who, in stark contrast to the middle class, are in pivotal positions to make decisions having major consequences.

Practical interest

Common-sense reality and everyday existence, which is basic to the study of ethnomethodology; concept gives rise to *indexical expressions*.

Principal of least interest—George Homans

The person who has the least interest in continuing a social relationship is the best able to dictate the conditions of the relationship.

Proposition

A statement of relationship between two or more variables or concepts that is used to build a theory.

Quasi group—Ralf Dahrendorf

Potential groups that would develop around as-yet-unrecognized latent common interests (see also *manifest group*).

Rational model of decision making—Amitai Etzioni
A decision-making model that makes an exhaustive survey of all relevant alternatives and calculates the respective alternative outcomes in order to best meet a set of preselected goals (see also *incrementalism* and *mixed-scanning decision-making*).

Realistic conflict—Lewis Coser
Those conflicts that arise from the frustration of specific demands within the relationship and from the estimates of gains of the participants, and that are directed against the presumed frustrating object; for example, the use of an economic boycott to protest the unfair hiring practices of a company.

Reality—Peter Berger
A quality appertaining to phenomena that we recognize as having a being independent of our own volition (as we cannot "wish them away").

Reductionism
The practice of explaining the whole by simply analyzing the parts that comprise it; more specifically, using one discipline (e.g., psychology, physics) or natural phenomenon (e.g., climate, geography) to explain social behavior.

Reflective sociology—Alvin Gouldner
An approach to the sociology of sociology that analyzes the development of sociology within its socio-historical-cultural milieu.

Reward
Anything that a person receives during the exchange process that he/she values.

Role distance—Erving Goffman
A pointed separateness between the individual and his/her putative role.

Role embracement—Erving Goffman
A person's admittedly expressed attachment to his/her role; the degree of attachment to one's social role.

Role set—Robert Merton
The complement of the role relationships in which persons are involved by virtue of occupying a particular social status; for example, the principal of a school, by virtue of that status, will be involved in role relations with teachers, students, office staff, custodial help, and so on.

Routine—Erving Goffman
The preestablished pattern of action that is unfolded during a performance and that may be presented or played through on other occasions.

Rule of might—Gerhard Lenski
Coercive rule characterized by a forcible seizure of power by a new elite. It involves an initial phase of violence.

Rule of right—Gerhard Lenski
Constitutional rule; reduction of force and increase in reliance on persuasion to maintain rule.

Safety valve—Lewis Coser
A mechanism, including a social institution or practice, that allows the steam of hostilities to escape without destroying the structure.

Scientific law

The final stage in theory construction, which consists of a precise statement of relationship among the facts that have been repeatedly corroborated by scientific investigation and is generally accepted as accurate by experts in the field.

Scientism

The attack made by some humanistic sociologists in sociology regarding a misuse and misunderstanding of the scientific nature of sociology; an approach that is preoccupied with scientific rhetoric rather than the pursuit of scientific knowledge; pseudoscience.

Sectlike groups—Lewis Coser

Those groups that select membership in terms of special characteristics. These groups tend to be limited in size and lay claim to the total personality involvement of their members.

Self-fulfilling prophecy—Robert Merton

A false definition of a situation that evokes a new behavior that makes the originally false conception come true.

Self-indication—Herbert Blumer

A moving communicative process in which the individual notes things, assesses them, gives them meaning, and decides to act on the basis of the meaning.

Sensitizing concept—Herbert Blumer

A research tool of using concepts that give the user a general reference and guide in approaching the empirical world; for example, culture, institutions, norms.

Social forecasting—Daniel Bell

An approach to theorizing about society that attempts to outline the probabilities of an array of historical tendencies; assumes regularities and recurrences of phenomena or persisting trends whose direction can be plotted.

Sociological imagination—C. Wright Mills

A blend of the molecular and macroscopic research ways that combines a concern for relevant sociological theory with a knowledge and use of history and biography as data sources.

Sociologizing mode—Daniel Bell

The effort to judge a society's needs in a more conscious manner than in the economizing mode, doing so on the basis of some explicit conception of the "public interest" (e.g., cost of air or water pollution, destruction of the environment's beauty).

Sociology of sociology

A subdivision of the larger perspective of sociology of knowledge that attempts to study, using the sociological method of research and analysis, the development of sociology itself (see also *reflexive sociology*).

Stigma—Erving Goffman

A handicap that disqualifies a person from full social acceptance; may be either discredited (or readily visible) or discreditable (or not immediately apparent).

Structural functionalism
An approach to sociological theory that studies society as a set of relatively stable and patterned social units and the adjustment of these parts to the whole; views society as being made up of interdependent and interrelated parts, with norms guiding status roles, statuses being interconnected to form institutions, and institutions being interdependent in larger society.

Structure
A set of relatively stable and patterned social units or a system with relatively enduring patterns (e.g., social institutions).

Symbolic interaction—Herbert Blumer
Action that involves a stimulus, an interpretation of the stimulus, and a response based on the interpretation; differs from nonsymbolic or simple stimulus–response actions.

System
Organization of interdependent parts into a functioning whole; for example, electrical system, biological system, social system.

Team—Erving Goffman
Any set of individuals who cooperate in staging a single routine for the benefit of an audience.

Theory
A systematically related set of statements—including some lawlike generalizations—that is empirically testable.

Total institution—Erving Goffman
A place of residence and work where a large number of like-situated individuals, cut off from the wider society for an appreciable period of time, together lead an enclosed, formally administered round of life; for example, mental hospitals, jails, nursing homes.

Typification—Peter Berger
Reciprocal but patterned role behavior that marks the institutionalization of conduct.

Universal functionalism
A prevailing postulate in pre-Mertonian functionalist theory that holds that all standardized social or cultural forms have positive functions.

Universalistic standards
Status attributes that are generally valued by those who have them as well as by those who do not; for example, wealth, health, beauty.

Utilitarian relations—Amitai Etzioni
An ideal type of social relations based on the principle of social exchange (see also *normative* and *coercive relations*).

Value—Peter Blau
The medium through which transactions occur within and among institutions; may be oppositional, universalistic, or particularistic; that is, sharing the values of an organization is a medium for cohesion among people who may never engage in direct, face-to-face interaction.

Value—George Homans
That which elicits reward in the interaction process.

Value generalizations—Talcott Parsons

The evolutionary process by which newly emergent structures and resources are legitimated or couched through a value pattern at a higher level of generality than in a less evolved situation in order to make it relevant to a broader range of exigencies; for example, the value of "individual rights" has been used to legitimate the Western practice of mate selection, the unrestricted ownership and use of guns, the legalization of abortion laws, and so on.

Zero-sum game

An approach to games where both players know the fixed rules of the game and have freedom of choice within the rules, and where choices are made without knowledge of the opponent's choice of action. Most parlor games are illustrative of the zero-sum model. (See also *non-zero-sum game.*)

Index